DEEPENING
PSYCHOTHERAPY
WITH MEN

DEEPENING PSYCHOTHERAPY WITH MEN

FREDRIC E. RABINOWITZ
SAM V. COCHRAN

AMERICAN PSYCHOLOGICAL ASSOCIATION
WASHINGTON, DC

Published by
American Psychological Association
750 First Street, NE
Washington, DC 20002
www.apa.org

To order
APA Order Department
P.O. Box 92984
Washington, DC 20090-2984
Tel: (800) 374-2721, Direct: (202) 336-5510
Fax: (202) 336-5502, TDD/TTY: (202) 336-6123
On-line: www.apa.org/books/
E-mail: order@apa.org

In the U.K., Europe, Africa, and the Middle East, copies may be ordered from
American Psychological Association
3 Henrietta Street
Covent Garden, London
WC2E 8LU England

Typeset in Goudy by Monotype Composition, Baltimore, MD

Printer: Data Reproductions Corporation, Auburn Hills, MI
Cover Designer: NiDesign, Baltimore, MD
Technical/Production Editor: Jennifer L. Macomber

The opinions and statements published are the responsibility of the authors, and such opinions and statements do not necessarily represent the policies of the American Psychological Association.

Library of Congress Cataloging-in-Publication Data

Rabinowitz, Fredric Eldon, 1956-
    Deepening psychotherapy with men / Fredric E. Rabinowitz and Sam V. Cochran.
        p. cm.
    Includes bibliographical references and index.
    ISBN 1-55798-833-1 (alk. paper)
    1. Psychotherapy.   2. Men—Psychology.   3. Men—Mental health.   I. Cochran, Sam Victor, 1950- II. Title.

RC451.4.M45 R33 2001
616.89'14'081—dc21

British Library Cataloguing-in-Publication Data   2001022926
A CIP record is available from the British Library.

Printed in the United States of America
First Edition

To Janet, Karina, and Jared Rabinowitz
Fredric E. Rabinowitz

To Sam V. Cochran, Jr. (1925–1997),
Lucy Choisser, and Katherine Choisser Cochran
Sam V. Cochran

CONTENTS

Preface ix

Acknowledgments xi

Introduction.. 3

Chapter 1.   Understanding the Problems Men Bring to
              Psychotherapy.. 9

Chapter 2.   Theoretical Foundations for Deepening Psychotherapy
              With Men 33

Chapter 3.   Practice-Oriented Foundations of Deepening
              Psychotherapy With Men.. 51

Chapter 4.   Early Phases of Deepening Psychotherapy With Men..... 89

Chapter 5.   Entering the Working Phase of Deepening
              Psychotherapy With Men.. 117

Chapter 6.   Working Phase Through Termination of Deepening
              Psychotherapy With Men.. 137

Chapter 7.   Deepening Group Psychotherapy for Men.................... 157

Chapter 8.   A Question-and-Answer Session With the Authors:
              Some Final Words 177

References.. 193

Author Index 203

Subject Index... 205

About the Authors 215

PREFACE

It was in the fall of 1980 that we met each other in a graduate course called "Structured Groups for Consultation and Psychotherapy" at the University of Missouri–Columbia. As our major fieldwork project for the class, we designed and led a self-esteem group for women who were serving life sentences in the state women's penitentiary. The intensity of the stories the women told about abuse, rape, and murder led to many hours of discussion in the car on our way to and from the prison and resulted in a deep and enduring bond between us.

One of our many discussions turned to the challenges we faced as men. In the prison, the women seemed to both love us and hate us. In our own lives we found similar but less intense dynamics in our relationships with women. Women's liberation issues were paramount. Women were uniting, feeling their power, and letting us men know that we had better not treat them as objects or second-class citizens. Much anger was directed toward men, especially those of us who were willing to listen and hear what the women were saying. We agreed with many of their complaints but also wondered why men didn't talk to each other about their own lives.

In response to our recognition that many men did not talk in much depth about their lives, we decided to see if there would be some interest in a men's consciousness-raising group. With the support of Drs. Puncky Heppner, Helen Roehlke, and Dick Caple, and the sponsorship of the university's counseling center, we advertised for our men's group. After getting very little response, we found out about a film called "Men's Lives" and decided to invite the university's students to a screening of the movie. To our surprise, more than 100 people showed up, more than half of them men. We recruited some of our friends to help us lead small group discussions afterward to talk about the issues raised in the movie. We also gave out a questionnaire and on it left a space where a man could indicate that he was interested in joining a men's group. After the discussions, we had the names of 15 men interested in the group. Of these, 8 eventually became a part of the first experiential men's group at the University of Missouri–Columbia.

The rest is history. We not only led a series of semester-long men's groups while graduate students but we videotaped them, collected research data, and presented these findings at national conferences. We both became interested in working with men in individual and group therapy, an interest that quickly became the focus of our careers as clinicians, researchers, and theorists.

Of course, there was a selfish aspect to this work. Our own development as men was being profoundly affected by our personal explorations. We read the early books on men's issues and are indebted to Herb Goldberg, Joseph Pleck, Bob Brannon, and Warren Farrell, who broke the ground on popularizing men's issues. In the academic realm, we read Murray Scher's insights about working therapeutically with men and Jim O'Neil's early work on gender role conflict. On the national level, we joined the National Organization for Men Against Sexism (at the time called the National Organization of Changing Men), the Standing Committee for Men of the American College Personnel Association, and eventually the Society for the Psychological Study of Men and Masculinity of the American Psychological Association. In each of these groups we were invited to join in the ongoing discussion, research, and personal camaraderie of fellow men who were challenging the gender role stereotypes of masculinity.

Fred was hired by the University of Redlands in California as a professor, and Sam went to the University of Iowa as a staff psychologist in the University Counseling Service. Although we traveled separate roads, we maintained our contact through our work on men's issues. Each of us maintained clinical practices that specialized in working with men in therapy. Our academic careers included researching, theorizing, and writing about men's issues. We spoke on the telephone; roomed together at national conferences where we presented our findings; wrote articles about men through long-distance computer disk sharing and electronic mail; and collaborated on two books: *Man Alive: A Primer of Men's Issues* (Rabinowitz & Cochran, 1994) and *Men and Depression: Clinical and Empirical Perspectives* (Cochran & Rabinowitz, 2000). The present volume is our attempt to share the therapeutic perspective that we have developed from our many hours of discussions, clinical practice with male clients, research, and personal experiences as men challenging traditional masculinity in our own lives.

ACKNOWLEDGMENTS

We are indebted to many people who have supported us, taught us, and allowed us to be a part of this wonderful field. We are especially thankful that we have had the unconditional support of our families. For Fred, his partner Janet and his two children Karina and Jared have enriched his life more deeply than they can ever know. He is also fortunate to have grown up with two great brothers, Mark and Josh Rabinowitz, who have continued to stay close and connect him to his roots. For Sam, his spouse Lucy and his daughter Katherine have given him an abundance of love, support, and emotional grounding, providing him the base from which to explore the frontiers of his own and his male clients' lives.

In our professional lives, we are deeply indebted to the men from our consulting rooms. Through their struggles and therapeutic journeys, they have taught us much about masculinity, psychotherapy, and life. We are also grateful to the faculty at the University of Missouri–Columbia, who encouraged our work from the beginning, especially Puncky Heppner, Paul King, Helen Roehlke, Wayne Anderson, Joseph Kunce, Corrine Cope, and Dick Caple.

Fred is especially fortunate to have been able to lead men's groups for the past 13 years with two of his best friends, Tom Elliott and Jim McFarland. Without their loving, supportive, and creative notions of how to work with men, he would be less effective in his ability to understand, empathize, and intervene with the variety of male clients he has encountered in his practice. He is also thankful that he was able to work with Ben Shapiro, a bioenergetics therapist who taught him about the power of body-oriented interventions. He is deeply grateful to his mentor and friend, the late Frank Blume, who showed him the value of being honest in all encounters and not regretting speaking from the heart. Sam is fortunate to have worked with a supportive and talented staff at the University of Iowa, including Gerald Stone, Cheryl McNeilly, Julie Corkery, Audrey Bahrick, Martha Christiansen, Kathie Staley, and Scott Stuart.

We have also appreciated the encouragement of our academic and clinical work by many of our fellow members in the Society for the Psychological Study of Men and Masculinity of the American Psychological Association. This wonderful "think tank" for understanding the psychology of men has given us a warm and friendly professional home that has helped us stay on the cutting edge of the field. Fred was also lucky to have been given the academic "go-ahead" intellectually and financially for his work from the University of Redlands and Sam, likewise, from the University of Iowa. We have had terrific editorial assistance and direction initially from Margaret Schlegel and, more recently, from Edward Meidenbauer and Jennifer Macomber of APA Books. We are eternally thankful to the reviewers of our book, who gave us critical feedback, good advice, and encouraging comments about our work.

Finally, we are indebted to our parents, Sam and Bobbi Rabinowitz and Sam and Marilyn Cochran, who have always supported our endeavors and raised us to follow our own paths.

DEEPENING

PSYCHOTHERAPY

WITH MEN

INTRODUCTION

Then wilt thou not be loath to leave this Paradise, but shalt possess a
Paradise within thee, happier far. Let us descend now, therefore, from
this top of speculation.
        —Milton, *Paradise Lost*, 1667/1951, Book XII, verse 585

Much has happened in the study of men in the past 25 years. David
and Brannon (1976), Farrell (1975), Fasteau (1974), Goldberg (1976), and
Pleck and Sawyer (1974) were among the first to critique traditional male
sex role behavior in response to the women's liberation movement. Many of
these early writings in the 1970s on the psychology of men provided an
impetus for the men's liberation movement. This movement was devoted to
challenging society's scripts for men and women, believing that the future
held egalitarian liberation for both sexes. Whereas profeminist men continue to support this goal through social activism, in the 1980s the "men's
movement" split into factions with their own agendas. Notable among these
were the men's-rights movement and the mythopoetic men's movement.

The men's-rights groups, who have taken a legal tactic, were formed
mainly by men who felt betrayed by the concept of egalitarianism. They perceived themselves as victims of child custody and alimony laws that clearly
favored mothers over fathers in the aftermath of divorce. Political advocacy
and activism became a primary means by which proponents of this movement pursued their goals.

The mythopoetic men's movement was led by poet Robert Bly. He
articulated an appealing and honorable vision of masculinity that served as a
salve for the confusion and pain stirred up in men reacting to the changes
occurring in women's roles in society. The men who affiliated with the
mythopoetic groups were drawn together by a desire to expose and heal their
wounds in the supportive atmosphere of other men.

As scientists, we have noted that in the academic world theorizing
about men has evolved in many directions informed by various philosophi-
cal, empirical, and conceptual underpinnings. Notable among these were
the psychoanalytic developmental viewpoint, which focuses on the inner
emotional and relational worlds of men, and the gender role strain perspective, which concentrates on how cultural, economic, and family structures

affect men's lives. Tension between these two perspectives, in writings on the psychology of men, is reflected in what could loosely be called the *social constructionist worldview* and the *identity development worldview*.

As practitioners, we have been disheartened to notice that men have been reluctant psychotherapy clients. They make up only one fourth to one third of most clinicians' practices (Vessey & Howard, 1993). The psychotherapy process, with its emphasis on personal sharing and self-disclosure, is foreign to many men who have been raised to avoid intimacy and vulnerability. Even though many men have endured wounding and shaming since they were boys, they are wary about opening up this cauldron of pain to anyone, especially a psychotherapist (Osherson & Krugman, 1990; Scher, 1979).

Some clinicians have even expressed doubts about whether men can actually engage in more traditional psychotherapy processes and have suggested that therapy be modified so that it fits a more masculine framework (Shay, 1996). Some men have difficulty engaging in the classic psychoanalytic or client-centered process, with its emphasis on client revelation to a mostly passive therapist. For men who struggle with generating verbal material on their own, a more active, structured therapy can lead to increased depth and meaning.

We have found that experiential interventions that allow a man active expression of his feelings and behavior enhance the therapy process and work well in combination with traditional psychotherapeutic strategies. No intervention or strategy with men will work, however, without empathy for and sensitivity to a man's personal and cultural history and how it has affected the way he navigates his world.

Even though a man may have initial difficulty with the structure, format, or relational quality of psychotherapy, these challenges do not mean that the therapy won't work. In fact, by focusing on the relational difficulty of the situation in therapy a man may unlock many of the factors that contribute to his psychological suffering. We make the assumption that all men have psychological depth, but for many men this terrain has been obscured by years of neglect and active avoidance inspired by our culture.

Traditional gender role socialization is a powerful force that inhibits and restricts knowing this internal terrain for many men. This socialization comprises the parental, peer, and social rules of what it means to be a man (Levant, 1995; Pleck, 1981, 1995). This set of proscriptions on how to think, feel, and behave has urged men to avoid getting too close to their feelings. Instead, men have been encouraged to take a more active, problem-solving approach to life's dilemmas. As a result, this conditioning frequently lends itself to finding quick solutions to uncomfortable affective states.

Although surely multidetermined through biological, psychological, and cultural pathways, we believe some aspects of what is today considered the traditional male gender role originally had survival value (Jones, 1999;

Stewart, Stinnett, & Rosenfeld, 2000). Aspects of the traditional male gender role may have allowed men to transcend their fears and emotional misgivings to settle new lands, to fight wars, to hunt for food, and to earn a subsistence living. However, it also has spawned unintended consequences for men, such as channeling emotional turmoil into anger, avoiding self-reflection, ignoring mental and physical health, and being less communicative of internal thoughts and feelings in relationships.

Anxiety about one's place in the world has led to behaviors that have the purpose of providing safety. Some men worry excessively about money or how much they can accomplish, with the fantasy that if they work hard enough or accomplish enough, they will be free of this "demon." Other men escape these pressures by engaging in addictive behaviors that temporarily reduce feelings of inadequacy and lack of control. Some men trudge through their lives in a state of emotional hibernation that blunts these same feeling states. Others avoid intimacy, as if to say "If I don't let anyone close to me, I can't be hurt or pressured." Some men strike out violently at those about whom they care and, later, feel sorry for doing so.

A common theme in all of these behavioral outlets is that they can be used to soothe uncomfortable affective states. However, the bottom line on all of these maladaptive manifestations is that they are hard to change. They are self-reinforcing and become substitutes for opening one's heart to the depth of a life abundant in choices and intimate relationships.

The deepening approach to psychotherapy with men described in this book involves working with a constellation of common masculine-specific conflicts. These conflicts have varying salience for any individual man. The first conflict concerns the relational aspect of a man's life, specifically the dynamics of a man's ambivalence about independence and dependence in his significant relationships. The second involves the prohibition placed on men in our culture against assuming the *depressive position*—the emotional state that accompanies the many experiences of grief, loss, and disappointment that occur across the life span and to which many men are vulnerable. The third involves issues organized around masculine aspects of a man's self-structure. These include aspects of a man's identity developed from the influence of early family interpersonal interactions and the gender role demands of masculine culture. The fourth is the conflict many men experience between "being" and "doing." Men tend to have difficulty staying with a feeling or body awareness before wanting to move into an action mode to change the experience or problem solve. Psychotherapy often involves slowing down the movement to action in order to "be" with a feeling or awareness.

Viewing men's psychological difficulties through lenses that are sensitive to these masculine-specific conflicts affords clinicians greater understanding of and empathy for many of the problems for which men seek help. Many men who come to therapy have been challenged in ways that expose one or more of the above issues. This challenge, often experienced by men as a narcissistic wound, is the catalyst to seek help and, if responded to carefully by the therapist, may become a window into greater emotional depth for the man.

PURPOSE AND PLAN OF THIS BOOK

This book has been written to give therapists, clinicians, and counselors new ways to creatively conceptualize and intervene with the men whom they are treating. Through the therapy relationship, a man can be challenged, confronted, and stretched to untangle the web of defenses that he has created. In the process, he may learn to view himself with more psychological and emotional depth. Applied with empathic understanding, interventions that stem from a deepening perspective will reconnect men who are distracted, empty, addicted, anxious, violent, and frozen to emotional places that have been suppressed and long forgotten. We suggest that the therapist's role is to give men the tools and courage to traverse the darkness of their inner emotional worlds. Through the therapy process, men with varying adaptation styles might be able to feel their depth and trust that the most authentic and healthy choices they will make can emerge from this strong foundation of self.

The remainder of this book is divided into eight chapters covering aspects of understanding men, the issues that bring them to the consulting room, and the process of working with men in deepening individual and group psychotherapy. Because the actual process of therapy is not as neat or clean as the theories imply, we have included abundant clinical material to give readers a sense of how theory translates into practice. The cases are composites of clients we have seen. This is to protect the clients' confidentiality and to give readers a wide breadth of material to consider.

In chapter 1 we discuss the problems of the men who come to therapy. We delineate varying maladaptive styles that men bring to the therapy situation that are rooted in their psychological and cultural histories. These histories consist of the impact of early separation and relational trauma; the prohibition on feeling loss, grief, and disappointment; a masculine self-structure based on traditional male gender role norms; a primary mode of doing versus being; and the recent wound that has catalyzed the help seeking.

In chapter 2 we build a theoretical rationale for deepening psychotherapy with men based on a creative synthesis of the psychoanalytic and gender role strain perspectives on men and masculinity. Tracing the development of these two theoretical lines of thought furnishes the basis for an integrated psychotherapy for men. We have built on these rich theoretical foundations to further develop ideas about how best to help men who visit therapists' offices. The deepening model of psychotherapy with men emerges from understanding this critical mix of psyche and culture.

In chapter 3 we provide a practice-oriented rationale for deepening psychotherapy. By reviewing the writings of master psychotherapists from varying theoretical frameworks over the years we have distilled many of the essential elements of practice that best deepen the psychotherapy process with men. Freud, Jung, May, Yalom, Kohut, Rogers, Moreno, Perls, Reich, and Lowen, among others, have provided insights into how to deepen psychotherapy in general. We use their work as a basis from which to expand the practice-oriented aspect of our deepening model for working with men.

In chapters 4, 5, and 6 we take an in-depth look at the individual psychotherapy process by "listening in" on the sessions of the same two men over the course of a year. Through this extensive case material, derived from an application of the deepening psychotherapy perspective with these two men, we illustrate how theory and practice weave together into a coherent fabric of psychotherapy with men. In chapter 4 we delineate the features of the early phases of therapy, including how men can be helped to tell their stories, how a relational connection can be established, and how the therapist can listen for and respond to masculine-specific conflicts. In chapter 5 we depict the emergence of the working phase of therapy. Included is an analysis of the resistance and shame that are precursors to men going deeper in their self-exploration. Case studies illustrate strategies on how to navigate this difficult part of the deepening therapy process. In chapter 6 features of the working phase are depicted, including the working alliance and dealing with masculine-specific concerns that have roots in familial and cultural upbringing. We also describe the dynamics and practical features of responding to a man's decision to terminate therapy.

In chapter 7 we outline with extensive case examples the deepening group therapy process. This chapter illustrates how group interventions can deepen psychotherapy in a way that is both effective and powerful for many men.

In chapter 8 we anticipate and respond to questions that clinicians might have pertaining to deepening psychotherapy. This chapter allows elements of theory and practice to be broadened and applied to a wider range of modalities and concerns.

TERMINOLOGY

Throughout the book we have used the masculine pronouns *he* or *him* to indicate references to male clients, because this book is about working with men. Where appropriate, we have referred to therapists with both the masculine pronoun *he* and the feminine pronoun *she*, because both male and female therapists work with male clients.

Deepening psychotherapy, as we have developed it and come to understand it in these pages, is both an articulation of a process of therapy and a description of a kind of therapy. It is a process of therapy in that we describe a movement through levels of socially imposed and personally constructed defenses to those deeper levels of human experience. We have come to recognize that men are often dissociated or distanced from these levels of experience and use various defensive maneuvers to avoid touching these levels. Thus, the deepening process helps them to move toward these deeper levels of experience and knowledge. Deepening is also a description of a kind of therapy in that it relies on specific techniques and operations that have been developed over the years by a number of therapists to "deepen" the therapy process. In our work, these techniques have been particularly revealing in that they provide a means to gain access to the deeper levels of experience in the men with whom we have worked.

CONCLUSION

For us, this book is the culmination of our many discussions, research endeavors, and personal reflections on what it means to be the best therapist for the men who visit us in our consulting rooms. We hope that the book raises questions for readers, challenges some assumptions, and sparks therapists to get excited about working with male clients in a creative and depth-oriented way.

1

UNDERSTANDING THE PROBLEMS MEN BRING TO PSYCHOTHERAPY

Character structure, then, is the crystallization of the sociological process of a given epoch. (Reich, 1949/1976, p. xxv)

Men who seek the services of a psychotherapist have taken a first step toward deepening their understanding of themselves and their lives. A loss is often the experience that leads a man to make an appointment with a psychotherapist and could be the end of an intimate relationship, the loss of a job, a death of a friend or loved one, or a perceived failure. Through the experience of opening himself to the full meaning and impact of loss, a man's inner emotional life may come alive to him. A psychotherapist who is versed in the new psychology of men and sensitive to men's emotional vulnerabilities is equipped to guide a man through the emotional process that we call *deepening psychotherapy*. In this chapter we outline the kinds of difficulties that bring men to psychotherapy, detail an integrated psychological and cultural perspective for understanding these problems, and apply this conceptual model using several case examples.

ENTERING PSYCHOTHERAPY

Nick, a strong and handsome 27-year-old electrician, was attending his third session of psychotherapy. He had come at the urging of his long-term girlfriend Kristin, who was concerned for his well-being. She believed he was depressed and capable of hurting himself. Although she had declined an invitation to come with him, she made it clear that she was very close to leaving the relationship.

Kristin and Nick had been in couples therapy a year ago. They had attended only a few sessions. The therapist had concluded that they each needed to do some of their own individual work before they could work through some of their relationship issues. Kristin had entered therapy 9 months ago and was finding it helpful in her process of understanding some of her own abusive childhood. Nick, on the other hand, had demurred and avoided seeing a therapist until 2 months ago, when Kristin made it a requirement if they were to continue seeing each other.

Nick had grown up in an abusive family in which his father regularly beat him and his mother. Nick has a history of abusing alcohol and marijuana to soothe his ever-present agitation and anxiety. He claims to have stopped using substances, except cigarettes, because Kristin won't permit it in the house they currently share. He admits to having hit his previous girlfriend, but he has never been physically abusive with Kristin, although he often has felt the urge.

Nick was edgy and evasive at the start of this session. He rarely made direct eye contact with his therapist. Despite being uncomfortable initially, Nick soon became more animated as he revealed some of his inner thoughts and emotions in response to empathic probing from his therapist.

Therapist: So, what has been happening with you since we last talked, Nick?

Nick: Not much.

Therapist: What do you mean, not much?

Nick: You know, the same old bullshit.

Therapist: The same old bullshit has been pretty intense when you've talked before in here. What's been going down with you?

Nick: You mean, specifically?

Therapist: Yeah, specifically.

Nick: Well, for one thing, I think she's still screwing around on me. I thought I saw Kristin with that guy from her work when I drove past there yesterday.

Therapist: What were you doing driving past her work?

Nick: I just don't trust her. I can tell something is up. She got home about 20 minutes late and couldn't look me in the eye.

Therapist: What does that mean for you?

Nick: It means she's trying to hide something.

Therapist: How did you come up with that?

Nick: I remember when my stepfather used to do that to my mother. He was always messing around on her. You know what my mother did? She used to smell his shirt to see if he'd been with someone else.

Therapist: You saw this happen?

Nick: Uh-huh. It was almost a nightly occurrence. That asshole would come home late, smelling of liquor, and my mom knew. So did I. Maybe that's how I know something is going down with Kristin.

Therapist: Nick, you're still angry at your stepdad. He betrayed you and your mom.

Nick: Brilliant, Einstein. You're damn right I'm still angry. He didn't only fuck around on her. He hit her, too. She didn't deserve that.

At this point, Nick becomes more animated. His posture becomes straighter, and his pupils have enlarged. This is the first time he has made eye contact. The therapist hands Nick a rolled-up hand towel and asks him to squeeze and turn it with both of his hands as he speaks. This seems to give him a physical outlet for the anger he is feeling and allows him to continue with his past memories.

Therapist: No one deserves to be hit. So what did you do when this was happening?

Nick: When I was little, I just hid and got out of the way. When I was a teenager I used to get pissed off and let him know. At first he beat the shit out of me. Then, when I got bigger, I took him on and got the best of him.

Therapist: Keep squeezing the towel, Nick. How did that feel? To take him on and get the best of him.

Nick: It felt good to be able to help my mom and get that asshole to stop the beating.

Therapist: Anything else?

Nick: You mean like afterward?

Therapist: Yeah, like afterward.

Nick: I used to feel pretty sorry for myself. I thought I had the shittiest life possible.

Therapist: You must have felt pretty alone.

At this point, Nick puts down the towel. His eyes are watering slightly. His breathing has slowed, and his body is less rigid.

Nick: I still do.

Therapist: You mean the same feelings are with you now?

Nick: Yeah. Why is she doing this to me? What did I do to deserve this shit? I love her, and she just keeps pulling away from me. (Nick's lower lip begins to quiver.)

Therapist: What do you feel you've done to deserve it?

Nick: I've been pretty possessive, I guess. I've always been afraid that she would leave me. I mean, I treat her well, but I guess I knew it wouldn't last.

Therapist: How could you know this?

Nick: I've never had a girlfriend who didn't eventually want to leave. I thought Kristin would be different. She really seemed like she loved me.

Therapist: Nick, what makes you so sure she doesn't love you?

Nick: I told you. I can sense her pulling away. She's been awfully friendly with this guy at work. They spend a lot of time together; you know—business trips and stuff like that.

Therapist: You seem pretty threatened by this guy.

Nick: Well, Kristin has always told me that I should make more money or go back to school and get more education. I've never let on that it bothers me when she says that. I just suck it up.

Therapist: You just suck it up. What does it feel like? On the inside?

Nick: Lousy! Like I'm a failure. School has always been hard for me. I think I probably have some kind of learning disability. I was lucky to get through high school. College blew me out of the water after a semester.

Therapist: You feel inferior to this guy.

Nick: Well. I think I could beat the shit out of him, but yeah, he's got like a master's degree and makes a lot more money that I do. I know it sounds lame, but I just don't measure up.

Therapist: And you think Kristin knows this?

Nick: Well, how could she not? I still get into my funks where I feel sorry for myself.

Therapist: When does that happen?

Nick: Usually it happens when I've been drinking or I get reminded in some way that I don't have what other guys have.

Therapist: How do you act toward Kristin when this is happening?

Nick: I get loud and say hurtful stuff like "Why do you even like me? There must be something wrong with you to go for someone like me."

Therapist: Actually, that sounds more hurtful toward yourself.

Nick: Well, it is, but I can see how much it pains her. I always apologize, but I think she is just sick of my shit.

Therapist: Seems like you are sick of your shit. You ready to do something about it?

Nick: Well I'm here, aren't I?

Therapist: Yeah, you're here because Kristin said that if you didn't come there would be no more relationship. Are you ready to be here for yourself?

Nick: I'm tired of the way things are. Something's got to give. I've pretty much lost her anyway, I think. At least that's the way it feels.

Therapist: Is that a yes?

Nick: I feel like I'm volunteering for the military or something.

Therapist: It might feel that way. I'm concerned that you are just going to keep repeating this pattern with Kristin or the next woman if it is not her. The effort to change needs to come from you, not your girlfriend.

Nick: I'm ready to change the pattern. I'm just not sure if I can. I've had a lot of years of screwing my life up. I'm just being realistic.

Therapist: I hear you. It takes a lot of guts to make the effort and not just blame everyone else for your problems. So are you in for you?

Nick: Yeah, I'm in.

Like Nick, most men are reluctant visitors to a psychotherapist's office. Only about half as many men as women are seen in most clinical settings (Vessey & Howard, 1993). Some inroads have been made in efforts to assist men in surmounting the barriers that exist to their seeking help. Nonetheless, it is uncommon for men to seek the services of a psychotherapist. Notable exceptions to this are men who are seen in alcohol and drug abuse treatment settings and men who are incarcerated. This is not surprising, because recent epidemiological surveys have found that men experience higher incidences of alcohol and drug problems (Hanna & Grant, 1997) and create legal difficulties for themselves because of antisocial behavior patterns (Black, Baumgard, & Bell, 1996).

Problems such as alcohol and drug addictions and legal difficulties lead many therapists to conclude that men are mainly unsuitable for, and untreatable with, psychotherapy. A common assumption among some therapists is that alcohol and drug problems as well as antisocial behavior patterns are manifestations of underlying character pathology that often remains untouched by the more traditional psychotherapy venues. Perhaps therapist attitudes such as these are one reason why the numbers of men seen in psychotherapy are low.

However, with increased sensitivity to men's problems and a gradual shifting of cultural norms and values toward accepting men's vulnerability, men like Nick may meet a receptive therapist. A new psychology of men has developed over the past 20 years that has articulated a male-friendly, empathic understanding of the issues with which many men struggle. This new psychology of men has also led to increased sensitivity by both male and female psychotherapists and a greater receptivity by these therapists toward helping men.

EMPIRICAL FINDINGS ON THE PSYCHOLOGICAL PROBLEMS OF MEN

What kinds of problems do men who come to psychotherapy bring to the therapist's office? One approach to understanding men's problems is to examine the epidemiological findings regarding the prevalence of psychological disorders in men. Epidemiological surveys have yielded findings indicating that most men's psychological suffering is expressed mainly through problems related to alcohol and drug abuse and dependence. Major depression, social phobia, and antisocial personality behavior problems are the next most frequent psychological maladies afflicting men in samples of the general population.

Results from two of the most widely reported epidemiological surveys indicate lifetime prevalence estimates for alcohol and drug abuse and dependency of approximately 30% in men (Kessler, McGonagle, Swartz, Blazer, & Nelson, 1993; Robins & Reiger, 1991). This means that almost 1 in 3 men will experience problems with alcohol or drug abuse or dependence at some point in their lifetimes. These problems occur at almost three times the rate of the next most prevalent psychological difficulties: Major depression occurs in men at about a 10%–15% lifetime prevalence rate, social phobia occurs at about a 10% lifetime prevalence rate, and antisocial personality behavior occurs at about a 5%–8% lifetime prevalence rate.

Many researchers have speculated on what might be the cause of these particular problems of men. Biological, psychological, and cultural underpinnings have all been implicated. This composite profile, which includes alcohol and drug abuse, depression, difficulties in social relationships, and antisocial behavior, is commonly associated with what some authors have noted as a male tendency to externalize psychological distress through action, distraction, and compulsive acting out (e.g., Cochran & Rabinowitz, 2000).

Another approach to understanding the kinds of problems that men bring to treatment is to actually survey the presenting problems of those who seek treatment. A recent survey of presenting complaints of applicants for psychological services reported that men and women present to therapists with generally the same kinds of problems (Burstein, Loucks, Rasco, & Green, 1993). Both men and women were found to present most frequently with concerns about interpersonal difficulties, followed by depression, uncontrolled behavior, anxiety, identity issues, general stress, family and interpersonal difficulties, substance abuse, physical complaints, academic concerns, and child abuse concerns. Presenting concerns that men endorsed more frequently were issues related to job stress and to gender identity.

In general, surveys of presenting problems have tended to find men's presenting concerns to be somewhat at variance with what one might expect if one were to extrapolate from the epidemiological survey findings. One would expect most men to be in treatment for alcohol or drug abuse problems or behavior problems, if one used the epidemiological surveys to guide one's anticipations. Also, it is possible that many of the presenting concerns of men who ultimately seek the services of a psychotherapist may actually be a result of the problems detailed in the epidemiological surveys. For example, a drinking problem may lead to interpersonal conflict and job-related problems, which might in turn be the problems presented to the therapist.

CLINICAL REPORTS ON THE PSYCHOLOGICAL
PROBLEMS OF MEN

In addition to these empirically based reports detailing the kinds of psychological problems afflicting men, several clinical case reports have also appeared. In general, these reports tend to confirm the above findings related to the presenting concerns of applicants for psychological services. However, because empirical reports are typically based only on verifiable diagnoses, clinical case reports tend to provide greater breadth and depth to the kinds of problems that men experience and that bring them to consulting rooms.

One of the main problem areas that often lead men to seek the assistance of a therapist is interpersonal conflict (Brooks & Silverstein, 1995). Rejection experiences, divorce, and ongoing relational conflict may become a pattern in a man's life that might lead him to seek the help of a psychotherapist. Often, many men are "persuaded" into therapy by a partner, friend, family member, or employer. A concerned partner might request greater intimacy or commitment, and when this does not occur he or she may suggest individual therapy for the man or conjoint therapy for the couple.

At the extremes of interpersonal conflict, interpersonal violence may erupt and bring a man to a therapist's door (Hamberger & Hastings, 1991). This can occur through self-referral once the man realizes he has anger-control problems that need to be addressed. However, it often occurs more commonly through court-mandated referral as a sanction against a man who has been adjudicated guilty of domestic violence or assault.

Presenting concerns related to interpersonal issues are consistent with research findings that suggest that men frequently experience increased interpersonal conflict in conjunction with symptoms of depression and anxiety (Heifner, 1997). Many men who report depression also report increased levels of conflict between work and family (Good & Wood, 1995). Furthermore, the numbers of men who experience alcohol and drug problems suggest that such difficulties will frequently be played out in familial and relational contexts, resulting in increased conflict in these domains.

In addition to these more obvious examples of interpersonal conflict, some men request help regarding issues of shyness, loneliness, and difficulty establishing an intimate interpersonal relationship. Usually, this experience emerges as a man begins his journey out of his family of origin and enters the world of work or enrolls in a college or university (Good & May, 1987). Once he establishes a foothold in these environments, lack of interpersonal relatedness often emerges as a missing element in his life. Such a realization may lead a man to consult a psychotherapist.

Several case reports have also been based on problems of men who formally get into trouble with legal authorities or who are sanctioned for antisocial behavior in communities or workplaces (Aston, 1987). These difficulties might include, but are not limited to, difficulties with anger management, alcohol and substance abuse, depression, or other symptoms that interfere with social and occupational adaptation. These problems, too, frequently result in a third-party suggestion that the man obtain help. Often, retaining employment or status in some social or community activity will be contingent on receiving help. Although this is problematic in that the male client who presents in this manner may be perceived as lacking motivation, therapists should be prepared to respond to such presentations in an empathic and respectful manner.

Often related to legal or occupational difficulties are problems with compulsive or addictive behaviors (Diamond, 1987; Hanna & Grant, 1997). These problems can include difficulties with alcohol and other mood-altering substances. In addition to these substance-based addictions, some men will experience addictions to work, gambling, computer games, sexual activity, sports, television, or any number of outlets that ultimately serve to deflect a man's attention away from the content and quality of his inner, emotional life.

Another problem area detailed in recent clinical reports on men is depression (Cochran, 2001; Cochran & Rabinowitz, 2000). Many men, after experiencing loss, react by plunging into a depressive episode (Cochran & Rabinowitz, 1996). In fact, several recent popular and professional reports have drawn attention to the problem of undiagnosed and untreated depression in men (e.g., Pollack, 1998; Real, 1997). Because many men may use alcohol, other mood-altering substances, and other compulsive or addictive behaviors to medicate themselves, the problem of underlying depression for many men who seek the services of a psychotherapist must be addressed.

At the extremes of depression lie difficulties associated with suicide and homicide. Given a tendency toward action and externalization, men are much more prone to aggressive acting out of their depressed mood. This tendency may lie, in part, at the root of empirical findings indicating that suicide is a significant mortality risk for depressed men (Moscicki, 1997). This risk rises dramatically with increasing age (Kennedy, Metz, & Lowinger, 1995). In addition to suicide, homicide is associated more frequently with men than with women. Homicide, too, often occurs in conjunction with a depressive episode. Careful assessment of the risk of both suicide and homicide is warranted when working with depressed men.

Concerns related to identity may bring a man to therapy (Lazur, 1987). Career and work concerns connected to the meaning of work in a man's life may precipitate discontent with a chosen career direction. Other elements of identity conflicts may include concerns about sexual orientation, relationships with one's family of origin, relationships with friends, and choice of lifestyle.

In contrast to empirical findings on the problems of men, clinical case reports reveal a broader and more complex array of psychological problems with which men may struggle. Psychotherapists who work with men will benefit from a conceptual scheme that incorporates many elements of men's experience to adequately understand this diverse array of presenting concerns. Such a conceptual scheme will also equip psychotherapists as they prepare to intervene with male clients.

CONCEPTUALIZING THE PSYCHOLOGICAL PROBLEMS OF MEN

Is there a conceptual framework that draws together these seemingly disparate psychological difficulties of men? Men experiencing these typical problems have lost their ability to balance their inner emotional lives with the demands of culture, family, and loved ones. An adequate conceptual understanding must balance sensitivity for the inner lives of men with recognition of the challenges presented to most men by American culture's traditional notions of masculinity.

Many of the difficulties men experience may be conceptualized by examining four psychological dimensions or dynamics. These dimensions of male psychological conflict emerge from an integration of two important viewpoints informing the psychology of men: the psychodynamic developmental and gender role strain viewpoints. The first dimension is related to conflicts regarding dependence that for many men often lead to difficulties in interpersonal relationships. A second involves problems resulting from internalized cultural prohibitions around emotionality in men in general and against grief and loss in particular. The third is related to the often-problematic construction of a masculine-specific self-structure or gender role identity. The fourth is derived from a masculine tendency for "doing" and a discomfort with "being" that may lead a man away from intimate knowledge of his and others' deeper inner worlds. We believe that viewing men's presenting difficulties through these lenses enhances therapist sensitivity and empathy and provides a firm foundation on which to build treatment plans.

The Pull of Dependence

A significant component of men's conflict in interpersonal relationships is rooted in the frustration of basic dependency needs the male infant may experience in his relationships with his mother and other caretakers (e.g., Chodorow, 1999; Pollack, 1995b). This relational discontinuity, the pushing from the maternal relational orbit, is inevitable in light of our culture's child-rearing practices. Mothers and fathers have been exposed to many problematic and conflicted expectations about masculine gender role behavior. They naturally and innocently bring these attitudes and values to the child-rearing task. These attitudes, values, and behavioral expectations take shape in the interpersonal milieu of the family and are transmitted to the young boy through child-rearing practices.

One child-rearing practice shaped by our cultural values is a tendency to push boys away from connection and toward independence and autonomy. This frequently results in a preference for self-definition through autonomous, motor-minded activity. However, this tendency to push boys away from connection at early ages can create powerful conflicts regarding intimacy and relatedness. How many times are a young boy's needs for connection, soothing, and dependency frustrated in service of conformity to basic child-rearing norms that reinforce the gender role norms that are prevalent in our culture?

At preverbal levels young boys may thus experience and internalize powerful conflicts around their natural dependency needs in interpersonal relationships. This is frequently manifested in the adult man by a difficulty with commitment in relationships, a tendency to pull away from emotionality or intimacy, and a dread or fear of being engulfed or of "losing" oneself in a relationship. Boys and men develop a "defensive autonomy" (Pollack, 1995b) to protect themselves against the emergence of these relational anxieties and conflicts.

To illustrate, we introduce the case of Bill, age 30 and single, who requested therapy after being asked to move out of his cohabiting relationship with his partner Anne. After a 10-month courtship they had decided to live together and had been sharing a house for the last 2 years. They shared many common values, and Bill described to his therapist how he perceived them as being very happy together. Bill and Anne each had professional jobs, and they enjoyed a comfortable living.

As Bill's sessions unfolded, though, he described a "dance" he and Anne would perform in which she would make a request for deeper commitment to the relationship. This was often in the form of planning more quality time together or, ultimately, asking for a commitment to marriage. In response to these bids for greater commitment Bill would either avoid commitment altogether or would buy time by saying he would "have to think about it." Finally, Anne's frustration outweighed her own commitment to the relationship, and she asked him to move out of their home.

In therapy, Bill had a hard time explaining his behavior from a rational framework, as illustrated by this short exchange with the therapist.

> **Bill:** I don't know why I couldn't commit. She was everything I wanted in a woman. I don't get it.
>
> **Therapist:** You feel regret now about how you pulled away.
>
> **Bill:** I feel terrible. I wish I could have made the commitment. It was like something in me felt repelled, like I was going to suffocate if I let her get any closer. I didn't know how to tell her how I felt because I didn't understand it myself. It scared me.

Bill's situation is a common one for many men seen by psychotherapists for help with relationship problems. When asked for greater involvement, commitment, or to demonstrate their love or caring, some men simply draw a blank. They are at a loss as to how to respond to such a basic, elemental relational situation. Frequently, men's loss of voice in this situation is felt as withholding or rejecting by their partners. This, then, leads to increased frustration and disappointment with the relationship for both partners. Out of frustration, a man may thus be referred for therapeutic consultation.

The roots of this dilemma lie deep for many men. Basic ambivalence around dependence and intimacy often lies at the heart of this dilemma. This ambivalence is played out in a relational context that recapitulates the earliest experiences of dependency and relational holding with the mother and father. Adult intimacy is often associated with vulnerability and, ultimately, with disconnection as the man unconsciously remembers his connection, then disconnection, with his earliest love object. The "blank" that many men draw when asked for deeper relational commitment is simply the present-day enactment of this fundamental relational dilemma.

Internal Prohibitions on Grief and Sadness

A second area of conflict for men involves the expression of emotion in general and the experience and expression of grief and sadness in particular (e.g., Cochran & Rabinowitz, 1996). From an early age, little boys are presented with both overt and covert messages suggesting they suppress their emotional experience and their expression of emotions. "Crybaby," "keep a stiff upper lip," and "gut it out" are but a few of the admonitions given young boys to deny, disavow, and suppress outward expression of their emotions of sadness or vulnerability.

One consequence of the internalization of such admonitions regarding emotionality is the creation of powerful, often unconscious, internal prohibitions against the experience and expression of such feelings. This is especially problematic in light of the fact that young boys experience, as do young girls, losses and sadness from birth onward. Just as girls are often perceived as being more comfortable with these emotions, boys are often frightened of them. As a result, boys frequently dissociate themselves from these emotions and repress them deep into hidden realms of their inner lives.

Such repression creates conditions that invite self-medication and acting out to relieve the discomfort caused when these emotions threaten to break through into consciousness. Perhaps it is in this dynamic that we can understand why so many men experience alcohol and substance abuse problems and tend to distract or act out many of their emotions in benign as well as destructive ways. Here, too, is one of the important elements of the deepening model of psychotherapy with men, namely, that the unavoidable, inevitable experiences of loss that many men experience and that many men repress and deny must be uncovered in the psychotherapeutic situation and addressed directly.

Consider the case of John, age 34 and never married, who sought therapy to address his feelings of boredom and lack of motivation for his work. He had been employed as an assistant professor for 2 years and was experiencing serious work inhibitions. He felt uninspired and bored in his classroom teaching, writing, and work with students. As he described his situation to his therapist, he began talking about his childhood and experiences as a boy growing up in his family.

John's father was a practicing alcoholic who was away from the home much of the time when John was a boy. His mother was a grade school teacher who overfunctioned in this role as well as in the role of homemaker. He had a sister who was 2 years younger. John recalled a great deal of conflict in his relationship with his sister and his mother. He recalled being the brunt of many "man jokes" and being criticized in most of his activities by his mother and sister. Adding insult to injury is that he felt little support from his father, who was hardly ever home.

As a result of this family-of-origin experience John felt he had never developed a healthy, positive sense of himself in general and as a man in particular. He longed for a more positive childhood and at the same time would chide himself for "crying over spilled milk." In discussing these feelings with his therapist John would simply dismiss his longing by saying it was "in the past" and that he should "just get over it."

John: I feel like a big whiner. Plenty of people have had rougher childhoods. No one hit me or abused me.

Therapist: Maybe no one hit you, but you feel like you missed out on something important when you were younger.

John: What do you mean I missed out? What am I missing? You mean like my father?

Therapist: Does that fit for you?

John: I sure wish he had been more there for me. Living with my mom and my sister was pretty brutal at times. I guess those are the breaks.

(Pause)

Therapist: You're doing it again.

John: Doing what again?

Therapist: Trying to rationalize your way out of the feelings you have of missing your dad. You're pulling away from looking at your sadness about this.

John: I know. I just don't like to admit it to myself. I keep thinking I can redefine myself and get on with my life without acknowledging his absence.

Therapist: That doesn't seem to be working very well. You still get down on yourself.

John: I wish I could just let out all this damn emotion and be done with it. I want to feel free. I want to move on.

John's experience is not unusual. Many men who were born and raised by the post-World War II generation were reared in a milieu that stressed traditional gender roles. For the fathers, this meant being good providers. Being a good provider often meant being away from the home for much of the time. John's situation was complicated by negative interactions with the women in his family, who did not support him emotionally and who were highly critical of him. As a result, John left home with a poorly defined sense of self, highly negative associations about his masculinity, and a pattern of negative interactions with women.

John's emotional life during these years was stifled, dissociated, and repressed. His longings for connection with his father, his needs for support of his own growing interests, and his poor interpersonal experiences with women left him deeply wounded and sad. As he made his way through secondary school and then college he began to be acknowledged for his sharp intellect and his biting wit. This carried him until he was faced with the self-activation required of him as an assistant professor. As a result of this activation, his repressed sadness and longing for more intimate and meaningful connection broke through into consciousness, overwhelming him with grief that he was unaccustomed to managing.

Masculine-Specific Self-Structures

A third conflict zone for many men is related to the acquisition of masculine-specific elements of a gender role that have proved maladaptive or outlived their usefulness. The construction of gender is just one aspect of a man's identity. To be sure, it is a central component for most men and, if asked, many men will have a great deal to say about what it means for them to "be a man." However, there are aspects of the traditional masculine gender role, as embodied in our culture's media images and cultural narratives, that are problematic for many men.

Several social scientists have outlined the underlying elements of problematic masculinity in our culture. For example, David and Brannon (1976) outlined the elements of masculine-specific self-structures in their four values regarding the problematic construction of masculinity in our culture, represented as "the big wheel," "the sturdy oak," "give 'em hell," and "no sissy stuff." O'Neil, Good, and Holmes (1995) described four elements of masculine gender role strain and conflict that are prevalent in our culture: conflicts related to restrictive emotionality; problems related to restrictive sexual and affectionate behavior between men; preoccupation with success, power, and competition; and conflicts between work and family relations.

Men are influenced, to greater or lesser extents, by these values and their emotional and behavioral implications. Overall, as we examine the stereotypes of masculinity in our culture, it is easy to see how the uncritical adoption of many values or aspects of contemporary masculinity might eventually lead to problems for many men (Levant, 1995).

We now present the case of Craig, age 43 and in a committed gay relationship, who came to therapy to discuss several problems he was having both at work in his career and at home in his relationship with his partner Jim. He was referred by his company's employee assistance program (EAP) after he had sought advice on how to deal with an apparent ongoing conflict with his supervisor. Craig described his approach to things as "straight ahead." "I see what I want and I go get it," he explained to his therapist. After exploring the elements of his problem it became apparent that Craig was oblivious to the impact of his aggressive style on both his coworkers and his supervisor, who was a woman and who approached her supervisory duties through teamwork and collaboration.

The immediate incident that brought Craig to the EAP was a situation in which he had given some valuable team information to a potential customer, who had then used it to negotiate a better purchase price with a competitor in the industry. Craig's supervisor had confronted him with the negative consequences of his indiscretion and told him she expected him to change his ways of doing things or to apply to join another team in the firm. Craig's partner Jim, although sympathetic, could see the supervisor's point of view, because Jim often felt that Craig was impulsive and self-serving in their relationship.

> **Craig:** I am tired of hearing all this bullshit about me not being sensitive to other people's needs. I work hard and do what I think is right. I may have screwed up, but at least I was trying my best. I was taught that you take a stance and follow through. I'm not going to back down when things get rough.
>
> **Therapist:** You sound angry.
>
> **Craig:** My dad taught me to be strong and trust my instincts. All this corporate sensitivity to how others feel really runs against my upbringing.
>
> **Therapist:** Your instincts seem to have gotten you into some hot water at work.
>
> **Craig:** Yeah. It happens at home, too. Jim tells me I come on too strong sometimes. I don't take his needs into consideration. That's not good. I'm not sure what I can do. The rules I learned don't seem to be working these days.

Craig's dilemma is a common one for a man who has adopted the take-charge and get-results elements of our culture's definition of masculinity. He was confused and angry. He noted the similarity between his supervisor's complaint and Jim's feedback to Craig about Craig's tendency to just take charge and not include Jim when making plans. Craig was genuinely stumped by the consequences of his actions. Craig's attitude toward and behavior of what it means to be a man conflicted with his good intentions at work and at home. It is apparent that an exploration of his masculine self-structure, made up of his gender role history and the messages he incorporated in his development as a man, will be a significant part of his therapy.

Men's Doing and Being

A fourth conflict zone that underlies many men's difficulties is a preference for "doing" and a discomfort for "being." Winnicott (1987) used the terms *being* and *doing* to describe a person's basic tendency toward activity and externally directed focus and toward a more process-oriented, contemplative, inward focus. For Winnicott, being precedes doing. Being provides a firm foundation from which an individual constructs his or her life through activities in the world. As Winnicott (1987) wrote,

> (Holding) gives the baby the opportunity to be, out of which there can arise the next things that have to do with action, doing, and being done to. Here is the basis for what gradually becomes for the infant the self-experiencing being. (p. 7)

Although each person contains elements of both of these preferences for being and doing, Winnicott felt that a being approach was more characteristic of a feminine attitude and a doing approach more characteristic of a masculine attitude. Indeed, our culture tends to emphasize the doing aspects of a boy's personality, perhaps at the expense of a firm foundation of being.

Sometimes, though, the doing approach can lead to unintended and negative consequences. The outward focus of doing is consistent with a more action-oriented approach that is preferred by many boys and men. This preference is noted on the playground as well as in the boardroom. Boys, and men, take action, they do things, and they solve problems. As an adaptive coping style this can have advantages and can yield positive results. The often-unrecognized disadvantage to such an approach is that boys and men do not focus on their inner experience or how their actions affect others. Instead, they tend to rearrange external components of their environment to achieve their goals.

Such a tendency is consistent with the action-oriented approach of the antisocial or sociopathic individual who is interested in manipulating external contingencies for the fulfillment of personal needs. At the extremes, this tendency, when coupled with a corresponding lack of superego development, results in the frank antisocial personality who manipulates, uses, and abuses others with no empathy for the suffering of those around him.

A related aspect of the doing-versus-being dilemma is that men who prefer the doing modality lose touch with their inner lives. Our inner lives form the basis of dreams, expectations, and values that give meaning to life.

Therein lie feelings and wishes from which to make connections with others. Such disconnection from one's inner life, which often parallels the many relational disconnections that boys may experience at an early age, prevents a boy or man from truly knowing himself and from acting in a genuine and authentic manner when faced with life's challenges.

This disconnection from one's inner life characterizes the case of Dave, age 37 and never married, who sought therapy after his third offense of operating a motor vehicle while intoxicated. He had been arrested while driving home from a party at a friend's house. Dave relished his reputation as the "life of the party." He had many friends and engaged in many sporting activities. Some of his activities, such as motocross racing or white-water rafting, were considered dangerous or risky.

As Dave told his story to his therapist, he described how he enjoyed "pushing himself to the limit" and how he got a thrill out of mastering dangerous situations. Although he had many friends, Dave also disclosed his frustration at not having a more permanent or serious significant relationship. He had dated a few women in college, but now, 15 years after graduation and with several failed relationships behind him, he was unhappy and worried. He began to notice the double-edged nature of his preference for "doing"—namely, as he was active and busy, racing his bicycle and going on camping excursions, he avoided close interpersonal connection with any potential partners.

> **Dave:** I've noticed that a lot of my old friends don't want to hang out with me much anymore.
>
> **Therapist:** What do you think that might be about?
>
> **David:** You're the therapist. You tell me. (Pause) Only kidding.
>
> **Therapist:** Seriously, this is your life, Dave. What do you think is going on?
>
> **Dave:** I probably have scared them off. I'm still doing the crazy stuff we used to do when we were younger. These days it seems like everyone's married or settled down.
>
> **Therapist:** How does that feel?
>
> **Dave:** It feels kind of lonely, to tell you the truth. I really do miss my friends.
>
> **Therapist:** It feels lonely. Do you think your need to do the crazy stuff, as you put it, is worth this lonely feeling?
>
> **Dave:** I'm beginning to wonder. I really feel lonely a lot of the time. I just don't have the same connections I had when I was younger.

Like many men, Dave had been socialized to be active, outgoing, and fun loving. He did not immediately perceive any particular costs to this lifestyle; however, as his sessions unfolded it became clear to both Dave and his therapist that his high-intensity, risk-taking lifestyle left him devoid of intimate interpersonal contact. He simply moved "too fast" for anyone to ever get close to him. This downside of his lifestyle became more and more apparent as he began to recognize how most of his old friends had "settled down" and were beginning to establish their own families of choice. Dave was still the fun-loving, fast-moving guy, but he was beginning to recognize the limitations that his lifestyle imposed on his efforts to fulfill his emotional needs.

Each of the cases presented in this chapter represents themes that are common for many men. Interpersonal issues, represented by the case of Bill, may take many forms. Difficulty with commitment, avoidance of intimacy, diminished sexual desire, and frequent arguments, are but a few of the ways that interpersonal dynamics play out in the problems of men. The deepening approach to psychotherapy with men emphasizes the underlying conflict around dependency that leads to these multiple interpersonal issues.

Masculine prohibitions related to emotionality, grief, loss, and sadness can result in an emotionally desolate landscape on the surface for many men. Underneath this calm exterior, however, may lie many unresolved losses and a deep well of sadness. As in the case of John, this deeper emotional material broke through as he entered a professional role and was faced with defining his "true self" in his workplace. He was forced to articulate a line of research, to make choices about how he spent his time, and to create new courses based on his own interests. The challenge activated in John a powerful internalized sense of loss and neglect associated with his true self. This emotional tone had its origins in a childhood in which he received little support for his own unique ideas or aspirations.

The problematic construction of masculine-specific self-structures, represented by the case of Craig, is frequently a central component in psychotherapy with men. Increasingly, men are recognizing the impossible demands imposed by our culture and, by extension, by the important people in their lives. Many men in treatment frequently report contradictory and inconsistent expectations. Men recognize the difficulty of being sensitive yet strong, of being in control yet spontaneous, of being a good father yet a good provider. Of course, none of these values are inherently mutually exclusive yet, more and more, men are recognizing the maladaptive and costly nature of many of these masculine values inherent in our culture.

The spectrum of externalizing defenses, the "doing" way, manifested through dangerous, reckless, thrill-seeking behavior, represents the male tendency for doing as opposed to being. This can result in relatively more socially acceptable problems such as workaholism or other compulsive activities. It can also, as in Dave's case, result in more dangerous compulsive activities that include reckless thrill seeking, sexual promiscuity, and episodes of alcohol and substance abuse meant to numb an inner state that may threaten to emerge in the absence of such thrill-seeking activities as outlets.

DISCOVERING A PORTAL: OPENING MEN TO THE DEEPENING PROCESS

In any journey, there is a beginning point. The four psychological conflict zones described in this chapter provide the signposts for both the therapist and client as they navigate the terrain encountered in the deepening process. The concept of a portal to the deepening process is based on the idea that most men do not readily or easily reveal their inner worlds or emotions to a psychotherapist. This is not to be interpreted as an indication that no inner world exists, merely that gender role–related restrictions and prohibitions have accumulated that often render this inner world inaccessible. It is through the portal that the therapist and the male client gain access to this rich inner world. The portal is the window to entry, the pivotal point from which the deepening process unfolds.

Identifying a Portal

What we are calling the *portal* has a connection to what other writers on short-term psychotherapy have called a *central* or *focal* conflict (e.g., Davanloo, 1980; Malan, 1976; Mann, 1973; Sifneos, 1987; Strupp & Binder, 1984). We view the portal as both a way to organize thematic elements in the male client's narrative as well as an entry or key to the deeper, emotional elements of the client's inner psychological life. The portal is a constellation of images, words, thematic elements, emotional associations, and bodily sensations. It is a holistic organizing principle. It is, therefore, much more than simply a "theme" or a "focus."

The portal is identified through empathic listening as the male client tells his story. In any psychotherapeutic encounter, the therapist listens and responds to material presented by the client. In the deepening process, the psychotherapist listens for elements of the story that signify emotional association. For example, a client may be catapulted into treatment after the end of an intimate relationship. The portal material will, most likely, be organized around themes of rejection, loss, or inadequacy as a partner. In another instance, a client may seek treatment after a failure experience in the world of work. In this situation, the portal material will most likely be organized around themes of failure, incompetence, or inadequacy.

As we have noted in other writings, for many men loss experiences are often core elements in both developmental narratives as well as precipitating events that might prompt a man to seek psychotherapy (Cochran & Rabinowitz, 1996). In line with this, grief and loss themes often emerge as a portal to the deepening process.

A key to locating the portal is the capacity of the therapist to listen carefully to those elements of the client's story that have significant emotional resonance. This can be accomplished not only by careful, empathic attunement but also by intuitive as well as countertransferential modes. Empathy provides the most direct means by which the therapist and client can locate the portal. Intuitive listening may illuminate an image or seeming random association to the therapist. Such material and response may well point the way to the portal. In addition, countertransference reactions that are based on similar life experiences or woundings can also serve as a means of locating the portal.

Wounds as a Portal to the Deepening Process

What we call *woundings* challenge a man's basic sense of self. Some have called this experience *narcissistic wounding*. In addition to these kinds of wounds, life serves up many experiences that may be felt as wounding simply because they are painful. Deaths of family and friends, the inevitable confrontation with aging and physical decline, or the reconciliation of one's life dreams with reality's limitations are often felt as wounds to men. In conjunction with cultural prohibitions of the experience and expression of sadness and grief, these normative life experiences often trigger intense emotional conflict for many men and often are an important portal location.

Most, if not all, problems that men present to a psychotherapist have an element of wounding. *Wounding* here refers to the nature of the experience that has precipitated a visit to the therapist. Interpersonal conflict and rejection, failure experiences, and frustrations with not meeting expectations of life all can be construed as wounding experiences for many men.

The wounding nature of these experiences is based on the assumption that the particular experience brings to awareness for the man shortcomings or perceived failures to live up to his or his culture's masculine ideals. Such perceived shortcomings are felt as a failure and as such are experienced as a wound to the ego or sense of self.

A rejection in an intimate relationship has an obvious element of wounding. The man who is rejected often enters therapy feeling confused, hurt, angry, and unable to completely understand what may have gone wrong. The man's sense of adequacy as a partner, both sexual and social, has been challenged. His view of himself must be reconciled with his partner's view of himself. The realignment of self-perception and another's perception is frequently a painful one for many men.

Failure at work is a similar wounding. A man who is laid off from his job or who is fired experiences a sense of failure and inadequacy. A process of realignment, similar to that which occurs in the rejection in an intimate relationship, occurs in which the man must reconcile his own perceptions with another's perceptions. In addition, his identity as a provider is challenged.

Using the Portal to Facilitate Deepening

Identifying a portal is a key element in the deepening process. By listening and identifying the specific nature of the portal the therapist can begin to incorporate elements of the portal into the ongoing therapist–client interaction. Choice of word, identification of meaningful body language, and verbalization of significant emotional content all provide means for the therapist to use the portal to facilitate access to deeper levels of communication with the client. Thus emerges a process of associations, a shared experience of discovery, and a deepening experience of intimacy as the deepening process unfolds.

The therapist can use verbal content to make the portal explicit to the client. For example, a therapist may verbally track and highlight the word *stupid* with a client who is struggling with being terminated from a job and who keeps referring to himself and his actions as *stupid*. A therapist may actively respond to the words "I don't know what to do—I'm just lost" with a client who has been rejected in an intimate relationship and is attempting to put his life back in order.

Emotional content may also often provide direction to locating the portal for a man. A man may discuss his anger at being passed over for an important promotion at work. The therapist might note this and ask him to reflect on the meaning of this anger for the man and his life. A man experiencing intense anxiety as he discusses conflicting feelings of whether to make a deeper commitment to a relationship might be asked to give voice to the concerns that the anxiety might signify.

An additional means of locating the portal to the deepening process is through the identification of specific body language. A man may sit forward with his brow furrowed and a scowl on his face as he discusses his frustration with his current employment situation. The therapist may ask him to notice his posture and to reflect on the meaning of his facial expression. The therapist may further request the client to verbalize what his expression might be intended to convey. Tears may pool in a man's eyes as he discusses the death of his father with his therapist. His therapist may make note of this to the man and ask what his tears "might be saying if they could talk."

In each of these situations, the important element for the deepening process is for the therapist to be attuned to the convergence of emotion, body, and content and to explore this conjunction as a potential portal. Often it is only after exploring the conjunction that the portal will be fully revealed. It is through this exploration of this salient material that the deepening process is carried forward. The portal is the entry point to the deeper levels of connection between and among the elements of the man's presenting concerns and their meaning in his life.

A MULTIDIMENSIONAL CONCEPTUAL FRAMEWORK

The deepening approach to psychotherapy described here outlines a perspective for understanding the problems men bring to their therapists. Using the interacting, overlapping dimensions of four psychological conflict zones in conjunction with locating a portal to deeper exploration and understanding of the male client's psychological difficulties offers a conceptual model for therapists to work with their male clients.

The model described here comprises four interacting, overlapping dimensions of male psychological experience. The clinical use of these dimensions involves combining them in a synergistic manner that merges the male client's psychological history, formative experiences, cultural upbringing, and current functioning. The portal focuses the client and therapist on the elements of the client's life that will serve as the window into deeper, more integrative levels of his psychological functioning. Together, they provide a framework for conceptualizing male psychological difficulties and intervening in these difficulties from the deepening perspective.

Multiple conflict zones are apparent in the case of Gerald, age 29, who sought consultation with a therapist after he and his spouse Sarah had decided to discontinue marital counseling. Gerald, Sarah, and their couples therapist had concluded that until Gerald made some decisions about his level of commitment to the marriage and his willingness to work on joint issues that couples counseling would be of limited benefit. In the dialogue that follows, Gerald outlines the problem areas that he perceives in his relationship with Sarah as he meets with a new therapist for an initial consultation.

> **Gerald:** We don't seem to agree on much at all, especially when it comes to how we spend our time together.
>
> **Therapist:** What do you mean?
>
> **Gerald:** Well, she wants to just sit at home on the couch and rent a movie and make some popcorn. I just get real edgy and feel claustrophobic when we do that. I can't stand it, really. I would prefer to do something.
>
> **Therapist:** You get edgy and claustrophobic?
>
> **Gerald:** Yeah. Edgy. I don't know. I can't explain it very well, but I just get real uncomfortable. And Sarah can pick right up on it, then she gets frustrated and hurt, and then we usually just get into a fight.
>
> **Therapist:** You said you get real uncomfortable?
>
> **Gerald:** Yeah, it's just an anxious feeling. Like I want to sit down and have a nice evening, but then like I don't. I feel like I just want to leave and go drive around in my car or something.
>
> **Therapist:** What do you think would happen if you were to sit down with your wife and eat some popcorn and watch a movie?
>
> **Gerald:** I don't know, but I just haven't felt like being close or intimate with her lately. I just don't feel very warm. I guess I would have to level with her about how I'm having so many second thoughts about our marriage and how I don't really want to be with her. Ugh. This makes me feel uneasy just talking about it.

Therapist: Uneasy? What do you feel the uneasiness is telling you?

Gerald: I feel like I'll get pinned down, like I'll have to say what I really feel and own up to it. And the fact is that I just don't know if I'm in love with Sarah any more. And I think that would just devastate her. I don't know if she could take it.

How are the conflict zones illustrated in this clinical example? We might view a major element of Gerald's presenting conflict to be associated with the first psychological dimension: conflicts regarding dependence. Gerald is straightforward about his hesitation and second thoughts regarding his marriage and his relationship with Sarah. We might expect that this conflict would have significant emotional and historical underpinnings that could be further explored. Yet he is stuck in a position of not having brought his feelings out in the open with Sarah, for fear of how she might react and his concern that she would not be able to "take it." This reveals his own ambivalence and projection of his own dependency conflicts onto Sarah. Further exploration might help Gerald to integrate these feelings and examine his own feelings of depending on Sarah and his own fears of what would happen if he were honest with her about his feelings.

The second psychological dimension, prohibitions against emotion in general and sadness in particular, is illustrated by Gerald's avoidance of honesty with Sarah and his holding back of his real emotional experience with her. At this point we do not know the roots of this particular conflict, but we wonder how they might be rooted in Gerald's own gender-based restrictions on emotional expression in the context of an intimate relationship.

The third psychological dimension, a problematic masculine-specific self-structure, could be reflected in Gerald's overall inhibition of emotional expression with Sarah and with his tendency to escape intimacy through involvement in a solitary activity. Restrictive emotionality in men and avoidance of intimacy and emotional expression have been found to be common themes of male psychological conflict.

The final psychological dimension, comfort with doing and discomfort with being, is clearly illustrated by Gerald's anxiety and discomfort with the possibility of "just sitting" with Sarah on the couch and enjoying a movie together. His fantasy of escape involves going and driving around in his car, clearly a "doing" mode as opposed to a "being" mode. What might be the threat associated with "just being" for Gerald? How does the escape into an apparently solitary "doing" activity serve him?

One portal to Gerald's inner life may be found in one of several possible locations. First, the anxious feeling that Gerald gets when he thinks about sitting down with his spouse on the couch and watching a movie represents a bodily manifestation of what appears to be a core conflict for Gerald. Further exploration of this feeling on both the cognitive as well as the emotional and physical levels may reveal the portal to Gerald's deeper ambivalence about intimacy and connection. Another portal could be discovered by following the feeling of being "pinned down" and how Gerald feels he might have to be honest with Sarah about his true feelings. Through any of these portals Gerald and his therapist will discover his authentic, true feelings about himself and his life.

SUMMARY

In this chapter we have outlined a multidimensional perspective on how to assess a variety of male presenting problems, understand typical zones of male conflict, and begin to intervene with the men who come to the therapy. We believe that clinicians who can see men's presenting concerns through the lenses of conflicts around dependence in relationships; internalized cultural prohibitions around emotionality, and against grief and loss in particular; the problematic construction of a masculine-specific self-structure or gender role identity; and the masculine tendency for "doing" and discomfort with "being" will enhance sensitivity and empathy and provide a firm foundation on which to build treatment plans and intervene with male clients. By helping a man find the portal that has been exposed by life's woundings, the therapist and the male client can begin to access an often-hidden inner emotional world.

2

THEORETICAL FOUNDATIONS FOR DEEPENING PSYCHOTHERAPY WITH MEN

We refer to them as "fallen heroes," not because they ultimately failed in their quests, but because "falling" is an inevitable part of being a real man. In contrast, we believe that the predicament of many men today is precisely due to their inability to face their limitations—they seek to deny death and the inevitability of loss. (Betcher & Pollack, 1993, p. 21)

The rationale for deepening psychotherapy with men is based on recognition of the important intersection of two major conceptual models that have informed the field of psychology of men (as well as many other disciplines) over these past 30 years. These two lines of thought are drawn from two distinct and, at times, seemingly incompatible intellectual and theoretical traditions: the psychoanalytic developmental viewpoint and the gender role strain viewpoint. Theoreticians and practitioners informed from each perspective have shown that they each have a great deal to offer the understanding of why men are the way they are, how men experience psychological distress, and the problems that men bring to psychotherapy.

However, much of the recent work in the area of the psychology of men has been based on a belief that these two traditions are often incompatible or contradictory, frequently resulting in devaluation or dismissal of one by the other. Social constructionist theorists, representing the gender role strain model, and identity theorists, representing the psychoanalytic developmental model, often posture as if they are at odds with one another. We believe that an approach to psychotherapy that integrates these two perspectives will provide deeper, richer, and more complex conceptualizations of men and the problems that men face in their lives.

Integrating the psychoanalytic developmental viewpoint with the gender role strain viewpoint may at first seem like trying to mix water and oil. The psychoanalytic developmental viewpoint has focused mainly on inner experience and early childhood development, whereas the gender role strain viewpoint has concentrated mainly on the external world of society and how cultural trends mold and shape important aspects of behavior. More specifically, the psychoanalytic developmental viewpoint has examined how young boys and girls forge an identity, including a gender identity, and how this identity is shaped, expressed, and modified over the life span. The gender role strain viewpoint has examined how cultural practices, often based on economic factors and family structure, determine individual constructions of gender and how these external forces impinge on this individual fashioning of a gendered self.

In spite of these apparent divergences, we feel that the merging of these two traditions offers the optimal means by which to more fully understand men's lives. Each, in isolation, describes only a limited aspect of men's (and women's, for that matter) experience. Like the ancient depictions of the yin and yang symbols, combining these two traditions results in a holistic, comprehensive way of understanding men. Together, these perspectives more completely convey the complexity and diversity of the male experience and the meaning of masculinity for men. Together they also provide a means for psychotherapists to develop a better understanding of the psychological aspects of men's lives and to gain an empathic conceptual basis from which to formulate interventions to help their male clients.

In this chapter we outline some of the important theoretical advances each of these viewpoints have contributed to our understanding of the psychology of men, and we articulate important areas of convergence of these viewpoints. It is from struggling with this convergence in an effort to integrate the individual and the cultural that we have come to appreciate how each perspective enriches the other.

PSYCHOANALYTIC FORMULATIONS

Although Freud, Horney, Adler, and many other early psychoanalytic pioneers addressed in various ways important differences in the psychological functioning of men and women, it was object relations theory that truly laid the groundwork for a gender-informed psychological understanding of men and women. The British school of object relations, including Klein, Fairbairn and, later, Bowlby, Winnicott, and Guntrip, all emphasized important aspects of the infant child's relationship with the mother and father. Later, American psychoanalysts Mahler, Kohut, and Kernberg provided important refinements and elaboration on these ideas. Chodorow integrated the object relations perspective with a socio-anthropological analysis of how family structures shape and influence (dare we say *determine*) women's and men's psychological development. Most recently, Pollack has extended Chodorow's important theoretical advances and related them specifically to the psychological and emotional development of boys and men.

The First Wave: British Object Relations Theory

Optimal navigation of early developmental tasks, including biological separation from the mother, adaptation to the extra-uterine environment, and the beginning development of a sense of self that heralds the infant's "psychological birth" are dependent on the provision of a "good-enough mothering" relationship for the developing child. This quality of good-enough mothering consists of both physical "handling" and emotional "holding" of the infant (Winnicott, 1965a, 1965b). Good-enough mothering is comfortable with dependence and supports the child's growing independence, thereby laying down the capacity for relational interdependence in the developing child. It is during this stage of development that

> the infant is dependent to a high degree on the capacity of the mother or the mother-substitute to adapt to the infant's needs, a feat which she manages only by an identification with the infant that arises out of her attitude of devotion. (Winnicott, 1965a, p. 104)

Bowlby's (1988) attachment model of human development further underscores how continuities and discontinuities in this earliest relationship with the mother provide the basis for expectations and experiences in later interpersonal relationships. In addition, these continuities and discontinuities may relate specifically to the later development of psychological symptoms and problems in living. Bowlby's perspective asserts the importance of the emotional quality of the child's tie to the mother in those earliest, preverbal months and years of existence.

Although there are subtle variations in these two thinkers' themes, they and other object relations theorists emphasize the importance of normative dependency as a critical aspect of the developing child's experience. The child enters the world profoundly dependent on his (or her) caretakers for survival. In the context of the biologically programmed unfolding of the capacity for upright locomotion and speech and the provision of good-enough mothering, the originally dependent child develops into an individual in his or her own right. Emphasizing this complex interplay of nature and nurture, Winnicott (1965a, p. 19) wrote that "development is a matter of the inheritance of a maturational process and of the accumulation of living experiences; this development does not occur, however, except in a facilitating environment."

The Second Wave: Separation, Individuation, and the Self

In the United States over the past 30 years several important theoretical developments have built on these early ideas of the British object relations theorists. These refinements and extensions of the earlier object relations theories have been developed through psychoanalytically informed infant observation studies pioneered by Mahler and her colleagues and by retrospective reconstruction of early childhood experiences derived from material reported by analysands in psychoanalytic treatment. The result of this work is an increased specificity of the developmental tasks of these early years of life.

Mahler's separation–individuation theory has mainly confirmed the propositions of the British object relations theorists. Mahler and her colleagues (e.g., Mahler, Pine, & Bergman, 1975) have outlined the important stages an infant must negotiate in the development of a healthy sense of self. Like the British object relations theorists, Mahler described the infant's initial dependence on the mother. She used the terms *autistic* and *symbiotic* to characterize what is thought to be the nature of the child's inner self and object representations at this early stage of development.

From this initial stage of self–object merger and dependence the child begins to gradually explore his or her environment and to move further away from the mother. Catalyzed by the advent of upright locomotion and increased interest in his environment, the child begins to develop an increased sense of mother and father as distinct from himself in his inner mental representation. Through an oscillating process of movement away from (practicing) and then movement back toward (rapprochement) the mother and other caretakers, the developing child gradually establishes emotional and representational separation and develops an increased sense of individuality (individuation), including a gendered individuality.

This model emphasizes the importance, as did the British object relations theorists, of initial attachment as well as the ongoing, reciprocally influencing interaction between the mother and child. Many psychoanalytic theorists who have built on Mahler's discoveries have confirmed the general outlines of this separation–individuation process and its dramatic impact on the ultimate development of a stable sense of self and the capacity for emotional health (e.g., Kernberg, 1985a, 1985b; Masterson, 1981; Rinsley, 1989).

This separation–individuation perspective also suggests an important role for the father (or surrogate father) in a young boy's development. As a boy begins to move from the intensity and exclusivity of the maternal relational orbit, the father is often present to facilitate this emergence. The father is often the first external object who embodies—literally, behaviorally, and symbolically—cultural values around masculinity and the male gender role. Because the father exists as a separate, distinct figure he often assists the developing child as he begins to draw distinctions between "me" and "not me" in his movement out of the maternal orbit. As Mahler et al. (1975, p. 215) pointed out, "We have the impression that identification with the father or possibly with an older brother facilitates a rather early beginning of the boy's gender identity."

Mahler's insights have extended those of the earlier object relations theorists in that she has described the oscillation of separation of the infant from the mother and early caretakers with the return, or rapprochement, for emotional support to assuage separation anxiety. Mahler's discoveries have provided added detail to the particularly fateful rapprochement period of development. Her studies have confirmed many observations about young boys during this phase of development, including the observation that young boys are active, "motor-minded," and take great pleasure in motor functioning. Mahler (1975, p. 214) noted that "the little boy, in the rapprochement subphase, also shows soberness and increased hypersensitivity about his separateness from his mother, (and) also pursues his own motor and perceptual–cognitive activities with more or less confident tenacity."

Criticisms have been leveled against this separation–individuation model of development because it is perceived to place separation or autonomy at the apex of psychological development and to devalue dependence and relatedness. In general, we do not agree with this particular criticism. Mahler and her colleagues emphasized the importance of both relatedness and separateness and defined psychological and emotional health as the capacity for both. Indeed, Mahler's paradigm is a dialectical one that describes a lifelong oscillation of connection and disconnection in human growth and development. Such dialectic, it seems, more accurately describes the nuance, the give-and-take of emotional and relational development, through the life span. *Separation* in this model refers not to physical independence or autonomy but to the intrapsychic separation of the self-representation from the maternal (object) representation. It is both a cognitive as well as an emotional process that is characterized by the capacity to tolerate increasing physical separation and separation anxiety from the mother and to comprehend the existence and persistence of the internal maternal object in spite of her physical absence.

As a complement to Mahler's theories of separation and individuation, Kernberg (1985a), Kohut (1977, 1984), Masterson (1981), Rinsley (1989), and others have outlined the development of the self and disorders of the self resulting from a breakdown of these normative developmental processes. These advances represent an intermingling of the object relations paradigms with the separation–individuation paradigms. Kohut, like advocates of both the object relations perspective and the separation–individuation perspective, emphasizes the critical importance of the developing child's relationships with the mother, father, and early childhood caretakers. In his model, a "bipolar self" ultimately develops from experiences of support and validation (empathic responsiveness) as the child gradually expresses a creative, unique self. These experiences of support and validation are viewed as empathic "holding" in the child's early relationships with both mother and father. Such empathic holding (good-enough mothering?) provides the foundation for the coalescence of a cohesive self-structure based on internalized functions that both the mother and the father provide. Echoing Winnicott and Mahler, Kohut (1977, p. 85) wrote, "The child that is to survive psychologically is born into an empathic–responsive human milieu (of self-objects) just as he is born into an atmosphere that contains an optimal amount of oxygen if he is to survive physically."

According to Kohut, gross, consistent failure of empathic holding results in fragmentation of the self and a resulting difficulty in maintenance of adequate self-esteem and compromised capacity for relatedness with others. Kohut viewed this deviation from optimal development as resulting in a basic disturbance of self-structures (compensatory and defensive structures) that produce characteristic interpersonal patterns and emotional responses.

The separation–individuation and self psychology theorists teach that individual identity, that sense of self that is composed of a gendered component, is forged out of the complex interplay between the developing child and those other significant people who comprise the developing child's interpersonal milieu. Identity, a coherent, stable sense of self and other, is developed in the context of ongoing, intimate, emotional relationships. The quality of these relationships as they unfold over the early years of childhood has profound implications for the healthy acquisition of aspects of a gendered identity.

The Third Wave: Postfeminist Psychoanalytic Constructions

The developing child participates in the creation of a gendered self within the context of close interpersonal relationships with first the mother and father and, later, with other important persons in the child's interpersonal milieu. Such deeply personal, unique, emotionally charged relationships provide the basis for the development of the boy's conceptions of what it means to be a boy and later inform his notions of what it means to be a man. These formative relational templates are transmitted by the mother and the father, who each have developed their own unique, idiosyncratic notions about the meaning of gender that are derived from their own individual development.

Chodorow (1978) analyzed the implications of women's mothering for the development of gender identity in boys and girls. She emphasized the interpersonal transmission of cultural values pertaining to gender in the context of the maternal relationship:

> The different length and quality of the pre-oedipal period in boys and girls are rooted in women's mothering, specifically in the fact that a mother is of the same gender as her daughter and of a different gender from her son. This leads to her experiencing and treating them differently. (p. 98)

Using developmental object relations formulations Chodorow argued that young boys experience a gender-specific relational discontinuity in their developmental progression from attachment through separation within the mother–child dyad. In contrast to young girls, who experience connection with the mother and a joining of identity and relationship, boys join together separation and identity.

Although Chodorow's (1978) analysis clearly sketches out the complex interplay between cultural values and how their relational enactment influences basic psychological processes, Pollack (1995a, 1995b) has perhaps come closest to integrating psychoanalytic developmental insights with a gender role sensitive analysis. By extending Chodorow's (1978) analysis of the gender-specific vicissitudes of the mother–son relationship Pollack speculated about the subjective nature of young boys' experiences of differentness hypothesized by Chodorow. Might boys be pushed from connection to their mothers at an early age in conformity with our cultural values related to masculinity? Might boys further experience this ejection from the maternal orbit as a deep loss? For Pollack, such an abrupt, often premature separation experience is viewed as a

> traumatic abrogation of the early holding environment, an impingement in [boys'] development—a normative life-cycle loss—that may, later in life, leave many adult men at risk for fears of intimate connection. This traumatic experience of abandonment occurs so early in the life course that the shameful memory of the loss is likely to be deeply repressed. (1995b, p. 41)

Young boys' experience of loss of maternal holding is thought to result in a self-protective, defensive firming of ego boundaries as well as internalized conflicts related to relationships and dependency. Yet Pollack goes a step further and adds an emotional aspect to this earliest inner experience of young boys' sense of self and other when he said that this loss is "a normative male, gender-linked loss, a trauma of abandonment for boys which may show itself, later, as an adult through symptomatic behavior, characterological defense, and vulnerability to depression" (Pollack, 1998, p. 154).

This normative trauma has an important influence on a boy's developing sense of self. If this developmental trauma occurs early in the boy's life, he will experience a breakdown of empathic holding and will be vulnerable to developing narcissisticlike compensatory self-structures (Cochran & Rabinowitz, 1996; Pollack, 1995b, 2001). To the extent that such developmental trauma is normative for boys, they will emerge from this early childhood experience with a rather consistent accumulation of conflicts and defenses. Such compensatory structures are characterized, as we have seen, by firming of self–other boundaries, conflicts around dependency and relatedness, and an overvaluing of autonomy in service of preserving these structures.

Postfeminist psychoanalytic analysis of boys' and men's development has enriched our understanding of the masculine-specific strains characteristic of both normative and deviant developmental trajectories. These strains often result in what is commonly perceived as men's unique psychological characteristics: a tendency to prefer autonomy to relatedness; defensiveness about bids for intimate connection; and a deep-seated, if not unconscious, discomfort around interpersonal relatedness. Although these characteristics have often been called forth in service of criticizing men, psychotherapists must recognize their normative developmental origins and be prepared to work with them within the context of an empathic, supportive therapeutic relationship.

Conclusions From the Psychoanalytic Perspective

What, then, can we conclude from our efforts to understand male development from this psychoanalytic developmental perspective? Several conclusions that pertain specifically to the deepening approach to psychotherapy with men are warranted.

First, lessons from object relations and separation–individuation teach us that young boys enter the world in a state of complete dependence on the mother. This early relationship forms the basis of an ongoing, dialectical process of separation and reconnection with the mother. Through this oscillation, important aspects of identity are lain down. Over time, optimal psychological functioning is characterized by interdependence in interpersonal relationships, not simply defensive autonomy or dependence. Because there are important relational differences in the context of young boys' and girls' early childhood experiences, the experience of basic dependence will differ in important ways across boys and girls.

Second, the complex interplay of culture and individual development creates for boys a situation in which feelings of sadness, loss, and grief are learned to be unmanly. This learning, which is intimately intertwined with the separation–individuation process, creates conflict for the developing boy as he navigates his early experiences of attachment and separation and the inevitable loss experiences that accompany these processes. Excessive emphasis on disavowal of loss and grief may result in a compromised capacity for mourning that will affect later experiences of loss and grief.

One outcome of this learning about loss, sadness, and grief is that psychological growth for boys and men will often be played out in issues of grief and loss. Because boys' and men's experience of grief and loss is often suppressed or repressed in service to conformity with cultural expectations, natural mourning processes are truncated or aborted. Hence, psychological growth across many domains becomes a struggle to recover the memories and emotional experiences that were split off from a man's emotional life.

Third, these psychoanalytic models describe multiple, interactive processes of attachment, identification, and internalization. Through these processes, "identity" is constructed and reconstructed, in a relational context, on an ongoing, lifelong basis. Boys', as well as girls', identities are unique, privately as well as interpersonally constituted, and drawn from both emotional as well as perceptual and cognitive experiences within both parental relationships as well as relationships with important others in the developing boy's (or girl's) life.

Thus, the acquisition of masculine values and traits is a complex process that is mediated through the early childhood relationships with the mother and father. This development of masculine-specific self-structures is primarily based on the transmission of learning about gender from both the mother and the father. It is important to recognize that this learning is not just a cognitively, behaviorally, or verbally mediated process. It is heavily charged with emotional nuance. The meaning of masculinity for the young boy is always emotionally charged and joined with issues of both maternal and paternal connection, isolation, love, and rejection.

GENDER ROLE STRAIN FOUNDATIONS

For many years, a male identity development model of gender role acquisition held sway over social and behavioral scientists. This model was consistent with many early psychoanalytic conceptions of identity development. Such conceptions were usually based on stereotypes of healthy male or female development that granted superiority to the attainment of autonomy and the adoption of a heterosexual object choice. Identity in this narrow sense was viewed as the outcome or endpoint of development—something that could largely be completed—instead of a process that unfolded over the course of a life span and that was subject to ongoing revision.

The new psychology of men critiques this identity development model by offering in its place what has been termed the *gender role strain model* of the acquisition of masculine and feminine gender roles. This perspective contends that there is no essential, monolithic masculine gender role identity; rather, there exist multiple masculinities that are based on each man's appropriation of those elements of masculinity (and femininity, for that matter) that conform to his own highly personal, idiosyncratic conceptions of what it means to be a man.

Early Descriptions of Problematic Masculinity

Gender role strain models critique existing gender stereotypes by identifying those characteristics of gender roles that are thought to be exclusively the province of either males or females. Early critiques of the male gender role were relatively consistent in their analysis of the nature of the male gender role. They identified the often-contradictory, problematic features of the traditional male gender role as it was being challenged by feminist thinkers in the 1960s and early 1970s.

Goldberg (1976) identified several "impossible binds" or paradoxes that our culture imposes on men. Some of these binds included the bind to be strong and in control but to also be sensitive and responsive (the gender bind), the bind to be physical and active but also to be savvy and in command of oneself (the kinetic bind), and the bind to take risks and challenge oneself but also to care for and nurture oneself (the hero bind). Such language eloquently articulated the contradictory, paradoxical, problematic nature of the male gender role as it was embedded in late-20th-century American culture.

Fasteau (1974) and Farrell (1975) were two other early critics of the male gender role. Fasteau focused his critique around issues related mainly to men's relationships. He found that men experienced problematic messages from the media and culture in regard to relationships, sexuality, fatherhood, competition, work, and violence. All these phenomena played out in interpersonal domains, whether at work, at home, on the playing field, or in the bedroom. Farrell tended to focus most of his analysis on the impact of feminism on men's lives. He believed women's changing roles affected men's feelings of disempowerment as well as male–female interpersonal relationship dynamics. Farrell, like Goldberg and Fasteau, underscored the contradictions inherent in contemporary American culture's definitions of men and masculinity.

David and Brannon (1976) condensed these various observations about the problematic nature of the male gender role that were prevalent at the time. They distilled from them four preeminent values about masculinity that were inherent in our cultural enactments of masculinity. These four values were "the big wheel," "the sturdy oak," "give 'em hell," and "no sissy stuff." The value of being a "big wheel" is embodied in the importance of being successful, important, and in charge. The value of being "a sturdy oak" is portrayed in the masculine ideals of being tough, self-reliant, and confident. "Give 'em hell" means to be aggressive, competitive, and powerful both on the playing field and off, and "no sissy stuff" means to restrain from showing affection, emotion, or any behavior that might be construed as feminine.

Sex Role Strain

On the heels of these early critiques of the traditional male gender role, Pleck (1981) took to task those social and behavioral scientists who had subscribed to what he called the *male sex role identity* paradigm. This paradigm, as portrayed by Pleck, viewed healthy men and masculinity identity as unfolding from within. This male sex role identity paradigm portrayed men as striving to attain some ideal state of masculine identity. According to this perspective, "individuals must be fitted to traditional roles, and the problem of traditional sex roles is only that so many people fail to fit them, not the nature of the roles themselves" (Pleck, 1981, p. 4).

As an alternative, Pleck (1981) proposed the *sex role strain* paradigm, which views the male sex role identity paradigm as lacking in empirical validation and inadequate to account for the diversity of masculinities. The sex role strain paradigm proposed that it was the sex roles themselves that were problematic. Sex role strain implies the strain an individual has experienced as he tried to fit himself to various, often contradictory, cultural presentations of the male sex role. The sex role strain paradigm, unlike the sex role identity paradigm, incorporated the ambiguity and contradictory nuances articulated in the popular press.

Content of Gender Role Conflict

O'Neil and his colleagues have incorporated many of Pleck's notions about sex role strain into a research program that examined in some detail aspects of what is termed *gender role conflict*. O'Neil (1981) originally proposed six elements of male gender role conflict. These elements included restrictive emotionality; socialized control, competition, and power; homophobia; restrictive sexual and affectionate behavior; obsession with achievement and success; and health care problems. Later factor analytic inquiry (see O'Neil, Good, & Holmes, 1995) verified the existence of four discrete elements of male gender role strain: conflicts between work and family relations; restrictive emotionality; restrictive sexual and affectionate behavior between men; and success, power, and competition issues. Continued research has related these elements of masculine gender role strain to levels of psychological distress (Good et al., 1995), depression (Good & Mintz, 1990; Good & Wood, 1995), and avoidance of mental and physical health care venues (Good, Dell, & Mintz, 1989).

Beyond Gender Role Strain

Gender role strain paradigms have expanded the focus of inquiry within the psychology of men to include elements of socially constructed masculinity and the strain men experience as they attempt to fit or conform themselves to cultures' proscriptions about masculinity. The gender role strain paradigm implicitly assumes that there are a number of social roles that can generally be viewed as either masculine or feminine depending on prevailing cultural stereotypes of masculinity or femininity. Yet in today's postmodern 21st-century culture we feel that it is impossible to assign such valences to social roles in an unambiguous fashion. This creates a situation in which a wide range of social roles—some seen as masculine, some as feminine—may be incorporated into any individual's contextualized construction of his or her masculine gender role or feminine gender role.

The creation and enactment of social, including masculine or feminine, roles is a normative developmental task for all men and women. This construction begins with the earliest stages of awareness of self as distinct from others. Today's young men and women often seem more at ease adopting, then discarding, any number of social roles. Some of these roles have masculine valence, others have feminine valence. Men and women in today's culture appear capable of a relatively fluid movement between the masculine and the feminine without attaching significant importance to any particular role or whether it might be masculine or feminine. As such, concerns about what it means to be a man or a woman appear less salient.

INTEGRATING PSYCHOANALYTIC AND GENDER ROLE STRAIN FORMULATIONS

Where is the common ground between the psychoanalytic formulations of male development and the gender role strain formulations of masculinity? Several important convergences are noteworthy. Their exploration will help illuminate how, in boys' development, psychological and cultural elements interact in a continuous unfolding of an individually constituted, interpersonally related masculinity. The most significant of these convergences, we believe, are situated around issues related to the meaning of interpersonal dependence, the management of grief and loss experiences, the shaping of masculine-specific self-structures, and men's comfort with and preference for "doing" as opposed to "being."

Dependence in Boys and Men

In the developmental paradigm it is understood that both young boys as well as young girls begin their life journey in total dependence on their early caretakers, particularly the mother. Boys are dependent on these early caretakers for feeding, holding, and shelter as well as love and support. As we acknowledge this normative, universal human experience we must at the same time recognize that in American culture, dependence and its psychological meaning are often seen as problematic in the context of masculinity.

Constructions of masculinity in contemporary American culture emphasize independence, the capacity to "stand on your own two feet" and all that is associated with this particular psychological value. How does a developing boy, who is initially unaware of the way his culture devalues his dependence, negotiate this experience? Or, to state it another way, how does our culture's ambivalence about and disavowal of dependency in males become integrated into boys' and men's psychological lives?

Chodorow (1978) contended that this earliest experience of dependence on the mother has important implications for later experiences of relationships for both boys and girls. As she wrote, "it is aspects of the relationship to [the mother] that are internalized defensively; it is her care that must be consistent and reliable; it is her absence that produces anxiety" (1978, pp. 60–61). We further emphasize that this earliest relationship, characterized by dependence, longing, and (we hope) gratification, forms the basis for expectations in boys' and men's relationships with their own mothers and later with both men and women in their lives.

However, this longing and gratification that the young boy experiences are culturally devalued. In general, males are presented images and messages that they are unmanly and unhealthy if they experience gratification of dependency needs. Thus, from childhood onward, boys internalize contradictory, mixed interpretations of their experience of these important interpersonal relationships. On the one hand, they experience affirmation and gratification of dependency in their early relations with the mother and other important adults. On the other hand, they learn that such an experience is to be disavowed. The gratification of dependency is unmanly, unhealthy. Such learning occurs not only in the context of the maternal, paternal, and significant-other relationships but also in relation to peers, teachers, and several other important others in the boy's life.

In addition, such learning is laden with powerful affect. Disapproval and shame are often associated with this enactment and gratification of dependency needs. Cultural values related to men's independence are powerfully internalized by many boys, resulting in the painful disavowal of the most basic of psychological needs: the need to depend on another person for love, support, and nurturance.

The important conclusion for a psychology of men is that psychoanalytic developmental psychology emphasizes the emotional quality of the child's earliest interpersonal relationships. These earliest relationships are not just with "people" but with first a woman/mother, and later with a man/father and, later, other significant figures. Within these relationships boys experience a spectrum of powerful emotions. It is in the context of these early relationships that important learning occurs with respect to the meaning of masculinity for a young boy.

To fully understand the importance of these relationships to a growing boy's psychological development we must add the complicating impact of cultural norms, expectations, and stereotypes to the mix. We must understand and respect the manner in which each culture's norms regarding the propriety of male dependence and emotional neediness affect the both the content of what the developing boy learns about himself and others as well as how this learning is imparted. Such learning is imparted in the context of interpersonal relationships. As Chodorow (1999) observed, "Any gender-related category (man, woman, mother, father, sister, brother, femininity, masculinity) gains meaning not just from language but from personally experienced emotion and fantasy *in relation to a person connected to that label*" (p. 115, emphasis added).

As such, this learning is preverbal as well as verbal and carries emotional as well as cognitive and linguistic meaning. This learning thus creates conscious and unconscious memories and expectations of both self and other in a developing boy that are powerful forces that shape behavior throughout his life. Such learning also may result in the creation of enduring, conscious—as well as unconscious—templates of interpersonal expectations that have important implications for how a man experiences and acts in interpersonal relationships.

Negotiation of this cultural, interpersonal, and emotional crucible provides the basis for several commonly observed male difficulties in interpersonal relationships. Two of these difficulties include problems with intimacy and difficulties associated with commitment to long-term relationships. The integration of the psychodynamic developmental perspective with a gender role conflict perspective offers insight into the nature of these difficulties and provides direction to psychotherapists who are working with men who may be struggling with issues related to these difficulties.

In the therapeutic relationship the conflict about dependence manifests itself in several ways. The fact that few men even make it to a therapist reflects the avoidance by men in our culture of involving themselves in a potentially dependent relationship, even if it is for their own good. Another demonstration of this conflict results in the devaluing of the therapeutic relationship, especially early in the process. Men in the initial stages of therapy often perceive it more as an impersonal psychological "tuneup" rather than an intimate relational process. The dependence conflict may also be manifest as a perceived lack of commitment by the male client to the therapeutic endeavor.

We believe that therapists often misinterpret the casual language, the hesitancy to share, and lack of emotional expression of a man as resistance to be overcome rather than an expression of the conflicting nature of dependent urges toward the therapist and therapy.

Prohibitions Against Sadness, Grief, and Mourning

In the nexus of separation and individuation we find another convergence of the psychoanalytic developmental paradigm with the gender role strain paradigm. We, and others, believe that the optimal outcome of the separation and individuation processes described by Mahler and her colleagues is intimately related (if not tantamount) to the development of the psychological capacity to mourn. This capacity is often compromised in many men because of both masculine-specific vicissitudes of early development as well as cultural prohibitions on men's sadness. The convergence of these forces often results in interference with full awareness and acceptance of loss experiences and the accompanying grief and sadness.

As we have seen, young boys, as they grow and develop, learn important cultural values about gender-appropriate behavior in the context of their early interpersonal relationships. Gender role strain critiques have taught us that a constellation of cultural values about masculinity are organized around the prohibition of emotional awareness and expression in general and the prohibition of sadness as a mood and crying as a behavioral expression of that mood in particular. We all know that "big boys don't cry" and that little boys are often told to "shut up and quit whining; don't be a sissy." Such values, often unconsciously imparted by parents and other caretakers, profoundly shape a growing boy's interpretation of his experience of loss and grief and have a long-lasting impact on the manner by which he eventually learns to mourn his losses.

However, our cultural values around masculinity and emotionality, as they are embodied in the interpersonal relationships with the mother and father, and later with peers on the playground, are mixed at best. At times, boys may experience affirmation of their emotional reactions; at other times, they may be shamed or ridiculed. Thus, a developing boy may learn to dissociate himself from aspects of his emotional experience, specifically from any feelings of sadness. In this way, dissociation, as a defensive psychological process, compromises natural mourning that occurs as a result of the making and breaking of intimate emotional attachments to others throughout the life span.

Complications arise in the manner in which a growing boy may negotiate the depressive position. As we have noted, contradictory signals regarding sadness and mourning become internalized as powerful elements of the boy's internal psychological makeup. The holding of the (male) child in the early maternal and paternal relationships is an important element in the successful navigation of the depressive position. When this normal process of grieving is truncated and thrown off course, anger, shame, and control-oriented defenses often arise as a means of self-protection. Here, in these mixed messages around sadness and grief, many men develop powerful and ultimately problematic defenses around the complete and healthy resolution of what is in fact a normative human experience: the experience of loss and sadness that arises from the making and breaking of human bonds.

In the therapeutic relationship, issues of grief and loss and the accompanying emotional experience of sadness may be elusive or difficult to acknowledge. A male client may describe a loss experience and take a "what can I do about it now?" attitude instead of moving toward the emotional level of experiencing the loss. Similarly, a male client may minimize the impact of a loss experience, saying "it's no big deal, I can handle this." Often, when a therapist openly addresses loss and grief issues, many men find a new and rich level of emotional experience (e.g., Cochran & Rabinowitz, 1996).

Problematic Masculine-Specific Self-Structures

As a result of contemporary child-rearing practices individual psychological development is intimately intertwined with conscious and unconscious transmission of cultural values regarding masculinity and femininity.

Such learning occurs mainly in the context of relationships with early care-takers (mother and father), but it also occurs in relationships with siblings, other relatives, peers, teachers, and other people who have a formative impact on a developing boy. Because these processes occur in a context of intense, emotionally significant interpersonal relationships, aspects of masculinity and femininity are often assigned "good" and "bad" valences. Young boys, as they develop, are given mixed and incongruous messages about how important others view their masculinity. Such messages often conflict with their inner experiences of emotional need and desire. The development of a coherent sense of self with a positively valued facet of masculinity is thus a significant challenge for many boys. As boys emerge from latency and venture forth into puberty, problematic aspects of their masculinity have been well learned and suppressed, resulting in an underlying emotional tone of sadness and loss that must also be hidden from others.

These cumulative experiences that result in disavowal of self are tanta-mount to the lack of empathic holding that Kohut (1977) identified as contributing to the development of a narcissistic disorder of the self. We have speculated elsewhere (Cochran & Rabinowitz, 1996), consistent with Pollack (1995a, 1995b, 2001), that narcissistic compensatory structures are normative in boys' and men's personalities. Indeed, our current diagnostic criteria for narcissistic personality are practically universal caricatures of exaggerated masculinity. Many boys and men exhibit many of the behavior patterns and traits that are subsumed under this narcissistic-disorder category. For some, these operate merely as defenses and can be relatively contained without causing serious disruptions in relationships and work. For others, these defenses contribute to chaotic relationships; a deep sense of despair and depression; and a loss of meaning, purpose, and direction in life.

As boys begin the project of constructing masculine-specific self-structures they must balance how others view certain aspects of masculinity with their own acquisition of various aspects of masculinity. Often, others' views of masculinity conflict with inner needs, wishes, and values. A young boy who is hurt and needs a hug is sometimes admonished to stop crying and "take it like a man." Over time, such contradictory and mixed admonitions result in the creation of a facade of problematic masculine-specific self-structures designed to hide vulnerability and apparent weakness. Such self-structures include a tendency to restrict emotional awareness and expression, a tendency to distance oneself or withdraw from interpersonal connection, a discomfort with depressive feelings and corresponding expression through tears, and a tendency to show force or action when encountering a personal problem.

Problematic masculine self-structures are often the reason a man may consult a therapist. Denial of sadness and loss, retreat from intimacy, compulsive competitiveness, neglect of physical health, and other traditional masculine ways of being often have detrimental consequences to a man as well as to his relationships with those he loves. Ultimately, the creation and eventual dismantling of these self-structures must be addressed directly in any gender-sensitive psychotherapy for men.

"Doing" Versus "Being"

A common observation on playgrounds around our country is that in general boys tend to be busy "doing" while girls tend to be busy "being." Boys are often involved in competitive, active play within larger groups. Girls are often involved in smaller groups of more relational, cooperative play. These sex differences appear to persist and are thought to reflect externalizing defense styles (Gjerde, Block, & Block, 1988), distracting response styles (Nolen-Hoeksema, 1990), or externalizing ego defenses (Levit, 1991).

Winnicott (1988) emphasized the importance of "being" as a universal developmental milestone that is accomplished through the union of a good-enough environmental (maternal–paternal) adaptation with the infant's physical and emotional needs. It is out of this elementary experience of being held and nurtured that the capacity for true "doing" arises. Doing corresponds to the spontaneous, joyful emergence of the real self and the actions taken to activate and express this real self in reality. However, such a capacity is based on, or evolves out of, the basic capacity for simply being that is characterized by an absence of restlessness secondary to need frustration.

Winnicott (1971) assigned a feminine valence to the capacity for being and a masculine valence to the later developed capacity for doing. He believes that all humans possess both capacities in a basic "bisexuality" that is differentiated out over the course of development.

If we take these two elements of human personality and apply them to a developing boy's experience, we can see at once how he would learn to dissociate himself from the elemental capacity for being and move more quickly toward the doing mode. Cultural values, as imparted through the early caretaking environment, tend to differentiate these two human capacities into masculine and feminine elements and to value one over the other in boys (doing) and girls (being).

Boys' preference for doing over being can be observed in several ways. As noted, a young boy may prefer active, physical play on the playground with his friends at an early age. In addition, boys, and men, appear to prefer more action-oriented means of problem solving that can have both adaptive as well as maladaptive consequences. Adaptive doing is seen in the active problem solving, willingness to take risks to protect others, and capacity for hard work that characterize many men. Maladaptive doing is seen in unseemly risk taking; overt and destructive acting-out behaviors that often serve as distractions from unpleasant emotional states; aggression; and problems with various kinds of addictions, ranging from substance abuse and addictions to compulsive gambling, sexual promiscuity, and workaholism.

The tendency for doing, and a discomfort with being, are often essential components of many men's emotional and relational difficulties. As the unpleasant and destructive consequences of a life that is based on an overreliance on doing accrue, many men recognize the value in cultivating their capacity for being and strive to strike a balance between doing and being. Relational bonds that have occurred through productive doing can be strengthened by a therapeutic approach that intertwines activity in the therapeutic relationship along with a focus on being with the feelings that emerge. The familiar doing approach can act as the doorway to the being world. With an appreciation of the meaning of both of these elements for men, a sensitive psychotherapist may be better able to facilitate the attainment of this balance.

SUMMARY

In this chapter we have outlined a conceptual model that integrates two important perspectives that have contributed much to the psychological understanding of boys and men: the psychoanalytic developmental approach and the gender role strain approach. We have summarized each perspective and distilled their unique contribution to our psychological understanding of men.

This integration offers both insight into and empathy for men's psychological development. It further adds culture-sensitive specificity to these important developmental processes. A positive benefit of this integration is that therapists, working with both of these perspectives to guide them, will increase their empathy for men's difficulties and have greater clinical resonance with men's struggles and will thereby have greater conceptual clarity to inform their clinical practices with men.

3

PRACTICE-ORIENTED FOUNDATIONS OF DEEPENING PSYCHOTHERAPY WITH MEN

> While clients often initiate therapy because of a painful symptom, they quickly begin to discuss their lives—the complex fabric of who they are, where they are going, and what is present and what is missing in their lives. Once clients enter this deeper process, it is almost impossible to convince them to do what they consider to be "gimmicky" techniques or homework assignments directed only at symptom alleviation. They sense that they have embarked on a journey that will not only alleviate their symptoms but will also lead them to a deeper, more meaningful life. (Elkins, 1998, p. 181)

Even when a man has crossed the threshold and entered psychotherapy, he often faces numerous obstacles to inner exploration. His reaction to the intense interpersonal nature of psychotherapy may stir up his conflicts about dependence and force to the surface uncomfortable feelings of grief and sadness. Adherence to traditional male gender role rules of conduct will be challenged by the intimacy demanded in the interpersonal situation with the psychotherapist. A man's preference for immediate problem solving will often be in conflict with his psychotherapist's orientation toward staying with feelings and body sensations. The emotional wound that has brought the man to psychotherapy will feel uncomfortably exposed, and he will be asked to approach, rather than avoid, its presence. The task that lies ahead of the psychotherapist is not an easy one. He or she will need not only to understand his or her male client's presenting concerns but also to be well versed in a wide range of deepening interventions in order to guide the man toward his emotional depth.

In this chapter we highlight the classic psychotherapeutic foundations of the practice of deepening psychotherapy and how these methods can be applied to psychotherapeutic work with men. Although we use the term *deepening* more broadly, it has traditionally been aligned with the psychology of Carl Jung, whose followers called his clinical work *depth psychotherapy* (Douglas, 1995). As Jung was a disciple and collaborator with Freud, it is best to begin with Freud's (1917/1961) psychoanalytic conception of the unconscious as the first contribution to deepening therapy.

Freud's emphasis on uncovering repressed and forgotten emotional trauma from an individual's past serves as one of the first models for an intensive deepening approach within the therapeutic relationship. Psychoanalysts who came after Freud added to the technique and theory without abandoning the depth-oriented emphasis. For instance, Jung (1958) and his followers expanded the depth of the unconscious to also include elements of a more universal collective unconscious. May (1961) and Yalom (1980), existential psychotherapists, expanded depth to include an analysis of one's place in life, one's choices, and an increased awareness of one's mortality. Kohut (1977) and Rogers (1951) have emphasized the importance of focusing on the individual's phenomenological world by mirroring and reflecting his or her words and feelings in a nonjudgmental manner. For them, deepening involved the empathic connection of therapist to client in a way that facilitated the individual's natural inclination toward psychological growth. The experiential approaches to psychotherapy of Moreno (1946) and Perls (1969) involved an integration of perceptual and body awareness, behavioral practice, and emotional expressivity that could give clients a more holistic and immediate deepening perspective of their lives. The transpersonal and spiritual approaches of Elkins (1998), Hillman (1975), and others, which streamed intellectually from the writings of Jung (1968), Maslow (1968), and Eastern approaches to human understanding (see Walsh, 1999), provide rich metaphorical language and descriptions of the experiential results of the deepening therapy process. Finally, Reich (1949/1976) and Lowen (1975) have connected depth to the physical body with its intimate and direct symbiosis with the mind and behavior.

PSYCHOANALYSIS AND THE BEGINNINGS OF DEPTH-ORIENTED THERAPY

The goal of psychoanalysis is to help the patient achieve resolution of internal conflicts through insight and corrective emotional experience (Alexander, 1932). Psychoanalysis as a therapeutic technique emphasizes the patient engaging in a process of free association to connect current events with those from the past that have been forgotten or repressed. The idea is for the patient to freely verbalize whatever comes to mind while the psychoanalyst listens for discrepancies and defensive maneuvering that can be interpreted to the patient in a nonjudgmental manner. Freud (1917/1961) believed that many repressed traumatic events involved sexual and aggressive material, the outward expression of which would be socially unacceptable.

Dreams, believed to be forbidden expressions of wishes, desires, and impulses, were often used as starting places for free association. Early free-association technique included the use of a couch on which the patient would lie while the analyst sat out of sight of the patient. This encouraged a detachment from external reality and movement toward the reverie of the unconscious for the patient. The reduction in stimulation created a state of consciousness similar to hypnosis.

Freud discovered that repetitive contact with the psychoanalyst, who revealed little of his personal life in the therapeutic interaction, created a special transference relationship between the psychoanalyst and patient. Often the patient would experience strong emotional feelings toward the analyst, as if the analyst were a significant individual from the patient's past. A variety of reactions, such as a desire to please; fantasies of being together; as well as anger, disappointment, and dependency could be aspects of the transference relationship. These reactions often represented a regression to earlier relational encounters with parents or significant others.

The deepening level of self-understanding that accompanies the repetitive interpretations of transference and resistance has been termed *working through* (Greenacre, 1956). The analyst encourages the patient to amplify and elaborate on associations and verbalizations of feelings pertaining to the transference relationship. Rank (1947) believed that the main focus of analysis should be entirely on the transference, primarily on the inevitable separation and loss of the therapist by the patient. The working through of guilt, fear, dependency, and control recapitulates the separation from one's mother. The analysis of the transference provides the patient with a means to accept his ambivalence about separation and strengthen his ability to individuate in his current relationships and live a more creative life.

A working through of resistance to exploring unconscious material also occurs continually throughout treatment. An individual in therapy may use a variety of mechanisms to avoid talking about core issues or conflicts. Some of these mechanisms include isolating oneself from feelings, missing sessions, changing topics, remaining intellectual, or introducing important material at the very end of a session with little time to elaborate. The psychoanalyst uses these situations to interpret the resistance and help the patient find out why the issues are so threatening. Although impasses often precede breakthroughs in insight and awareness, resistance must be continually challenged in the psychoanalytic therapy process.

Intellectual insight, a by-product of hours of analysis, is not necessarily enough to change long-standing patterns of behavior but does give the individual the possibility of making better choices (Freud, 1917/1961). It might take hundreds of sessions to loosen the patient's defensive structure enough to allow for deeper, more lasting change. Behavior change is more likely after what Freud (1926/1961) termed *catharsis*.

Catharsis happens when an event long buried in the unconscious is recalled after many hours of psychoanalysis and is accompanied by a strong emotional release. Freud initially thought that just the recall of a traumatizing event was enough to remove a psychological symptom, but he found that it would take a cathartic emotional charge accompanying the re-experiencing of the memory to disable a presenting symptom. Often it involved fear, grief, or anger that could be fully experienced in the presence of the accepting therapist without fear of retribution.

Alexander (1932) emphasized that the therapist, who also served as a projective object, be a supportive surrogate parent, because most individuals in therapy had been traumatized by poor parenting experiences. He termed this a *corrective emotional experience*, the purpose of which was to counteract the original trauma. The analyst could provide support instead of the original negative reaction that might have caused or worsened the trauma. This permitted the patient to be more self-accepting. It also allowed him to relive and master the conflicts that he did not have the skills or defenses to handle as a child.

Eventually, the deepening process of psychoanalysis leads an individual to grasp the origins of his conflicts and to challenge the attitudes and behaviors that have served him since childhood. The working through of resistance and the transference relationship with the psychoanalyst releases the need to maintain debilitating symptoms, permits an expansion of one's sense of self, and allows for a greater repertoire of relational and behavioral choices.

Here are some of the primary psychoanalytic approaches for working with men.

Free Association

Ken, age 50 and divorced, feels as if he has nothing much to talk about, so the therapist asks him to just say what comes to his mind, even if it seems inconsequential.

Therapist: Let yourself go. Just say whatever comes into your head.

Ken: I don't know. I have a picture of walking my dog this morning, and he's sniffing every dog that walks by, and its strikes me as kind of strange.

Therapist: Why is that?

Ken: It made me think about how I deal with people. In a way, I wish I could sniff all the people coming by me also, but then I'd have to get out of my shell and actually make an effort to make contact with them.

At this point, several avenues are open for further exploration. Free association is used to both generate potential material as well as to free blocks to more direct exploration. Sometimes, an invitation to "say whatever comes to mind" is perceived as less threatening than a more direct challenge to the defenses.

Dream Interpretation

In work with men, it is not unusual to relate dream content to early stages of psychological development, including separation from one's mother; the oedipal drama; or early memories of deprivation, fear, or threat. Lionel, age 28, talks about a dream in therapy that is about him being caught in a room with thousands of spider webs. He feels repulsed and can't seem to escape the room, leading him to wake up in a cold sweat.

> **Therapist:** What are your associations to the to the spider, the webs, or any of the other imagery?

> **Lionel:** I keep thinking about the webs. They are so disturbing to me.

> **Therapist:** In what way?

> **Lionel:** I wonder if the web is something I feel is going to trap me. Every time I like a woman, I find myself pulling away after a while. I don't want to get trapped.

> **Therapist:** When was the first time you can remember having this feeling?

> **Lionel:** I don't know when the first time was, but my mother was over the other day, and I had a strong sensation of wanting to stay out of her web.

Potential material for the therapist and client to follow is obvious here. Connections among relationship anxieties, the maternal relationship, and feelings of being trapped in relationships are often salient themes for many men who struggle with relationship issues.

Interpretation of Transference

Lance, age 41 and recovering from severe depression, is increasingly cutting and hostile toward the therapist after the therapist announced that he would be on vacation for 3 weeks in the summer. The therapist helps Lance become aware of the quality of his remarks and asks Lance if his anger has anything to do with the therapist. Lance eventually makes the connection that he is angry with the therapist for taking a vacation. On further association, Lance realizes that maybe his anger is connected to his feeling that his father abandoned him as a child.

> **Lance:** I hope you have a good time on your vacation. I hope you're not planning to go to the coast. I heard the weather is going to be really bad.

> **Therapist:** I didn't know that. Are you having any feelings about me being away on vacation?

> **Lance:** Not really. It must be important to have some time away from us crazies.

> **Therapist:** You sound pretty sarcastic. You feeling some anger?

> **Lance:** Actually, I guess I do feel some toward you. I wish you weren't going to be away.

> **Therapist:** Anyone else in your life who you wished hadn't been going away?

> **Lance:** My dad seemed to never be around. Could my anger at you be really about my dad's absence?

Material related to the absent father and a son's anger and grief emerge in this vignette. By relating this directly to the immediate dynamics of the therapist–client interaction the therapist is able to help Lance understand his tendency to harbor anger and to withdraw from conflict.

Working Through Transference

Saul, age 32 and recently separated from his longtime partner, finds that his therapist seems to not be as emotionally attuned to him as Saul would like. This leads to Saul's increasing frustration with the therapist and a sense that he is wasting his time in therapy. The therapist notices the emotional withdrawal and asks him if there is something going on in his feelings toward the therapist. When Saul verbalizes his frustration, he realizes that it represents the same issues he has had with both of his parents. The therapist encourages Saul to say what he would have liked to say to his parents.

Therapist: What would you have liked to say?

Saul: Pay attention to me. I don't like it when you are in your own world.

Therapist: How did it feel to say that?

Saul: I feel kind of whiny and weak. My parents told me never to complain.

Therapist: It's important to me that you say what you feel.

Saul: That's something I never heard. It feels good to hear that.

In this short vignette, again, the immediate effects of bringing a here-and-now transference phenomenon to light in the therapy setting move exploration of these dynamics to a deeper, more emotional, and more personal level.

Interpretation of Resistance

Alan, age 52, says that he has no time for a therapy appointment next week. The content of the therapeutic dialogue this week was about Alan's feelings of longing toward his father, who abandoned him when he was a boy. The therapist helps Alan make the connection between the emotional content of the session and the choice to have no time for therapy next week.

Alan: I'm probably not going to be here next week. I have some important things at work I need to do.

Therapist: I wonder if there is anything we have been talking about today that might make you less motivated for therapy than usual?

Alan: I don't know. I'm feeling pretty strange about talking about my dad here.

Therapist: What do you mean by strange?

Alan: The guy hasn't been in my life. Why should I still have these feelings like he's going to show up at my door some day and tell me he's sorry?

Therapist: The fact that he abandoned you as a boy might certainly bring up some strong feelings and a wish of his return.

Because men are often socialized to avoid or suppress strong emotions, especially feelings of sadness and loss, the therapist must often encourage the opening of emotionally difficult material. In this situation, by relating strong feelings of loss directly to an emergent dynamic in the therapist–client relationship, the therapist is able to help Alan relate his current life experience to important relationship issues from his past.

Working Through Resistance

Alan, in a later session, has begun to talk about issues he has with his father, who abandoned him when he was a young boy. He knows intellectually that it probably was painful, but he currently feels no pain attached to the experience. Instead he feels a numbness, as if it had happened to someone else. During one session he reports a dream about an older man who is trying to get into his house. Alan hears the man yelling to let him in, but in the dream he pretends he doesn't hear him. Alan's associations to the dream become connected to how he has suppressed memories of his father.

Therapist: What are your associations to the dream?

Alan: I really didn't like that man trying to get in my house.

Therapist: Is there anyone in your life who you might have that reaction to?

Alan: I don't think so. But he seemed really familiar. Do you think it is my father?

Therapist: What does it feel like to you?

Alan: I really do miss him, the bastard. (His eyes moisten.)

Corrective Emotional Experience

Saul, from an earlier vignette, screams at his therapist to stop screwing around and listen to him. He begins to feel shame after his outburst, wishing that the therapist would punish him as his parents would have.

Saul: I know I was wrong. I am sorry. I bet you don't want me as a client any more. I'm probably too high maintenance.

Therapist: Sounds like you're afraid I'm going to do something to you.

Saul: If I ever yelled at my parents like that, I'd be in deep trouble.

Therapist: What I hear is that you want to be heard and you would like to get some acknowledgment for your feelings.

Psychoanalytic techniques offer several means through which to deepen the psychotherapeutic process. First, the therapist is able to assist the client in exploration of difficult relationship themes by means of transference interpretations and illumination of here-and-now relational dynamics. Second, loosening of rational, intellectual mechanisms and encouragement of the more spontaneous say-whatever-comes-to-mind approach to session material can weaken the control these mechanisms often exert over the emotional aspects of a man's life. Third, taking a direct approach to difficult emotional material allows the therapist to affirm the emotional aspects of his or her male client's life, thus rendering it more acceptable to the client himself.

THE JUNGIAN APPROACH TO DEPTH

Carl Jung, a collaborator and disciple of Freud, expanded the realm of the unconscious by emphasizing its universal elements (Jung, 1958). He believed that the psyche, the inner realm of personality, was made up of a personal and collective unconscious. Although the personal unconscious was similar to Freud's conceptualization, the *collective unconscious* was Jung's term for the vast psychic resource shared by all human beings.

Images from the collective unconscious are represented by fantasies, dreams, symbols, and myths. The images, termed *archetypes*, are universal patterns of how humans perceive and order meaning in their lives. Archetypes predispose us to see the world in certain ways and allow us to share common visions and experiences. They permit us to relate our experiences to each other and to understand the lives of our ancestors. The archetypes are the structures that carry psychic energy from the collective unconscious into current consciousness and, eventually, into action. Accompanying archetypes are *complexes*, energy-filled clusters of emotion. For instance, the father or mother complex involves myriad conflicting associations of imagery, ideas, and feelings for most people.

Jung believed that, with age, individuals grow toward wholeness by integrating the conscious and unconscious aspects of the self. This process toward wholeness, involving the incorporation of the undeveloped aspects of self, is termed *individuation*. For example, an individual who has relied on the masculine aspects of the self may need to learn more about the feminine aspects to understand himself fully and move toward wholeness. A person who has tried to control may need to learn how to let go. The opposite of one's preferred mode is often a key to finding individuated wholeness.

Perhaps the most obvious dichotomy depicted by Jung (1968) is that of the *persona* and *shadow*. The persona can be described as the adapted, social mask that functions superficially with others in order to simplify and protect oneself in interactions with society. Many individuals identify themselves with this aspect of their personality and deny the depth and wisdom that comes with embracing other parts.

The shadow can be described as a portion of the unconscious self that has been forced to be denied or forgotten because of its incompatibility with social values and ideals. Often it involves repressed anger, hostility, sexuality, or curiosity. It may appear in dreams as a dark, frightening figure. The power of the shadow can be represented by secretive behavior involving antisocial actions (e.g., visiting a prostitute, gambling, taking drugs, having illicit affairs) in relatively "normal" individuals.

It is common for a person to project his or her shadow onto others by being critical and condemning of activities and behavior that conflict with an idealized public self-image. Jung believed that individuals became less dominated by the power of the shadow by acknowledging this darker, less noble part of themselves.

Jungian therapy takes on a unique form for each individual, emphasizing client expression through verbalization as well as through writing, art, music, and play. In many current Jungian forms of therapy the therapist is attentive to metaphoric images that arise in his or her own consciousness in response to the patient (Siegelman, 1990). Generally, the therapist is required to remain empathic, attentive to imagery, and willing to follow the patient's lead in the process of exploration.

Dreams are often used as markers for exploration in therapy (Jung, 1968). They are seen as dramas played out by the personal and collective unconscious to signal to the conscious self where to look for the source of conflict and distress. Unlike Freudian dream analysis, which involves deciphering the disguised code of the unconscious, Jungian dream analysis sees the dream as a manifestation of a creative, problem-solving, growth-oriented unconscious that seeks balance and integration.

A significant portion of many analytic therapy sessions is used to expand on the feelings, themes, and conscious associations to dreams. Sometimes a dream's meaning will be revealed only after examining a series of dreams, like acts in a play. In Jungian dream analysis the dreamer is asked to make his own interpretations with some prodding and support from the therapist. It is the therapist's goal to help the patient extract the wisdom from the dream (Jung, 1934/1966).

Jung (1968) also taught his clients a type of meditation technique called *active imagination,* which involves clearing the mind and allowing an image or scene to come through that can then be told like a story, acted out, or depicted in a creative or artistic endeavor. The images from the scene are used in therapy as material to understand and integrate from one's own personal or collective unconscious.

Ideally, the motivated client in Jungian-oriented psychotherapy moves beyond immediate personal concerns and uses the therapy process to live life more deeply in full awareness of the mythic and archetypal realities that exist in the collective unconscious. In a sense, the client in Jungian-oriented psychotherapy uses the wisdom from the psyche to make decisions and choices that reflect a balanced and holistic vision. The client is more comfortable trusting intuition and seems to experience life as a more poetic, spiritual, and creative endeavor.

Here are some of the primary Jungian approaches for working with men.

Imaging an Archetype

In therapy, George, age 32, talks about his unassertiveness in his work situation, especially when he is in the presence of male superiors.

Therapist: Who does your boss remind you of?

George: He is like a general, and most of the time I feel like I shouldn't even be in his army.

Therapist: Can you take a moment to close your eyes and imagine yourself as the "warrior" you had read about and notice how this feels?

George: (Closes his eyes and, after a few minutes, opens them.) I certainly like the image. I imagined myself as one of the knights of the roundtable. I do feel more strength as a warrior.

Therapist: Perhaps, in the presence of your superiors, you could try on this image before you go into a meeting with them.

George: It certainly would be better than always feeling inferior.

In this interaction, the Jungian-oriented psychotherapist connects George with elements of his shadow and with the image of a successful, assertive warrior. George is able to access this internal image of himself and to imagine becoming more assertive with his supervisor.

Exposing the Shadow

In a men's group session, the therapist turns off all the lights in the room except for one that casts a shadow on each member as they take their turn standing in front of the group. Henry, age 52 and recently separated from his wife of 25 years, at his turn, is asked to speak to his shadow. He expresses fear of his shadow self and wonders if he is strong enough to take it on. Directed to lie on the ground and become his shadow self, Henry initially hesitates. As a religious person who has a strong belief in God, this exercise is clearly moving him toward a line he has rarely, if ever, crossed. Finally, he lies on the floor where his shadow has been cast. He is encouraged by the therapist to feel the strength of the shadow. His voice becomes strong and clear.

Henry (Shadow): (Lying on the floor.) I am powerful and you are weak. I know that you don't like being pushed around. I am angry that you don't stand up for yourself.

Henry: (Henry switches places and sits up, looking at his shadow.) You don't know how it is. It is hard to tell people what I am feeling. They may use it against me.

Henry (Shadow): What are you so afraid of? They can't hurt you that bad.

Henry: I've been hurt, and I don't want it to happen anymore.

Henry (Shadow): Then align yourself with me. Together we won't let anyone hurt us like that.

The dialogue continues, with Henry taking on the role of both his conscious self and his shadow self. He emerges from the exercise with increased strength in his voice and clarity in his eyes. Other group members comment on the intensity of his shadow and their desire to see more of it in the group setting. Henry smiles and acknowledges a sense of feeling big and strong.

This simple interchange illustrates two important deepening processes. First, Henry is able to verbalize and externalize his shadow, that aspect of ourselves that is often dissociated and suppressed yet can play such an important part in our motivations, fears, and anxieties. Second, through the dialogue-with-self aspect of this session Henry is able to give voice to both aspects of himself and to thus realize how both of these parts of himself play a significant role in his definition of himself.

Reowning Projections

In a men's group session Zak, age 45 and a recovering alcoholic, finds that he is becoming increasingly irritated by the whining of one of the other members. He is directed to focus on what it is about the whining that relates to himself.

Zak: I was never allowed to whine in my house. My father used to beat me if he heard me do that. I've learned not to expect anything from anyone else, then I don't need to whine.

Peter (another group member): Aren't there things in your life that have caused you disappointment or that you wish were different?

Zak: Yeah, I guess. But I don't let myself focus on them.

Therapist: What if you go around the group and "whine" about something to each man? Maybe you will learn something about your expectations and disappointments doing this.

Zak: I hate whining, but if you think it will help I can give it a try.

Peter: Don't call it whining. Call it asking for what you want.

Zak takes a turn with each group member and with the leaders asking for what he wants. This owning of his projection, and the active acting out of this dynamic, leads to his deeper understanding of what it is that irritated him about another group member's whining.

Creative Expression: Art, Music, Writing, Making Collages, Movement

During a men's group session the members are given a stack of magazines, paper, scissors, and paste. They are asked to create a collage that reflects where they are in their lives right now. Each man produces a picture that includes images, words, and designs that reveal more about his inner worlds than many of his verbalizations. Joe, age 28, is asked by the therapist to talk about the meaning of his collage, which is dominated by a large dragon, a canyon landscape, and a small boy.

> **Joe:** I am the little boy, I think, waiting for the dragon to attack me in the barren landscape of the canyon.
>
> **Therapist:** What do you think the dragon represents?
>
> **Joe:** I'm not sure. I know that I am afraid of its strength and power to hurt me.
>
> **Therapist:** What would you say to the little boy if you were the dragon?
>
> **Joe:** Don't be afraid. I am your protector. You can count on me to take care of you when you are vulnerable. (He begins to smile.)
>
> **Therapist:** What is the smile about?
>
> **Joe:** I feel stronger knowing that if I take risks to be more open in here, I will be protected by "the dragon" part of me.

Creative expression using color images, storytelling, and collages is a powerful means by which to break through rational, verbally mediated experience. These creative venues allow deeper processing of experiences that uses verbal as well as nonverbal, textual, visual, and auditory channels.

Active Imagination/Guided Imagery

Active imagination/guided imagery is a meditation technique that encourages a patient to relax, shut his eyes, and imagine a scene that resembles a waking dream that can then be interpreted for meaning and unconscious wisdom. The therapist relaxes the men in the group with his words and tone, slowing their breathing with an imaginary rock they are asked to place on their chests. The therapist asks the group members to imagine themselves out on a road in the country where each is a 5-year-old innocent boy with his father. They are directed to encounter another boy who is mean, aggressive, and domineering. After the encounter they are asked to return to the arms of their fathers. Herbert, a recently divorced man in his late 50s, is visibly shaken by the imagined encounter.

> **Therapist:** Herbert, can you say something about what you have experienced in the imagery exercise?

Herbert: I haven't had such a vivid memory of my father in many years. In my imagery, my father is about my age now, and he is stroking my hair and telling me that everything is going to be all right. I could feel his touch. My dad has been dead for 15 years, and I've blocked out so many of my positive memories of him.

Therapist: You must really miss him.

Herbert: I really miss my dad a lot. (His eyes water.)

By combining age-old traditions of breath awareness with visualization the Jungian-oriented psychotherapist is able to activate powerful, emotionally charged images and memories. For many men, such activities are appealing because of their action-oriented and kinetic approach. At times, bypassing verbally mediated experience and accessing it through more direct means has a deepening impact on the therapy process.

Jungian Dream Interpretation

Bryan, age 30 and a recovering narcotics addict, had a dream about being caught in a room with thousands of insects. He feels repulsed and can't seem to escape the room. He woke up in a cold sweat. The therapist asks Bryan if he has had other dreams with this theme. Bryan states that in a dream earlier in the week, he was wandering through a large house, opening different doors. Each room was empty and cold. He had very little feeling.

Therapist: How does this insect dream connect to that one, do you suppose?

Bryan: The insects may be all my fears. I believe that I will be caught in their clutches and not be able to get out.

Therapist: How is this relevant in your life?

Bryan: I am torn in real life between getting messy and entangled in my relationship with a woman I am seeing and staying clear of it.

Therapist: So you have to choose between feeling cut off and feeling fear.

Bryan: Yes, and I can't find the middle ground.

Jungian approaches to deepening psychotherapy draw on the multiplicity of processing venues available to both the therapist and the male client. Nonverbal images, dreams, archetypal associations, storytelling, and other vehicles can "jump over" what are often defensively deployed verbal tactics. The end result is often a kind of action-oriented therapy that appeals to many male clients and that simultaneously offers them deeper and deeper levels of processing.

EXISTENTIAL PERSPECTIVES ON DEPTH

May and Yalom (1995) suggested that existential psychotherapy is perhaps the "deepest" of psychotherapies. Although it is not driven by technique, its emphasis is on how an individual lives his or her life. The therapist probes the client about all aspects of existence, including the choices he makes, his loneliness, and how he finds meaning in a life that he knows is finite. Existential psychotherapy focuses the client on who he is choosing to be and how he is choosing to encounter the life he has been given in terms of his relationships, work, and creative endeavors. Inherent in life is existential anxiety, a palpable feeling state that requires an individual to come to terms with his vulnerability, mortality, and choices. The existential therapist encourages clients to face this inevitable anxiety and respond to it with creativity, acceptance, and meaning. The client is challenged to let go of neurotic anxiety, the "what-if" fears that prevent risk taking and embracing full, ontological life experience.

Yalom (1980) proposed that there are four major issues that all individuals must face and that make up the core of existential psychotherapy: death, freedom, isolation, and meaninglessness. Perhaps the quality that most differentiates humans from animals is our awareness of the inevitability of our own death. Animals seem to have a survival instinct that doesn't carry with it conscious death awareness. Humans' instinctual motivation to stay alive is accompanied by a terror of death. We defend against this terror by denying death's existence and living as if we have forever to accomplish our dreams. In psychotherapy, an individual is forced to confront mortality, resulting in a fuller awareness of the limited time available, and to live life with passion and purpose rather than with passivity and fantasy. It is ultimately up to the individual to take responsibility for the quality of his short existence as a living creature.

Existentialists define *freedom* as the responsibility to make choices and author one's own reality. Whereas individuals without freedom in their daily lives crave it, those with freedom often feel burdened with the responsibility of choice. They frequently choose to abdicate responsibility to others to care and make choices for them. It is not unusual in therapy for a client to demand that the therapist fix or solve the problems for which help was sought. It is ironic that the therapist can use this encounter to remind the client of the issue of responsibility for life. The movement from awareness of one's choices to actually taking action is termed *will* (May, 1969).

Many individuals who come to therapy are overwhelmed by their choices or are afraid to act on the desires or wishes they have for their own lives. Often, taking action, even positive action, involves giving up something of life that is secure and familiar. It is not unusual to be frozen by the fear of losing a way of being, even if it is no longer functional or growth producing. In this situation the therapist encourages the client to consider the possible consequences of any decision. With full awareness of what might be lost, the individual is supported in taking action that enhances existence.

Isolation is the third major issue that an individual faces when honestly looking at his life journey. Not only are we often out of touch with other humans, but we also are out of touch with parts of ourselves. Therapy focuses on connecting the individual to hidden aspects of the self that have been denied, repressed, or forgotten. Therapy also helps an individual face existential aloneness. The existentialists believe that there is an ever-existing space between who we are as individuals and those with whom we are in relationships. Even the closest person to us cannot experience our perceptions or consciousness. Some people find it frightening to be in touch with this aloneness. Attempts to merge with another person by falling in love or fusing with a group or cause are ways to deny and distort one's ultimate aloneness.

Although it is healthy to be in a relationship with another person, to share one's experiences the best one can, it also is important to learn to accept one's existential loneliness. Awareness of this aspect of life can free an individual to take responsibility for existence and permit others their own phenomenological reality. Instead of seeking mergers, one can seek coexistence and interdependence with fellow humans.

The final issue to confront is that of meaninglessness. Because we are alone and eventually die, life often is a struggle to find a basis for meaning from which to live our lives. Often a person is tempted to take on the meaning of others through religion, education, work, or relationships. The existentialists believe that an individual's phenomenological reality must be sustaining. Structure and meaning must be understood for their own significance. There is a large difference between an individual who has never questioned the meaning of religion and an individual of the same faith who has explored, questioned, and chosen the religion as a foundation for spiritual beliefs.

Existential psychotherapy focuses the individual on discovering his own meaning from his experience and not relying on others to define it for him. For many men, desperation and despair are necessary pre-emptive stages to redefining that which has ultimate value. To the existentialist, life is a constant challenge to sustain meaning and connection while being simultaneously aware of the limitations inherent in one's existence.

Here are some of the primary existential approaches for working with men.

Existential Questions

One of the major tools that the therapist uses is to ask the client difficult questions about his existence. Often these questions arise in the midst of a discussion of a life dilemma or conflict. The therapist's role is to ensure that the client faces the dilemma of how the conflict and proposed solution affect his life in the large picture. What does he gain and lose by taking action to solve the problem? Rick, age 35, has been questioning in therapy whether he should stay married despite reporting that there is no warmth or love between him and his wife. She refuses to come to treatment with him and has often rejected his advances toward reconciliation.

> **Therapist:** So what do you get in your life from this relationship the way it is?
>
> **Rick:** I wish I could answer that with full confidence. What I get is the predictability. I know she will be there, but what else beside that? I don't know. It's really about security, I guess.
>
> **Therapist:** How would your life be different if you weren't in this relationship?
>
> **Rick:** I don't know. Maybe I'd be less secure. But maybe I'd be happier and freer. It makes me anxious to think about this.

Confronting Internal Discrepancies

An important function of the existential therapist is to confront a client's conflicts among what he believes, what he feels, and what he does. Often a client will bring up a dilemma that highlights how out of line these aspects of himself are. In therapy, Von, age 40, brought up his ambivalence about ending an affair he was having with a woman outside of his marriage. When asked about how he felt about her, he replied that he really enjoyed her company and her sexual energy. However, he also spoke of believing that extramarital affairs were definitely wrong and that he still had strong feelings of love for his wife.

> **Therapist:** So how are you going to reconcile your beliefs, your feelings, and your behavior?
>
> **Von:** I don't know. This is where I'm stuck. What should I do?
>
> **Therapist:** I can't answer the question for you, but it seems that this is the dilemma that is going to help you figure out who you are and where you want to go with your life. Where do you want to start?

In both of these short interactions we see how an existential attitude on the part of the therapist cuts, surely and simply, to the core issues and forces the male client to move beyond empty storytelling or intellectualizations and toward more authentic engagement with his psychological dilemmas. Such simplicity and direct honesty are often an appealing aspect of psychotherapy for many men.

Demystifying Life's False Promises

A therapist must be able to help a client discover the nature of his unrealistic expectations about life and to reclaim responsibility for how his life has turned out. Our culture often presents to men idealistic and unrealistic images of what will happen by following the rules set out by society. These images include a promise of wealth, power, and unencumbered relationships. Louis, age 43, sat in the therapist's office and complained about his position in life.

Louis: I did everything right. I went to a good college, got a good job, married a great woman, have neat kids, but I am stuck in a dead-end 9-to-5 job. What did I do wrong?

Therapist: Perhaps you had some expectations about what playing by the rules was going to get you?

Louis: Damn right. I thought I was going to be at least a corporate vice president by now and be making six figures.

Therapist: I wonder what choices you made that took you away from that dream? Did you really want to pay the price for that goal?

Acknowledging Death and Mortality

One of the core issues that all individuals must face is the fact that they will die at some point. Except for buying life insurance, it is rarely a topic that a man contemplates in depth unless he has experienced the death of a close friend or loved one or has been given a terminal diagnosis himself. Yet this death awareness significantly motivates much of a man's behavior and choices. It is not uncommon for a man in middle age to begin to notice that more than half of his life has already been lived. He may notice physical ailments and limitations that reflect the aging process. A therapist who works with a middle-aged or older man must help him face his mortality and loss of youth. Charlie, age 54, was in therapy dealing with periodic bouts of depression.

Charlie: I wish I was about 30 again.

Therapist: What would come with being 30 again?

Charlie: I wish I could still feel energetic, attractive, and look forward to my life.

Therapist: What stops you from feeling this way now?

Charlie: I'm getting old. Shoot, I might pull a muscle getting up from this chair. All I see down the road are more ailments and less energy.

Therapist: That may be true. Rather than focus on your memories of the past, how might you make the most of the time you do have left?

Charlie: It's so depressing. I hate thinking about the fact that I'm not going to live forever.

Confronting Freedom of Choice

One of the core issues facing all individuals is the freedom to make choices about one's life. Every choice a person makes means that there will be consequences to be reconciled both for choices made and those not made. Oftentimes in therapy a man regrets having taken action or not having taken action and uses the session to describe the anxiety that accompanies his decisions. The therapist's role is to normalize the experience of anxiety that accompanies the act of making choices about life. Michael, age 46, was worried that he made the "wrong" decision about leaving his wife and talks in therapy about how much he misses her.

Therapist: What were you thinking before you left her?

Michael: I thought my life would be freer, that I could go out with different women and not have to feel so hen pecked.

Therapist: Did you get what you wanted?

Michael: Yes, but I didn't realize all that I'd be giving up.

Facing Aloneness

The existential reality that each human being is ultimately alone often runs counter to our culture's emphasis on finding a partner with whom to share life. Sharing life is believed to take away loneliness but not necessarily the feeling of being alone. No one can get inside another person's body or mind but rather can only infer in a what-if manner what another person is experiencing or feeling. For men who have been directed by our culture to be individualistic, aloneness is often a normal state of affairs.

Marty, age 38, came to therapy complaining that no one would listen to him, not even his family.

Therapist: What are you needing from them?

Marty: I just want to know that I matter—that what I say has some validity.

Therapist: What makes you think it doesn't?

Marty: Well, they don't seem to respond to my suggestions or opinions.

Therapist: Sounds like you feel alone.

Marty: Yeah. I feel alone and cut off. I'm just looking for some sign that I matter.

Therapist: You don't want to feel like you are in this world alone.

Marty: I know I am, but I don't like it.

Therapist: It is hard to absorb that we are all separate. How might you approach your family in a different manner?

Marty: You mean like show them how much I appreciate them?

Therapist: Seems like a good place to start.

Existential psychotherapy provides direct and unflinching access to the "big issues" of life for a man. The meaning of life, mortality, acceptance of responsibility, and isolation are some of the content themes that are often addressed through existential approaches to psychotherapy. Many men resonate to many of these themes because they appeal to a man's sense of making meaning out of his life and living his life to the fullest. Existential themes often emerge in subtle and sometimes indirect ways from session to session. Therapists who listen carefully for themes that are derivative from these existential issues will find that addressing them directly deepens the emotional and personal content of therapy sessions.

SELF PSYCHOLOGY AND PERSON-CENTERED DEEPENING

Both Heinz Kohut (1977), the originator of the self psychology approach, and Carl Rogers (1951), the originator of person-centered therapy, realized the importance of a therapist being empathically attuned to a client's inner world. For Kohut, this meant being able to act as a "mirror" for the client in much the same way an ideal parent would with a child. Instead of arguing or judging, he accepted the client's interpretation of his own reality. For Rogers, empathy is the key to unlocking another's stunted human growth potential. By allowing himself to "walk in his client's shoes" he was able to get a sense of the individual's phenomenal experience. The result for the client from both of these approaches is a heightened sense of acceptance from a trusted authority that could then be internalized into self-acceptance.

Kohut (1977) suggested that the developing child has three major needs to be fulfilled if the self is to develop optimally. These include the need to be mirrored, the need to idealize, and the need to be like others. The need to be mirrored is best understood as the way that a child develops self-acceptance by having a significant adult validate (mirror) his or her best qualities. Parents, often through subtle gestures and verbalizations, make a child feel special, important, and desired. When parental mirroring fails, a child who has had significant parental support learns to create his or her own mirror. This process, called *transmuting internalization*, allows an individual to gradually create a self-structure, based on the accrual of mirroring experiences, that is stable and relatively positive. If a child does not get enough positive mirroring, he will have difficulty sustaining stable self-esteem. This failure of an internalized sense of positive mirroring results in feelings of low self-worth and is defended against by grandiosity.

In the normal child, grandiose needs are eventually fulfilled from resources drawn from within. In a child who lacks adequate self-structure, the need to be seen and validated becomes so strong it may completely overwhelm the ego structure. This leads to inappropriate exhibitionism to gain attention, resulting in only minimal gratification from external sources.

The need to idealize a parent provides a child with hope for the future. By looking up to parents, a child can identify with and one day imagine him- or herself as a competent and successful adult. If a parent betrays this trust and frustrates this idealization, the growing child is left with little in which to believe. In child abuse, the violation is obvious and overt. The damage sustained from the trauma makes it difficult for a child to believe that the future will be positive. Even subtle betrayals by parents can inflict passive trauma that, if not repaired, can lead to a sense of pessimism or negativity, the source of which is not consciously recalled.

Kohut's final aspect of self is based on the concept of *twinship*, or a need to be like others. This is the need to have a double or a playmate who is one's equal, so that the two are available to validate each other's feelings, thoughts, and interests. This often occurs in childhood and can lead to a strong sense of belonging with an individual or a group. If there has been abuse or neglect in the family of origin, shame, doubt, and secrecy may replace the openness needed for peer intimacy. The result is hollowness in relationship to one's peers and difficulty with functioning as a part of a group.

In a sense, Kohut's therapy is akin to reparative parenting, whereas for Rogers person-centered therapy is like an encounter with a trusted friend. Rogers (1957) identified the therapeutic relationship itself as the necessary ingredient in facilitating growth and change in therapy. It is interesting that Asay and Lambert (1999), in their analysis of several hundred empirical studies of psychotherapy, validated Rogers's declaration, finding that 30% of outcome variance is determined by the quality of the therapist–client relationship.

Rogers (1951) suggested that the therapist use empathic listening skills to really hear what a client is saying before rushing to diagnosis or judgment. Both Rogers and Kohut believe that for a therapist to be facilitative the therapist must keep his or her own issues out of the therapeutic interaction yet at the same time be authentic, congruent, and responsive to the client. More than parroting back what the client says, the essential element of this quality of relationship is about understanding the client's frame of reference at the verbal and nonverbal levels and reflecting it back to the client. Much like Alexander's (1932) concept of corrective emotional experience, the client may for the first time sense what it is like to be accepted unconditionally by a parental figure. Kohut (1971) warned that empathic acceptance is different than pure gratification. To be understood is a qualitatively deeper experience than being told "you are right" or "I will give you whatever you ask for."

Rogers's view of the individual is more optimistic and in line with the human potential movement championed by Maslow (1968). Rogers believed that each individual is biologically predetermined to grow not only physically but also psychologically. The process of being deeply understood allows the individual to break free of the negative, judgmental, and stifling experiences of the past that have stunted growth potential. Like existential psychotherapy, person-centered psychotherapy contends that the individual can make choices in his or her present situation that will allow him or her to transcend the past. To have a firm base of self-acceptance is seen as the key to taking risks for growth and moving beyond the security and mediocrity that many individuals come to accept as normal (Maslow, 1968).

We now discuss some of the primary self psychology and person-centered approaches for working with men.

Empathy and Mirroring

The significance of listening to what a client actually is saying about himself, his perceptions, thoughts, and feelings, is at the heart of psychotherapy. The mirroring process shows the client that he is really being attended to and acknowledged, not judged. The therapist accepts what the client is saying as the truth and reflects it back to him. Regardless of theoretical orientation, the therapist must be able to understand deeply the world that the client describes. For a male client, this level of deep understanding may make the difference to whether he continues with therapy. Christian, age 50 and recently laid off from his job, is questioning whether therapy is worth his time.

Christian: I don't know if this therapy stuff is working.

Therapist: You question whether talking about your life is helping you make any progress at all.

Christian: Yes. In all honesty, I feel like I am going to have to eventually solve my own problems and that this is all just intellectual bullshit.

Therapist: It seems that for you the therapy process has not really cut to the core of what is bothering you.

Christian: Nothing personal, but how can you really understand what I am going through?

Therapist: Maybe I can't, but I can certainly try to put myself in your shoes and try to see the world from your perspective.

Christian: That would be nice for a change. It doesn't seem to happen too often in my life.

Unconditional Positive Regard

This intervention is more of an attitude than a method or technique. It is an attitude on the part of the therapist that shows support for the client regardless of what the client is talking about even if it is something with which the therapist may disagree. It is one of the main ingredients for a strong working alliance between therapist and client. Philip, age 34 and having sleep difficulties, came into the therapist's office saying that he was having an extramarital affair but did not see that as his reason for coming to therapy. The therapist accepted Philip's perspective without judgment and made sure that Philip felt heard and understood. Privately, the therapist believes that affairs are not a good idea, but by first accepting the client's reality the therapist can begin to forge a trusting relationship in which the therapist might later be able to address the issue of the affair if it arises as an issue for the client.

> **Philip:** So, I am having this relationship outside of my marriage, but that is not why I am here. I'm here to make some other decisions about my work—whether I should stay or go.

> **Therapist:** The affair is not a big issue for you, but deciding whether to stay in your job is what is most on your mind.

Authentic Interaction in the Therapeutic Relationship

It is extremely important for the therapist to be him- or herself in sessions with clients. This means that reactions, feelings, and thoughts that arise in reaction to the client may potentially be shared with the client. Not everything must be shared, but an authentic response is deeply valued by a client. Self-disclosure in the present can help a client by modeling the type of expressiveness expected in the therapeutic relationship. Authentic interaction also strengthens the therapeutic alliance. In a therapy session, Ian, age 39 and referred by his family physician, describes the predicament he is in at his job. The therapist's honest disclosure validates the feelings Ian has and makes the therapist seem more human and understanding.

> **Ian:** On one hand, I have to answer to my immediate boss, but I must also answer to the owner of the business, who sometimes has a different agenda. It's hard to know what to do.

> **Therapist:** What a tough position to be in. I'm not sure I could live with all those double messages you are getting.

Focus on the Feelings Beneath the Words

Words are one of the main ways a therapist shows that he or she is attending to the client. The therapist's choice of words is significant and must, in some way, reflect the deeper feeling a client is trying to express. To be able to reflect back, without parroting what a client has said, shows a level of understanding that makes him feel seen and heard and encourages him to continue speaking about his life in more depth.

Luke, age 32, has been trying to describe to his wife how much he doesn't like his job. She seems to not want to hear this and often changes the subject. In therapy he speaks again about this.

> **Luke:** I really don't like my work. It has no soul. I feel like a robot going through the motions. I hate to think I am wasting my life there. But it is a job, and I do bring home good money.

Therapist: You feel almost dead doing your job, and it frightens you to think that this is how you spend a majority of your time.

Luke: Exactly. I have a hard time getting out of bed. I find the whole thing oppressive. But I have to do it for my wife.

Therapist: If you weren't so driven to please your wife, you would have been long gone from this soulless job.

Luke: I'm afraid that if I quit, though, she would just leave me.

Therapist: So you stay with the job out of fear of her abandoning you.

Nonverbal Attention

Although what the therapist actually says is important, a great deal of empathy, unconditional positive regard, and concern are communicated nonverbally. By making eye contact, leaning forward, and keeping the client as the main focus of attention a therapist can convey care and help build a trusting relationship with him. Claude, age 24, came to therapy anxious and fearful that he was "going crazy." As the therapist listened intently, leaned toward him, and made eye contact, Claude began to slow down and feel less anxious. He even settled back into his own chair and seemed less frantic and overwhelmed as he told his story.

Person-centered and self psychological approaches to deepening psychotherapy move toward the more intensely personal, core elements of a male client's sense of self, identity, and emotional world. Both of these approaches to psychotherapy rely on the healing and transforming potential inherent in a human relationship that affirms, at the deepest levels, the inherent value, dignity, and worth of the client. We may never know to what extent this healing attitude, especially in psychotherapy with men, derives some of its power from the fact that, in our culture, men are often encouraged to dissociate from these same aspects of themselves.

DEEPENING THROUGH EXPERIENTIAL PSYCHOTHERAPY

Although all psychotherapies can claim to be "experiential," in this section we highlight the approaches that make the therapy session itself a transformative experience. Rather than relying on the usual mode of talking about issues or feelings, these therapies use methods that encourage direct engagement of the senses, emotions, and intellect in the present. For experiential therapies, the goal of treatment is a "change in experiential knowing" (Bohart, 1993).

Experiential knowing is an immediate apprehension of one's life situation in a holistic manner. Like a gestalt, awareness of the self and the world is more than the sum of the parts. In experiential therapy, insights about one's issues and concerns often occur at a level beyond pure logic or reason. These insights are grounded in the body as well as the mind. Primary experience has more of an impact on an individual's gestalt of him- or herself than language, which has been described as a map of the territory rather than the territory itself (Wiener, 1999). Proponents of experiential therapy assume that the client possesses in his or her being all that is necessary for complete healing and that the therapist provides the structure for this to occur (Tallman & Bohart, 1999).

Jacob Moreno (1946) and Fritz Perls (1969) were pioneers in the use of experiential methods to facilitate client change. Both were a part of the early 20th-century Viennese intellectual and psychoanalytic movement influenced by Freud and his disciples. Both men took his concepts and translated them into therapies that were more actively engaging and quicker to approach core psychodynamic conflicts than the years of treatment required by psychoanalysis.

Moreno's therapy was called *psychodrama*, a term that reflects the use of improvisation and spontaneous theatrical techniques to engage an individual in all of his senses while working on a psychological dilemma. Perls, originally trained in psychoanalysis, along with his wife Laura, created Gestalt therapy, an approach that requires the client to interact with himself and the environment in an immediate, perceptual, and honest manner without excessive cognitive rehearsal. Both therapies encourage spontaneous risk taking that leads to a type of experiential knowing that goes far beyond intellectual insight.

Moreno, also considered by many as the father of group psychotherapy, used the theatrical stage as the place where his patients met as a group to take on various roles from each other's lives. Each individual would take a turn being the protagonist, setting up a psychodrama about an issue from his or her own life. Various other participants played the roles of family members, director, auxiliary ego, and audience. The auxiliary ego was like a double of the protagonist, who could show the protagonist alternative ways to handle a situation or express an emotion that the protagonist was fearful of expressing. Although the initial struggle might be outlined by the protagonist, it often shifted into the unconscious realm through spontaneous interaction with other actors and confrontations with parts of the self.

Blatner (1988) suggested that the advantages of psychodrama are derived from its creative engagement in the interpersonal world, which teaches listening, empathy, and honest interaction. It also actively engages various parts of the body through voice, breathing, movement, and heightened awareness of emotional shifts as the psychodrama plays out. Finally, cathartic emotional release occurs as feelings and repressed impulses are allowed to find active bodily expression. Following a psychodrama, the therapist, client, and other group members discuss the process that has just happened and solidify the experiential learning that has occurred.

Gestalt therapy contains many of the same elements of psychodrama, including the possibility of conducting it in a group situation and using members of the group to facilitate the growth of the designated client during his turn on the "hot seat." Perls (1969) assumed that the individual was holistically expressed in all aspects of his being, including his behavior, movement, thoughts, dreams, and interpersonal contact. Psychological problems were viewed as being caused by "unfinished business," aspects of the person's life that remained unresolved. Perls believed that the expression of this unfinished business could be witnessed in all elements of a person's being, from the movement of his hand as it scratches his knee to the hesitation that he might experience in his voice as he is asked to talk about himself.

The key to resolution is to focus on the bodily manifestations of anxiety or tension and engage in a spontaneous, verbal dialogue among the various parts of oneself. Perls encouraged his clients to experiment with new movements, new words, and new types of interaction with the interpersonal environment. He believed that there was a constant struggle occurring between the real, authentic self and the more superficial, social role that demanded safety, conformity, and a wish to please others.

Although Perls was known to be confrontational in his approach, most Gestalt therapists today are more accepting and empathic in their versions of Gestalt work (Wolfert & Cook, 1999). Clients are still encouraged to stay in touch with body tensions and feelings as they encounter parts of themselves through "empty chair" dialogues and other experiments. Resistance is not confronted but rather relabeled by the therapist as an expression of strength and power. The client can then be freed to explore what this show of strength means rather than be self-condemning or stuck in frustration. Eventually, the therapist's prodding of the client toward spontaneous action, experimentation, and dialogue in the present leads to both existential insight and resolution of an aspect of unfinished business that had been creating anxiety and holding him back from growth.

The following are some of the primary experiential approaches for working with men.

Staying in the Present

The ability to be aware of one's internal feelings as well as one's environment in the moment is a sign of psychological health. Many male clients are used to worrying about the future or obsessing about events that have already happened. Encouraging a man to try to remain in the present results in a shift of awareness and an increased sense of vitality. When directed to talk about an event in the past, like a dream, in the language of the present tense, the dream seems to come alive again, as shown in this excerpt from Greg's therapy.

Greg: I was running away from these hoodlums who were chasing me. I didn't know what to do.

Therapist: Try to repeat the dream imagery as if it was happening right now, using words in the present tense.

Greg: I am running away from the hoodlums. They are chasing me.

Therapist: How are you feeling now?

Greg: My heart is pounding. I really feel my fear.

Therapist: Stay with your fear now. It's something you don't often let yourself experience.

Psychodrama

Being able to play out one's life dramas in the presence of others gives a man another opportunity to see what has been going on emotionally and to make any necessary changes. Owen, age 42 and a member of a men's group, was feeling as if he couldn't stand up to his aging father, who was still treating him as if Owen were there only to serve him. Owen chose another man from the group to play his father. He also chose another fairly assertive group member to be his alter ego, to give him lines when he got stuck in the confrontation. Another man played his mother, and a fourth man played Owen as a little boy. All the characters were briefed on their roles by Owen, the protagonist. The therapist encourages the characters to embrace their parts fully and support Owen in dealing with the emotions that are aroused.

Owen: I'm not sure what to say.

Therapist: Check with your alter ego for a line.

Alter Ego: Just tell him that you are not here to serve him. That you have your own life.

Owen: (facing the member playing his father) Dad, I have my own life. I wasn't put on this earth just to serve you.

Therapist: How did it feel to say that?

Owen: I'm still shaking. I've wanted to say that for a long time.

Role Playing the Parts of Personality

A person often has internal conflicts among various parts of his own personality structure. For instance, there may be a part of oneself that wants to be more wild and spontaneous and another part that is more cautious and insecure. In therapy, a male client can be directed to have a dialogue between these parts as a way to give full expression to that perspective and to help with some sort of integration of the conflicting parts.

Carlos, age 49, feels that he often struggles with trying to be disciplined and hard working. This contrasts with another part of himself that wants to relax and feel comfortable. The therapist directs Carlos to speak first from the disciplined self toward the relaxed self sitting in an empty chair across from him.

Carlos 1 (Disciplined Self): You are a lazy bastard. All you want to do is sit around and feel good. You don't get anything done.

Therapist: OK, switch to the other chair and speak as the relaxed self to the disciplined self.

Carlos 2 (Relaxed Self): You call me lazy. I call you a workaholic. You don't know when to stop. You are never satisfied. All you want to do is work. Are we alive just to work?

Therapist: OK, switch again.

Carlos 1: Yes, I like work. It gives me a feeling like I am accomplishing something. I see you just sitting there vegging, and I'm disgusted. Work gives me meaning.

Carlos 2: You're a slave driver. You're going to kill us. I need time to relax and not feel guilty for not working.

Therapist: What have you learned so far from this inner dialogue, Carlos?

Carlos: I have really strong feelings about this. I wasn't so aware of that. I also realize how much I have defined my meaning in my life by work. That's all right, but I still need to also be able to rest and enjoy what I have earned.

Body and Perceptual Awareness

Therapy often involves helping an individual become more aware of how his actions, thoughts, and feelings are expressed in the body. The mind and body are connected, yet when one talks it is sometimes as if one is disembodied. Words lose their meaning when spoken in a flat monotone. In this manner, it is difficult to understand what a person is feeling. By doing awareness exercises in a psychotherapy session a man can become more aware of what he is feeling and sensing, resulting in greater sensitivity to the nuances of his own body's language. A man might be directed to close his eyes, sit back on the chair or couch, and become aware of his breathing. He might be directed to listen for any noises in the environment or to be aware of the images that are playing in his mind. There are many variations of awareness exercises that allow for an opening up of the senses and greater internal dialogue among parts of the body and a man's internal dialogue about issues that are significant to him.

Exaggeration

This is the intensification of a movement, a thought, a feeling, or even resistance to therapy. The intensification allows a person to experience more explicitly a conflict or aspect of the self that is unclear, ambiguous, or only partially felt. Exaggeration displays that which has been hidden and makes it more accessible for intervention. Aaron was talking and lightly banging his fist on the arm of the chair. The therapist asked him to exaggerate the banging. By doing this Aaron, who had come to therapy because of his anger, realized that what he had been talking about was angering him. In another therapy session, Ken, age 32, who presented with low-grade depression, was having difficulty coming up with something to say.

> **Therapist:** Can you physically exaggerate your desire not to say anything?
>
> **Ken:** (Looks confused, but then he starts to push his chair back away from the therapist until he is against the wall.)
>
> **Therapist:** What does this mean, Ken?
>
> **Ken:** I just think I'm overwhelmed by what we were talking about. Sometimes I need some space from all this intensity.

Once Ken had said this, it seemed that he was able to speak more spontaneously about what he was feeling. In later sessions, Ken used the "moving chair" as a signal to himself in therapy when he was feeling able to be close or needed more interpersonal space.

Playing the Parts of a Dream

The Gestalt method of using dreams in therapy involves having the individual play the various people, objects, or parts in his dream. The assumption is that all aspects of the dream have been created by the dreamer and thus must represent various parts of himself. Kyle, age 54 and recently divorced, had a dream about getting lost in a run down section of an unknown city. He was asked to give a voice to each dream element in order to find the message of the dream for him.

> **Therapist:** Kyle, try to imagine yourself back in the dream and speak in the present about how you are feeling.
>
> **Kyle:** I am lost and scared that something is going to happen to me. My heart is racing and I feel doomed.
>
> **Therapist:** All right. Now play the part of a run down building. What might it be saying?
>
> **Kyle:** Like the building can talk?
>
> **Therapist:** Yes.

Kyle: I am the building. No one has cared for me in years. I am abandoned and alone. No one cares if I am here or not.

Therapist: What are you feeling as you say this?

Kyle: I feel strange and in touch with how I haven't really taken care of myself. I think that I am afraid of how much I have neglected important parts of who I am.

Experiential approaches to psychotherapy, including Gestalt therapy and psychodrama, enhance intensity and depth by moving the male client to nonverbal and action-oriented modes of experience. One result of this movement is an intensification of emotional components of issues and conflicts. By acting out aspects of the self, splitting projections and embodying them in other members of a psychodrama or psychotherapy group, clients are able to fully experience the emotional meaning often attached to these dissociated aspects of life.

TRANSPERSONAL AND SPIRITUAL METAPHORS OF DEPTH

Most of the therapies already mentioned use methods and techniques to deepen clients' awareness of themselves as whole human beings. The hoped-for result in all of these psychotherapeutic approaches is a person who is more alive, spontaneous, and engaged in life.

The transpersonal viewpoint emerges from both Eastern and Western models of what it means to be fully human. Transpersonal theorists attempt to give words to human experience that is exceptional, spiritual, or transcendent (Fadiman & Frager, 1998). Maslow (1968) studied individuals whom he considered to be self-actualized and found that many of them had repeated *peak experiences*—powerful time periods where the self dissolves into a greater awareness of the universe and one's place in it. Many religious writings describe in similar words the ecstatic and mystical experiences of individuals who have achieved "nirvana" or "spiritual enlightenment" (Karasu, 1999).

In a sense, psychotherapy may be viewed as one path to spiritual growth. Once an individual moves through his own neurotic conflicts, he sees the world in a different way. It is very difficult to go back to a limited, mundane state of existence knowing that a more enlightened life is possible. The experiential manifestations of this life are senses of aliveness, engagement, and clarity. There is an awareness of one's limited time on the planet while at the same time a knowledge that life is to be revered fully.

Karasu (1999) suggested that an individual can live a "soulful" life if he makes his current life experience a "sacred" one. *Soulfulness* is the sense of rightness that is felt when one is following an authentic path in life (Hillman, 1975). *Sacredness* is the deep felt belief in one's whole being that there is inherent meaning in all life encounters and perceptions (Elkins, 1998). Even mundane experiences can be sacred if they are viewed with an eye to their uniqueness and potential for learning. When one is able to perceive the world from this perspective, every element of life—from the touch of the wind to a brief encounter with a stranger—is a stimulus for potential transcendence.

Soulfulness must be constantly nourished. It is elusive and easily lost in the daily demands of life (Moore, 1992). From this perspective, one is not finished with life's struggle after successfully working through core psychodynamic issues in psychotherapy. Instead, life requires an acknowledgment of its continued mystery and curiosity about how it will unfold. Because it is too easy to slip back into the dull perspective that permeates the social world, individuals on a spiritual path need to find others who share their beliefs and perspective.

Psychotherapy for individuals seeking soulfulness is often enhanced by interactive group experiences that use rituals, which are enactments of myths that acknowledge change and transition (Campbell, 1976). Participation in rituals provides individuals with ways to celebrate their changing perspective and reinforce its power in their lives (Roberts, 1999). It is not by accident that religions, families, and cultures are defined by rituals that mark occasions of great importance and bond their members to their beliefs and values.

Spiritually oriented psychotherapy uses rituals as rites of passage to remind the person seeking enlightenment of the journey he has undertaken. For instance, a men's therapy group might explore the meaning of "honor" by having each man in turn come to the center of the room and symbolically be knighted by the other members of the group. Each man might then express what the experience felt like and what personal meaning it had for his life.

Storytelling is another activity that can heighten the sense of depth for individuals. Often, listening intently and being witness to another's story of courage is a soulful event for all involved. The power of Alcoholics Anonymous to help in personal transformation has much to do with the listening to and identifying with stories that are told. Other groups read poetry, play music together, create collages, dance, or make masks as ritualistic ways to experience the sacred.

Because much of the world functions on a day-to-day, practical level that may clash with the values of spiritually oriented psychotherapy, this approach provides a sacred space and metaphorical language for individuals continuing to seek a deeper way of living. Although the therapy has no defined methods or techniques, it borrows from many of the therapeutic approaches described in this chapter. It also borrows from images, myths, and rituals of the world's religions. The ultimate goal is to help the individual transcend neurotic conflicts, socially constructed life constraints, and fear of change so that he may find his unique path and be supported on the journey.

Here are some of the primary spiritual approaches for working with men.

Storytelling

Storytelling is especially powerful in group therapy. A man might be asked to tell a story about his life as if he were the hero or protagonist. As the man tells the story and has the rapt attention of the group, the underlying message and themes can help define the issues of the life of the man who is telling the story and can be generalized to include universal issues that men face in life. In a men's group, each man was asked to tell a story that reflected his relationship with his father. After listening to several men tell stories of pain and hurt in relation to fathers, Rick told an uplifting story of how his father had taken him on a 2-week hiking trip in the mountains when he was 12. His father spent time listening to him and telling him about what it meant to be a man. Several of the men in the group acknowledged their envy of Rick's experience and wished that their fathers had made more time for them.

Reading Inspirational Passages

Another method to bring out universal themes for men is to begin a group session with a poem or passage from book that has strong images of men working through their life challenges. The images and metaphors can provide "grist for the discussion mill" about what it means to be a man or provide an image that can be acted out by men in the group. In one variation, the group leader read about Atlas carrying the world on his back. The men were then directed to pile several pillows on their backs and trudge around the room feeling the burden they often feel they carry with them. This led to an excellent discussion about the male gender role and its stringent requirements for men to be strong providers who don't complain about their burden and who just "trudge along their way."

Using Metaphors

The mythopoetic works of Robert Bly (1990) and Michael Meade (1993) emphasized the use of stories and images that resonate with a man's experiences in life. The metaphor is a powerful way that men connect with their emotions. Words that describe scenes or imagery seem to be readily applied to a man's emotional life. It is the language that has often seemed missing from the male vocabulary. It is a language of the outdoors and of objects. It fits with the more external, experiential orientation that many men have. Mario, age 48 and a member of a men's group, felt something inside him shift when he was asked to describe himself as an object in the outside world:

> I feel like I am a wall of granite that has been chipped away at over the years by weather and erosion. I am powerful, grounded, and defiant. You must climb me if you want to know who I am.

Drumming

Another powerful experiential method taken from listening to the stories of men from earlier times or from more technologically primitive cultures involves the creation of music from percussion instruments. It is a moving and opening experience for many men, often with no prior musical skills, to drum with a group of men (Hart, 1990). Often, the rhythm and beat change in synchrony over time. "I feel like I am a part of a real tribe. I can feel some of the spiritual power of men gathering together in a deeper way," said one man after a drumming session at the beginning of men's group. The shared activity, and the sensual feeling to which it leads, seems to create an open atmosphere for men to be more honest and authentic with each other.

Meditation

Like guided imagery, meditation allows a man to quiet the world around him so he can listen to his breathing, his body, and his emotions. A meditation can involve thinking about one particular idea or image and can be used at the start of a session to get group participants into a receptive space for dealing more intensely with each other. Shutting one's eyes enables a person to gain a focus on one's internal world that is rare for many men. This experience of quieting the body and mind can also be effective in eliciting spontaneous images and feelings from a man who is used to being vigilant, alert, and defensive. Jess, age 33, who had been in child custody court all day trying to get visitation rights for his children, was very agitated as he walked into the group room. The men were asked to shut their eyes, focus on an image of a flame burning in their minds' eyes while relaxing their bodies and regulating their breathing. As Jess came out of the meditation, he commented that the flame was a wonderful image for him:

> I feel like I need to keep my flame going. I need to take care of myself so that I can make it through this court deal. I have to remember why I am doing this and not lose perspective because of my anger and frustration.

DEEPENING THROUGH BODY WORK

As Jung expanded the concept of depth outward by exploring the universal archetypal elements of the collective unconscious, Wilhelm Reich (1942/1973) took Freud's teachings inward and applied them to the body.

Reich's style of therapy is rooted in psychoanalytic theory; he believed that the ego defended itself physically as well as psychologically. The instinctual forces of the id, representative of sexuality and aggression, were inhibited and contained by the body. The habitual patterns of defense, which he termed *character*, were manifested in an individual's muscular armoring, physical gestures, and movements.

Reich became a keen observer of the bodies of his patients and developed a classification system based on the correlation between the issues they raised in therapy and the way they looked and moved. Reich's therapy process involved in-depth psychoanalytic exploration combined with physical manipulation of the musculature in order to loosen the armoring of the body. The result was often a strong cathartic physical and emotional release.

Reich did not underestimate the strength of unconscious forces. He believed that he could cut short some of the length of psychoanalysis by dealing directly with the physical manifestations of neurosis. He firmly believed that *libido* was a palpable energy that gives life to the body. The physical blocks that prevent this energy from running freely throughout the body were thought to be connected intimately to one's psychological issues. Anxiety was interpreted as the containment of energy and the prevention of movement toward outward expression. Pleasure, in contrast, was the body's movement of energy from the core of the individual toward outward expression. The release of this energy he termed *orgasm*. Reich noted that the individual, freed from his body armor, would build up muscular tension and then, similar to a sexual orgasm, experience relief, relaxation, and pleasure following the body's releasing contractions.

Reich felt that "talking" psychoanalysis was amiss in not including the body as a part of the change process. By intervening at the body level he felt he was moving more honestly and deeply toward the blockages of life energy that were at the root of his patient's distress. Protection against sexual shame and trauma, and the general inhibition of instinctual processes by family and society, were often the basis of a patient's psychological and physical defenses. In psychotherapy, Reich used breathing exercises; putting physical pressure on tense, contracted muscles; and frank, open discussions with patients about the memories and resistance they were experiencing in the process.

Lowen (1975), a student of Reich's, refined and expanded on this approach and renamed the therapy *bioenergetics*. In contrast to Reich's primary focus on physical pleasure, Lowen found that a therapist was most effective if his or her goal was to open up the heart of the individual. The "heart" represented the patient's innate tenderness and vulnerability, which are crucial to being able to fully give and receive love. The heart was protected by layers of defense. On the outermost ring were the psychological defenses, followed by the muscular tension layer and then by the emotional layer, which contains suppressed feelings of rage, panic, terror, despair, sadness, and pain.

Lowen believed that effective therapy involved simultaneous attention to all three layers of defense. This entailed first contacting and manipulating the muscular tension layer and encouraging the patient to directly associate his psychological issues and dynamics with the rigidity and armoring of his body. From the muscular layer, the therapist could also encourage the expression of emotional release that would be not only cathartic but also connected to the psychological issues of which the individual was consciously aware. Repeated psychotherapy with muscular interventions allow for psychological awareness, muscular loosening, emotional release and, eventually, an inner softening and vulnerability. The end result is an individual with more fluid layering, who can function in society but also can be free to move gracefully, express emotion spontaneously, and embrace the opportunities the environment gives him to work, love, and play with energy and openness.

Body-oriented exercises should be done only after explaining their purpose to the client and asking about any physical problems that might cause harm or injury. If we are to use these techniques we ask the client to sign a waiver that states that the client has the responsibility to tell the therapist about any injuries pertinent to or reservations about doing the exercises. The client is allowed to decline participation in the exercises for any reason. After agreeing to an exercise under these conditions, the client releases the therapist from blame for any injury that occurs. None of our clients has ever experienced an injury. However, there is a chance for muscle soreness after doing an exercise.

Here are some of the primary body-oriented approaches for working with men. The reader is referred to Lowen and Lowen (1992) for illustrations and rationale for the exercises described in the following section.

Breathing Exercises

Deeper breathing facilitates the flow of oxygen to the brain, which in effect produces clearer thinking and increased energy. The therapist encourages the male client to close his eyes and breathe deeply from the diaphragm in long, smooth inhalations and exhalations. This exercise can be used at the beginning of a session to induce relaxation or when a client is feeling anxious to help him feel more centered and less emotionally overwhelmed.

Lee, age 30, came into his individual session directly from work. He was distracted and unable to concentrate on anything other than work-related worries. The therapist asked Lee to focus on his breathing and to extend his breaths so that he was taking in more air. Within 5 minutes, Lee reported that he felt calmer and that he felt more present for the therapy session.

Grounding Exercises

Grounding is an awareness of one's connection to the earth and to physical reality. The focus is on lowering one's center of gravity by allowing contact points to be made among the legs, feet, and floor. This allows a man to feel more centered and secure. The therapist encourages the client to stand without shoes, knees flexibly bent, and hands behind him on the small of his back, for several minutes, until his leg muscles begin to vibrate and shake. The vibrating and shaking keep the body awareness on the lower part of the body. Emotional release later in the session will be more contained and pleasurable if the man has grounded first. At the start of a men's group session all members were led in a grounding exercise. With his legs vibrating, each man was asked to literally feel the ground under him.

Otto, age 28, who had recently lost his 3-year-old daughter to a progressive disease, seemed especially affected by the exercise. Instead of speaking intellectually in an emotionally distant way, Otto began to weep as he told the group that this was the anniversary of her death. Several of the men supported Otto with verbal and physical reassurance as he spoke, but what was significant was that Otto stated that he felt more connected to his feelings about losing his daughter then he had since she died.

Eye Exercises

The eyes are believed to communicate much information about how a person is feeling and are one of the first sources of contact for a child with the mother. A bioenergetic therapist may ask a male client to open his eyes wide in terror, to relax and loosen his eye muscles, to dart his eyes back and forth, and to show various emotional expressions just using his eyes (although other parts of the body are likely to also engage at the same time). These exercises can stimulate a release of longing, sadness, or anger.

Byron, age 40, a man who had been severely abused as a child, was directed by the therapist to look at himself in a mirror during one of his therapy sessions. He was asked to describe what he saw in his own eyes and facial expression. Usually Byron had a blank, cold look to his face, but after doing some of the eye exercises his eyes moistened.

Therapist: What did you see in the mirror?

Byron: I saw myself first as frozen, but something feels like it has broken loose.

Therapist: What are you feeling?

Byron: I feel like I am going to cry.

Therapist: It's OK to cry here. You've been through a lot of pain.

Vocalizing Exercises: Guttural Screaming, Weeping, Laughing

The voice is a powerful indicator of tension, blockage, and energy. Inhibition of sound can indicate muscular blockage related to prior trauma, shame, or disuse. A therapist might encourage a man to use his voice in various fashions to release emotion. He is asked to breathe from the belly and have the sound make its way up from this point rather than just in the throat. Groaning can elicit feelings of hurt and pain. Screaming allows for a release of anger and frustration. Forcing a laugh can bring out a dark, shadowy, aggressive feeling. Encouraging vocalization while doing another body exercise can lead to releases of sadness, longing, and crying.

After being asked to open his eyes wide, smile, and force a laugh, Shawn, age 31, was encouraged to direct his expression toward one of the other members of the men's group and to say whatever came to his mind. "I am not afraid of you. You act tough, but I can see through your game. Heh, heh, heh." This was the first time that Shawn, who was typically shy and nonconfrontational, actually expressed some strong feelings toward another member of the group. The men in the group, including the man whom Shawn confronted, actually supported Shawn, proud of his directness and emotional honesty.

Kicking Exercises

Kicking is an expressive way to release anger, frustration, and negativity. The most powerful release comes if a client is asked to lie on a mattress or foam rubber pad on the ground and kick the mattress or pad, one leg at a time, in an alternating fashion. The whole leg should touch the mattress with each kick. By first starting slow and rhythmically, and then increasing the speed, a male client can begin to let go of his feeling of control. Combined with turning the head from side to side and having the arms alternatively pound, the man appears to be throwing a 2-year-old's temper tantrum. By adding the word "No!" or "Why?" the exercise can take a man back to childhood expressing his negativity toward his parents' control.

After doing the "no" exercise and kicking his legs, Jerry, age 37, felt like he was going to throw up.

Therapist: What's happening, Jerry?

Jerry: I felt like I was going to lose control.

Therapist: What would that mean?

Jerry: I don't know. If I ever told my father "no," he would have kicked my ass. I always had to be careful around him and do as he said.

Therapist: So saying no to him is like asking to be annihilated?

Jerry: Yes—in fact, I hardly ever say no to anyone because I'm afraid of what their reaction is going to be.

Therapist: What are you feeling now as you tell me this?

Jerry: Like I'm starting to break the spell, maybe.

Pounding Exercises

A therapist can help a man release anger and frustration in a cathartic manner using a tennis racquet, an 18-inch rubber hose, or even bare fists. The pounding can start out slow and rhythmically and get faster and faster. Vocalizations, such as "no, I won't do it!" or "fuck you," can be added to attach psychological meaning to the pounding. The therapist should have some pillows or soft cushions to have the man hit to reduce the risk of self-injury.

Stuart, age 41 and recovering from depression, was handed a tennis racquet in a men's group after he complained that he knew he should be angry at one of his coworkers but couldn't muster up any feeling. After hitting the pillow hard with the racquet for several minutes, Stuart was asked to put words into each of his hits. "Why did you screw me over? You hurt me. I trusted you!" he screamed. At the end of the exercise he was exhausted but had given voice to and expressed much of what he was feeling.

Twisting Exercises

A good exercise for expressing aggression and assertiveness toward others is towel twisting. By having the male client twist a towel with his hands tighter and tighter, while verbalizing a strong desire, such as "Give it to me!", he can experience throughout his body a full self-expression. This kind of full expression without muting is rare in the social world and can provide a significant bodily and emotional release.

Len, age 36, took the towel and twisted it tightly as he spoke of his feelings toward his ex-wife, who continued to complain and to harass him, even after 5 years of divorce. With maximum tension in his forearms, Len verbalized with intensity, "Leave me alone. I've already paid the price!", before collapsing into a pillow, weeping.

Reaching and Stretching Exercises

The reaching and stretching of the arms and legs can provide a loosening of muscular tension. Used at the beginning of a session as a warm-up exercise, this allows for body awareness and feelings of physical expansiveness. Stretching exercises with the arms used in session can elicit feelings of longing, especially if connected to a memory of reaching out toward a mother or father. Ryan, age 29, who recalls very few memories of his mother, who died when he was 5, was asked to lie on the floor and reach up toward the therapist. As he reached, Ryan was asked to open his eyes wide, look at the therapist, and verbalize his desire to be supported. Afterward Ryan, who allowed himself to feel his longing, was surprised to find that he had some vivid memories of his mother, especially ones in which she was holding and cuddling him.

SUMMARY

Although there are many paths to deepening a man's experiencing of himself, the diversity of therapeutic methods and perspectives often reflects the dynamic factors of the therapy situation. The timing of the intervention, the stage of therapy, the client's unique background, and the therapist's psychotherapeutic strengths form an ever-changing set of variables. Each man comes with his own unique character and interpersonal style that has been molded by family, culture, and individual life experiences. A therapy method that leads to deepening in one man at a particular stage of the process may not necessarily be effective with another. The successful deepening therapist must be sensitive to the nuances of the client's defenses and the changing interpersonal environment while being eclectic with the techniques that might nudge a man closer to the portal of his emotional depth.

The practice-oriented foundations of deepening psychotherapy involve a focus on exploring and exposing elements of the unconscious, including long-standing psychological dynamics, internalized emotions, and archetypal images. Connecting the psychological aspects of the self with the body's reactions in the context of an authentic and empathic therapeutic relationship also enhances depth. Existential concerns about the meaning of one's life in the context of a humanistic and holistic world perspective form another cornerstone of deepening therapy. These classic depth-oriented interventions, combined with the theoretical and clinical understanding of the new psychology of men, create a therapy process that is both expansive and eclectic. In the following sections of the book we provide readers with two extended case examples of deepening therapy with men that incorporate detailed attention to the actual dialogue of the sessions along with commentary about the therapeutic process.

4

EARLY PHASES OF DEEPENING PSYCHOTHERAPY WITH MEN

> Being in therapy awakens a man's early developmental experiences of shame. Feeling too guarded to reveal oneself, feeling like a dependent "mama's boy," loving an incompetent parent, as well as the confusion over needing attachment and the fear of feeling alone, are experiences evocative of childhood sources of shame which are then reactivated by being in therapy. (Osherson & Krugman, 1990, p. 328)

A man who comes to psychotherapy has somehow wandered off the road of traditional masculinity. He has either lost control of his life and burst through the "guardrail" of societal expectation, or he has been battered by the impossible demands of the masculine ideal and found himself in the back country, lost and confused. The former finds therapy only after family, friends, the law, or psychiatric authorities have caught him breaking the rules and have mandated his recovery. The latter, having bought into the culture's masculine ideals, wobbles into therapy feeling betrayed by the lack of reward or recognition. Both shamefully enter the therapy relationship with ambivalence and trepidation.

Psychotherapy is often seen as a venue for women or those too weak to take charge of their own lives (Brooks, 1996). It runs in direct opposition to the learned male role of remaining emotionally in control, rational, and bounded by ego considerations (Osherson & Krugman, 1990). In fact, men make up only 25%–33% of psychotherapy clients (Vessey & Howard, 1993). Although it may be more difficult to convince men to seek psychotherapy, the men who do encounter a therapist are just as likely as women to continue in therapy. Research has shown that men obtain successful therapy outcomes for many disorders, including both depression and anxiety (Cochran & Rabinowitz, 2000).

Brooks (1996, 1998a) has suggested that therapists should expect resistance in the first session and be prepared to "sell" men on the benefits of psychotherapy early in the therapy process or risk losing them. He has delineated two pathways to doing this, depending on the characteristics of the man in the office. The *hard sell*, which challenges the client to confront the consequences of his behaviors and coping style, is often most effective with a man who needs a jolt from an authority figure to take some responsibility for his predicament. The *soft sell* sides with a man's resistance to therapy and recognizes the difficulties and complexities of making changes. This pathway gives a man permission to trust his own pace and to count on the therapist's expertise to help him work through the barriers to change.

In the next four chapters we follow the deepening psychotherapy process of two men who come from different backgrounds and represent two of the common types of men who seek psychotherapy. To illustrate more clearly the therapy process of both men and to allow for comparison, the clients are presented in tandem, as they move through the therapy process at comparable rates. In actuality, the speed, intensity, and stage of therapy are apt to vary considerably from client to client. Identifying client information has been changed, and we have liberally used composites of therapy sessions to protect client confidentiality and give the reader a broad vision of the therapeutic work we do with men.

In the interest of narrative continuity, when the therapists in the following sessions refer to themselves in the session commentaries, the first-person singular "I" is used. Sam Cochran worked with the first client, Ron, and Fred Rabinowitz worked with the second client, Alex.

RON

After two canceled appointments, Ron finally found his way into my office. It was not easy for Ron to seek help. Within the last 2 years, this physically massive 42-year-old man had recently lost his job as a construction foreman, had his wife threaten to leave him, and lost his 19-year-old son in a car accident. On top of this, Ron's father, who had been physically and mentally abusive to him as a child and teenager, was dying of cancer in a nearby hospital. For Ron, the world was crashing in, and his usual coping style of denying psychic pain, working long hours, and drinking several beers each evening before bed was not working. Ron was seeking treatment to appease his wife, who had demanded he get help or say goodbye to her. Although he had very little awareness of how his life had become so tragic, he was growing tired of his own excuses, which placed blame for his problems on the external world. As he entered the office, Ron looked uneasy, shifting his eyes, with his head lowered as if he were a child being sent to the principal's office to be disciplined for bad behavior. I, as the therapist, greeted him warmly and allowed him to choose his chair in the room.

> **Therapist:** I know it hasn't been easy getting here. I'm not sure too many men would still be standing after being hit by all of the stuff you have. It sure takes a lot of guts to come to a place like this.

> **Ron:** Yeah. It's been a little rough. But I'll survive. I always do.

Therapist: I'd say that's understating it a bit.

Ron: No offense to you, Doc, but I'm not sure that anyone but me can get me out of this jam.

Therapist: Then why are you here?

Ron: My wife said that she's packing her bags if I don't come. She's about the only thing good left in my life, and I don't want to do anything that will push her away.

Therapist: So you are here for her primarily?

Ron: Yeah. I think if it was up to me, I'd probably try not to think about everything that has gone down recently. If it's not in your head, then I can almost pretend it's not happening to me.

Therapist: That style has worked for you, I'm sure, but with all that's happened I imagine its hard to pull it off these days.

Ron: It used to be easier, that's for sure.

Therapist: Is that how you have handled your son's death?

Ron: Sure. (Slight hesitation) I don't think his death has anything to do with me now. You have to move on. You know, shit happens.

Therapist: I'm not so sure I agree with you on this. Loss is a pretty powerful influence in most people's lives.

Ron: Listen, Doc. . .

It is apparent in this initial encounter that Ron is making sure that I know he is strong. His denial of pain conforms to a traditional masculine socialization model that precludes many men from appearing weak or vulnerable. His reference to me as "Doc" seems like an interpersonal distancing strategy that also emerges out of a traditional power model of masculine relationships. Because I am "the doctor," he must be "the patient." He responds to me as if I am judging him as a man, which is not an uncommon perspective in a relationship where men are sizing up who is stronger or higher on the "totem pole." From this perspective it is shameful to show weakness, and Ron is playing this out in our early interaction. As a male therapist, I must be aware of this dynamic and try to even the playing field, so to speak, if we are to get to the more substantive issues of his life.

Therapist: Hey Ron, you can call me by my first name if that's OK with you.

Ron: If you insist. What can you tell me about loss that I don't know? Once someone dies they are gone. Period. My mom used to say "Don't cry over spilled milk."

Therapist: You are comparing your son's death to spilled milk?

Ron: Of course not, but I can't bring him back to life. If I could trade places with him, I would in a second.

Therapist: Are you having any thoughts of taking your own life?

Ron: I think about it, but I couldn't do it. It would crush my wife. She already has been battered by Ronny's death. That would finish her off. What I need to do is to get back to work to take some of the financial pressures off her. I think that would help things a lot.

Therapist: You really care about her.

Ron: Yeah. She's probably my only friend in the world. If she left, I might consider following through, but I don't know how I'd do it or even if I would have the guts to do it.

Therapist: Sounds to me like you have a lot of your emotional self riding on your relationship with her.

Ron: I guess I do. I don't really like feeling that dependent, but I have no choice now. I'm not sure I can go at my life alone anymore.

It is crucial that a man who is laying himself vulnerable to a therapist feel that he is not only accepted and understood but also acknowledged as a hero for taking this courageous step toward his own emotional salvation. Even though a client's shame in admitting personal difficulties may be overwhelming, the therapist's attitude, posture, and words can convey respect and mirror strength rather than abject failure.

Perhaps I was premature in bringing up his son's death in the initial therapy session, but I also wanted Ron to know that speaking about his pain was not taboo in the therapy room. Most men are strongly defended against experiencing sadness and loss. At times, this initial exchange felt a bit competitive, with Ron showing me he could take pain without cracking and me challenging that assumption. It is not uncommon for a male therapist and male client to engage in some of this type of interaction as they test each other out. Male socialization has taught men not to show weakness, and in this vulnerable situation we both fell into some male posturing for power.

I find the balance between being too intrusive and ignoring a critical issue to be difficult. Ron's suicidal remarks needed to be followed up and assessed for lethality, yet it was important not to lose the flow of our interchange with a series of structured questions.

Ron's crucial admission in the last exchange let me know that a portal was open right now for him to see his life with depth, which would be a key factor in him being able to receive help and work in therapy. In his acknowledgment of his dependence and aloneness, Ron touched a core issue that defines his inner existence. It was imperative to seize the moment with Ron and engage him in a real discussion about his world. Anything less would have risked him shutting down further, validating his belief that no one could help or understand.

ALEX

Alex, a thin, handsomely dressed, 33-year-old, unmarried African American man, was referred by an old college friend of his who had had me as a psychology professor 10 years ago. Alex was the oldest of 5 children raised by both parents in a fairly rigid and restrictive religious family. His father was a minister, so Alex grew up around the church. He was expected to be a shining example to the rest of the congregation of goodness and responsibility.

Alex was required to disengage from his wants and desires as a child to please his parents as well as the extended church family. Recently he has found himself alternating between being angry and depressed. He has a well-paying job as an assistant hospital administrator, a position he took 2 years ago that involved him moving 200 miles from his family of origin. Alex claimed to have little time to date or engage in any relationships outside of work. His cautious approach to revealing himself early in therapy made me wonder what he might be hiding. I, as the therapist, observed and probed, noticing how protective he seemed to be of his current life situation.

> **Therapist:** I'm glad you made it in. How are you feeling about being here today?
>
> **Alex:** Kind of excited, actually. I have felt like I've been in a big rut.
>
> **Therapist:** Tell me what the rut is like.
>
> **Alex:** I don't know if I can describe it. It's like I keep myself busy, but I'm not happy. Do you know what I mean?
>
> **Therapist:** I'm not sure I do. Can you tell me more?
>
> **Alex:** It's like I used to think by the time I was 30 I'd be settled down, married, have a few kids. But I haven't even gone out in a date in the past 6 months.
>
> **Therapist:** So you feel like your life should be coming together, and it's not.
>
> **Alex:** Not exactly. My work life is good, but I have no personal life.
>
> **Therapist:** Is that a conscious choice on your part?
>
> **Alex:** Well, sort of. I've been having a hard time spending time alone with myself unless I'm focused on work.
>
> **Therapist:** Work must be really important to you.
>
> **Alex:** Yes, it is. I feel like I'm good at my job, and that lets me be OK with myself. I don't know what I'd do if I wasn't feeling like I was good at something.
>
> **Therapist:** So your self-worth is connected to being productive.

Alex: I know it's weird, but I still think that it's the only way to keep my parents off my back. They approve of my work, but I can tell they don't like me being single and living far away from them.

Therapist: How do you feel about your parents?

Alex: They are really supportive, loving people. Did I tell you that my dad is a minister?

Therapist: Yeah, you did, on the phone. Alex, you didn't answer my question. How do you feel toward them?

Alex: Well, they're good people. I love them, but... (silence).

Therapist: But what?

Alex: It feels really hot in here. Do you control the thermostat? (Beads of perspiration have appeared on his forehead.)

Therapist: Maybe the heat of your body is reflecting something important and relevant?

Alex: Do you think so? I still think you have a hot room.

Alex changed the subject when I persisted in asking for an emotionally honest response about his parents. He did look noticeably hot, with beads of sweat forming on his forehead. We were touching on something of deep importance, which his body was acknowledging in its intense heat. The temperature in the room had not changed, but this attribution allowed him to move away from his complex and contradictory feelings about his parents. Was my redirection back to the psychological significance of his body heat too intense for him?

Alex seemed to get a momentary glimpse of the possibility that his parents were a tough subject for him, even as he moved to save emotional face in my presence with his belief that the room had suddenly heated up. His responses to my probes left me questioning whether he could handle being exposed by my empathic responses this early in the relationship. Although I was giving him permission to be emotionally honest, I wondered, like I do with many male clients coming in for the first time, if I would ever see him again once he left the office.

LIFE-DAMAGED MEN AND SOCIAL CHAMELEONS

Ron characterizes the man who has been forced into therapy rather than one who has chosen it. For him, therapy is a maneuver to get back what he has lost or is in the process of losing. On entry, Ron has no idea how to use therapy except to know that the therapy process, whatever it is, will take the pressure off him. He naively believes that therapy will consist of him getting advice from some expert on people's problems. He doesn't see the interaction with the therapist as a potential relationship but rather as a life consultation to help him enhance his performance at home and work (Brooks, 1996). Chances are that relationships have not been particularly gratifying for him and in many cases have been downright painful. As a defense against feeling too vulnerable, a man like Ron will have a tendency to minimize his pain and show the therapist that he is strong and able to take care of himself (Scher, 1990).

In contrast, Alex represents the man who has a vague but nagging sense of dissatisfaction with his life. Overtly, he feels like he has nothing of substance to complain about. From a superficial perch, his life looks successful. On closer examination, however, there are a sketchiness and emptiness that he can no longer ignore. For Alex, it is the absence of intimacy that he is beginning to notice. Like many men, climbing the career ladder has provided him with a source of self-esteem (Levinson, Darrow, Klein, Levinson, & McKee, 1978). When he is not making progress on an achievement-oriented goal, life for Alex feels two dimensional, shameful, and depressing. For him, therapy will be more like an obstacle course on his attempt to discover his "real self."

Men like Alex find themselves caught in knots of guilt and shame about many aspects of their emotional lives. Anything that does not go as planned can breed self-recrimination for not having been in better control of the situation. For Alex, there is little forgiveness for the imperfections he sees in himself. There is little awareness about how this internal "judge" came about. He just knows that, internally, there is constant scorekeeping about his actions.

With little overt abuse or conflict, the problems in living have no obvious conscious thread of causation. Subtle identification with a perfectionist father or unconscious attempts to live up to an ideal are disguised by consciously heard words of love and support from parents. In public, these men are often smooth, charming, and energized in social situations. They confuse themselves as to whether the conflicting feelings they have are manufactured by faulty thinking or are real signs of something being amiss in their lives.

The Rons of the world appear to be *life-damaged men*; the Alexes appear to be *social chameleons*. Although there is always danger in generalizing, it seems helpful to characterize these two extreme variations of men who arrive for therapy. In reality, most men who come for therapeutic consultation are likely to have some shared features but often tend to resemble one of the types.

In the diagnostic language of the *Diagnostic and Statistical Manual of Mental Disorders* (4th ed., *DSM–IV*; American Psychiatric Association, 1994), life-damaged men, in their extreme form, are more likely to be recovering antisocial personalities in middle age (35–60 years) who have been in trouble with the law, may have had alcohol or substance abuse problems, or have worn out their welcome in social or employment settings. Earlier in their lives, psychotherapy would have been largely unsuccessful, because they would have blamed others for their problems. With age and a history of poor relationships, work changes, and possibly some time in 12-step or domestic violence groups, the life-damaged man is more likely to see himself as the common factor in his life problems and ready to accept assistance from a therapist. Although he may be in a position of power at work, often the life-damaged man has had to climb from an unprivileged background to achieve success. He may not have had support for intellectual pursuits and is more likely than the social chameleon to have had blue-collar family origins.

Life-damaged men are not subtle people. They wear their psychological bumps, bruises, and concussions on their sleeves. Usually one can see in a man's face and body how he has been battered by life. He may have some physical scars, perhaps a bad back, an overweight body, or an intense look in his eyes. He will speak in a direct, no-nonsense style, revealing some hard-earned cynicism and distrust of people in general.

Social chameleons, on the other hand, are disguised. Their life wounds are hidden behind good social skills; appropriate dress; and often professions such as lawyers, physicians, or business executives. They are less likely than life-damaged men to have had to deal with overt abuse in childhood and often have been born into more privileged families in which intellectual and financial success has been the norm. The social chameleons who enter psychotherapy often have a narcissistic self-structure that has been pierced in a significant way, leading to feelings of emptiness, deflation, or depression. A social chameleon's expectations of therapy are that he will receive support and regain the specialness he feels he has lost.

The social chameleon is sensitive to slights and will often retaliate with a cutting remark or a missed appointment when the therapist probes his narcissistic vulnerability. When asked questions, he seems to have a sophisticated answer and an uncanny sense of what the questioner might want to hear. It is difficult to know what the social chameleon really feels at times, because he has a strong need to impress with his words, deflect conflict, and be admired.

We have observed in the group therapy setting that life-damaged men have a keen sense of danger. They quickly home in on who they think is trustworthy. Their family backgrounds often are marked by tangible traumas, such as child abuse, sexual abuse, drug-addicted parents, divorce, death, and separation. Their adult lives often reflect unconscious choices that have run them into the same roadblocks as their parents, including their own run-ins with drugs, divorce, physical violence, or victimization. Their life journeys resemble country music songs about the down-on-your-luck side of life.

The life-damaged man can often "smell" a social chameleon a mile away. We have noticed that life-damaged men see social chameleons as unappreciative whiners who don't own their good fortune and who have let their intellect take precedence over their true feelings. It is not uncommon to hear a life-damaged man in a men's group say "Cut your intellectual bullshit and tell me how you really feel." Social chameleons, on the other hand, see life-damaged men as interpersonally dull, unsophisticated, and unable to defend themselves from life's misfortunes. By not learning the interpersonal subtleties of appeasing others, life-damaged men continually anger and frustrate bosses, wives, and potential friends with their "screw the consequences" emotional honesty. The life-damaged man's personality defense structure is usually fairly rigid and inflexible, putting him constantly in conflict with the fast-moving and ever-changing flow of interpersonal life.

Social chameleons are often dishonest with themselves and in their relationships to avoid conflict and pain. Many men like Alex have been reinforced for the "good boy" role in their families. Many times a social chameleon will side with his mother in a triangular relationship with the father. Instead of identifying with a distant or weak father, the social chameleon will identify with a present or strong mother who rewards her son with the intimacy that should have been extended toward his father.

When a social chameleon takes this role out into the world of men, he often finds that he is superficially accepted but not fully trusted. Even though there may be good reason for him to have sided with his mother, his betrayal of his father plays out with a subtle distrust of other men and more approachable friendships with women.

Although a social chameleon may be more comfortable with a woman, hoping she will emulate his mother in bestowing specialness on him, often he will be disappointed. He may end up being one of those "nice guys" whom the woman will want as a friend but not a lover. The good-boy dynamic assumes that others will see how "good" he is and thus afford him special favors and rewards. When he realizes that his specialness is not being appreciated, he will find fault with the other person. He may become passive–aggressive toward those who have betrayed him. Instead of overtly expressing his anger, he will be superficially nice but prone to unconscious betrayals of those close to him. He may renege on a commitment, have a secret affair, forget an appointment, or conveniently leave out an important detail that causes distress to a coworker, friend, or mate. He will later claim ignorance and apologize profusely.

In effect, the social chameleon persona is a sneaky and subtle defense against people who don't appreciate the social chameleon's specialness. After awhile, those who know the social chameleon realize that he is not quite trustworthy despite his Boy Scout appearance. The vague emptiness the social chameleon feels is of others pulling away from him while he is in need. His pain is that he doesn't know how to connect to others in an honest way despite all his efforts.

What the life-damaged man and social chameleon have in common is a sense of a life slipping away from them. Both types of men have worked extremely hard to overcome adversity, gain control over their lives, and try to do the right thing. No matter what they do it seems to them that life continually rips them off. For the life-damaged man there is always someone or something that interferes with his achievement of his dream. For the social chameleon there is a sense of falseness that accompanies his accomplishments and relationships. Both suffer from a lack of awareness of how they have adapted to and coped with the cultural forces that have shaped their development. It is not until an emotional wound pierces the male self-structure that conflicts about relationship dependency, losses across the life span, male gender role restrictions, and the tendency to avoid rather than face painful issues are exposed.

INITIAL THERAPY PROCESS ISSUES: BALANCING ASSESSMENT AND CONNECTION

One of the major tasks of the early sessions of psychotherapy with men is to balance assessment with the goal of building a strong therapeutic relationship. Although it is important to investigate the familial, cultural, and individual nature of the presenting symptoms, and to assess any suicidal or homicidal thinking, planning, or impulses, it is also important to listen to how a man presents his story. By tuning into subtle verbal and nonverbal communication the therapist can slowly start the process of connection through nonjudgmental reflections and genuine interest. The strength of the therapeutic alliance will correlate directly with the therapist being able to show explicit empathy for the male client's experience (Pollack, 1990).

We believe that assessment must take into account an understanding of core male issues from which a therapist can empathically understand and eventually intervene in a man's inner world. The first of these issues concerns the relational aspect of a man's life, specifically the dynamics of a man's socially learned tendency toward independence and his often-hidden dependence in his significant relationships. The psychotherapy process itself often reveals and highlights contradictions between giving in to dependent connection and fleeing toward independence and separateness. The intensity of this conflict is often mediated by shame-based defenses whose purpose is to reduce exposure and push away connection. An example of a shame-based defense is a man's minimization of any problems or the spinning of a story about the past that leaves the listener bored or wondering what emotions were left out.

The second core element involves the prohibition of men in our culture from assuming the *depressive position*, an emotional state that accompanies the many experiences across the life span of grief, loss, and disappointment. By listening carefully for these experiences a therapist can begin to assess how much defending a man has had to do in order to avoid feeling sadness and depression in his life. It is not unusual for a man to successfully defend against this type of pain for much of his life and then be overwhelmed by the breakthrough of feeling that accompanies an unexpected loss or trauma.

The third aspect to investigate is the nature of the masculine self-structure, a man's identity that has developed from the influence of early family interpersonal interactions, cultural factors, and the gender role demands of masculine socialization. Through history taking, and paying close attention to the way a man describes himself in his actions and attitudes, the therapist can begin to assess the impact of significant individual relationships as well as those that have been culturally learned. It is important to see all of these influences as being intertwined and related to fully understand their places in a man's life.

The fourth core element to attend to in assessment is the conflict for most men between being and doing. A therapist should listen to how a man has handled problematic situations and observe how anxious a man is about staying with a feeling or body awareness before wanting to move into an action mode within the therapy relationship. Psychotherapy often has the effect of slowing down the movement to action in order to "be" with a feeling or awareness.

Finally, it is important to investigate the nature of the circumstances that have brought a man to therapy. Often, a narcissistic injury or "wound" has pierced the defenses and precipitated a consultation with a therapist. This wound can be the catalyst for a man to seek help and move toward emotional depth. Because men rarely come to therapy on their own without having been emotionally wounded or threatened, it is the therapist's job to decipher how this wound has affected the deep structure of a man's identity.

In the early sessions, the therapist must act in a way that lets the male client know that he is welcome and appreciated, not only for his achievements but also for his life struggle to overcome adversity (Cochran & Rabinowitz, 1996). The therapist must balance connection with a measured respect for the man's tattered defensive structure. Too much overt empathy can be perceived by some men as threatening and shaming (Osherson & Krugman, 1990; Shay, 1996). The male client often struggles with the role of patient and his felt sense of being out of control in relation to the therapist (Scher, 1990). It is important for the therapist to be aware of this dynamic and use humor and self-disclosure to let the client know that the therapist is a fellow human, capable of collaborating with the male client (Cochran & Rabinowitz, 1996).

Male clients often come to therapy expecting the therapist to be an authority figure. Although this projection is inevitable in most cases, the therapist needs to be able to show his human side so that the environment feels safe. The therapist often has to explicitly give permission to the male client early on to speak about typically taboo topics (Scher, 1981). It is important for the therapist to use the client's style of language and pick up on his metaphors when engaging him about difficult and shameful topics (Cochran & Rabinowitz, 1996; Shay, 1996). Finally, it is useful in early sessions to help the client get used to making connections between his body and his self-verbalizations, because this will be the eventual gauge of truth for him in the therapy process.

In this initial therapy session both Ron and Alex have described their lives from a position of strength. As therapists, we are probing for information, but in an empathic way. We are less interested in getting all the data than we are in getting a feel for the way each man presents himself. In beginning the process of establishing a relationship, a therapist needs to be open to a man's interpretation of his situation yet willing to challenge him a bit to see how he responds. It is important to not minimize his issues. We know that even those issues presented in a low-key way by the male client may not necessarily be low-key issues.

It takes much courage for a man to overcome his shame and make it to the therapist's office. We are always genuinely impressed by a male client's effort, and we let him know that. Men need to know that they have not made a mistake by coming to talk with a psychotherapist. We want to give each male client the message that he is free to be himself in our office, that he will not be judged harshly, and that the therapist is someone with whom he can be safe. Even in the initial session, a reluctant male client will offer some test issues to see if the therapist is trustworthy and can truly relate to the client's state of being.

DEEPENING IN EARLY SESSIONS: THE PORTAL

> When the client feels understood, welcomed, received as he is in the various aspects of his experience. . . . then there is a gradual loosening of constructs, a freer flow of feelings which are characteristic of movement up the continuum. (Rogers, 1961, p. 137)

For the therapy process to deepen, several important relational factors must converge. The most important element is the therapist's openness to the client's internal perspective and his or her ability to reduce the shame that often occurs with self-revelation. Shame is often elicited from self-exposure that recapitulates negative relationship experiences. Kaufman (1992) suggested that a male child is often put into binds by parents in childhood that leave him feeling bad for having certain emotions, physiological drives, or relationship connection needs. Typically, the experience of one of these natural states is followed by a shaming parental response that leaves the boy stunned and wounded. With no one to speak to about his pain, the typical pattern for boys is to repress the experience and replace the pain of exposure with a feeling of blankness or nothingness. This blankness is sent up like a defensive shield whenever the boy re-experiences a situation of exposure in which he has been wounded. As the boy grows to adulthood he tends to respond to many of his own emotions, drives, and relationship needs with the disdain he received from his parents, having internalized their critical judgment. Psychotherapy, by its focus on these aspects of the self, elicits the gamut of shame-based defensive responses, including a cloud of repression that hangs over the origins of the original shaming.

Although a male client may have difficulty using words to describe his internal emotional state, the therapist must be able to translate, respond, and empathize with the gestalt of what is presented. This means that, aside from the actual words spoken, the facial inflections, physical movements, and silences, inferred meanings, metaphors, and projections must be understood and framed without overwhelming the client's defense system. The male client needs to feel safe enough to go into the fog of his past experiences and excavate the abyss of the unknown aspects of himself. He has to trust that his therapist will be there if he falls or gets lost.

Aside from being empathic, another important element that increases trust and reduces shame is the therapist's ability to maneuver through his or her own countertransference reactions to the client's issues. It is not unusual for the male client's major concerns to be similar to the issues that most men navigate in their lives. A therapist must be willing to revisit his or her own developmental crises and be open to exploring current issues as they are brought to the surface by the client's material. Separation from one's mother, the relationship with one's father, loss of innocence through abuse, creation of a false self, betrayal of one's own natural emotional reactions, counterphobic risk taking, death anxiety, loss of meaning, achievement, competition, feelings about love, sexual desire, hatred, anger, and rejection make up a significant list of issues that are likely to be stirred up in the therapist.

Unconscious responding by both male and female therapists to a man's pain is inevitable. What distinguishes a therapist who can go to the deeper levels with a male client is his or her willingness to wrestle with the emotional meaning of his or her reactions and use them to respond to the client. Countertransference cannot be avoided but must rather be embraced as the imprint of the intersection of the therapist's and client's relational worlds. In the feelings the therapist has toward the male client lies information about what the client elicits from others as well as a gauge of the therapist's current reactivity in the therapeutic relationship. Countertransference awareness is an invitation to the therapist to explore his or her own deeper crevices through his or her own therapy and supervision.

To facilitate the client's movement closer to his portal of depth a therapist must be willing to show the courage that he expects from his client. A client intuitively knows when a therapist is involved in his own growth process. The quality of empathy, the push to move further in the emotional realm, and sensitivity to discomfort in the client's presentation allow the client to sense the therapist's involvement. The therapist's sensitivity can be conveyed subtly by a nod, the use of an appropriate metaphor, a spontaneous facilitative therapeutic exercise, or a self-disclosure about how he might have felt had he been in the client's shoes at the moment being described in session. By sensing that he is with a man or woman who has done his or her own psychological work, a male client can paddle through the river rapids of self-exploration toward a deeper pool, knowing he has an experienced guide with him.

SESSION 2: BODY MEMORIES

As soon as possible, we like to bring a man's body as well as his mind into engagement in the therapy room. Too many men have split off their bodies from their intellect and minimize how much their bodies carry life's traumas. The body holds important emotional and psychological truths.

Ron

In this session, discussion about Ron's body leads to highly charged emotional memories from his childhood and adolescence. Ron recalls being bullied and shamed by his father as well as by his peers, and having to be his brother's protector. He begins to unravel the life damage that he has had to sustain to survive a rough, male cultural upbringing.

Therapist: Ron, tell me how your body has been holding up through all this stress.

Ron: I have always been a really big guy. I used to play football in high school. Now I'm getting pretty fat because I sit on my ass a lot. When I was a kid, skinny guys got pushed around, and I wanted no part of that. If anyone was going to do the pushing, it was going to be me.

Therapist: Do you remember when you were first pushed around?

Ron: Not really. All I know is that when I was walking to grade school, some of the older kids would make fun of the younger ones like me. They would call us babies and then push us backwards over another guy who was kneeled on the ground. One time I stupidly said I was going to tell my mom. Boy, was that a mistake! From then on they would mock me, "Why don't you go call your mother? Maybe she can save you." When I got older and some of the kids picked on my younger brother, I would protect him by acting tough. If I beat a few heads, then the bullies would back off.

Therapist: Sounds like a good strategy for protecting yourself and your brother. How did your dad react to you fighting with the other kids?

Ron: He would usually say that I was doing the right thing. He had no problem hitting me when I did something wrong. He thought that was how you made points to people who weren't paying attention. My dad was a bully himself.

Therapist: You must have had to watch yourself around him.

Ron: I avoided him at all costs when I was small. I protected my brother when I got big. My brother ended up moving away from the family when he finished high school. I see him every couple of years. (At this point, Ron's eyes drop, and his body, hunched forward, seems to go limp.)

Therapist: You looked kind of sad when you said that.

Ron: Yeah. We were really close as kids. He's out doing his own thing. Jackie doesn't want anything to do with the family here. I guess that's one way of taking care of yourself.

Therapist: What do you mean that's one way to take care of yourself?

Ron: That little fucker ran halfway across the country to escape our messed up family. I can't say I blame him.

Therapist: Are you angry that he got away and you didn't?

Ron: I love my brother. And he's doing a lot better than me right now.

Therapist: He may be taking care of himself, but you lost a brother you were close to.

Ron: I guess those are the breaks.

Ron has had many losses in his life that are unconsciously recorded in his body. I anticipate that this will be a major issue in our therapy together. The shift from talking about his father, bullies, and aggression to the loss of his brother demonstrates an unconscious link between these two powerful affects. For many men, anger is a learned defense against sadness and shame. Beneath anger is often a well of sadness that has often not been cognitively identified. According to the traditional rules of male socialization, anger is an acceptable emotion, whereas sadness makes one feel weak, vulnerable, and unmanly. A part of my role as therapist is to help Ron translate his anger into more differentiated emotional states. In this session I let Ron touch his sadness by reflecting what I see in his facial expressions and hear in his words and tone of voice. I am aware that he is likely to defend himself against falling too deeply into the emotional abyss by minimizing the impact of his losses.

Alex

In this portion of the second session Alex is talking about how he perceives his body, which leads him to reveal his strong need to stay in control in many areas of his life, including his interpersonal relationships.

Alex: I've always been pretty thin and athletic. I really have a fear of getting fat.

Therapist: What does having a thin and athletic body mean to you?

Alex: I guess that it makes me feel good when I look in the mirror. I hate when guys get a beer gut or let themselves go to pot. I swore I'd never get fat, because to me that would mean that I had lost control of myself.

Therapist: So your body is a reflection of how much control you are feeling in your life.

Alex: Yeah. I never thought of it that way, but it makes sense when you say it. I really do like to be in control. At work, it is superimportant to maintain order and control. I dread chaos. Maybe that's why I make sure my desk is cleaned off before I leave work every night. I hate coming in the next day and seeing stuff lying out random and disorderly.

Therapist: It seems important to be in control at work. How does being in control impact your relationships?

Alex: Funny you should ask that. My last girlfriend told me that I was impossible to please. She always felt like she was doing something wrong around me. I always thought I was doing what she wanted. We weren't very well matched, I guess.

The central issue of staying in control seems to have a profound impact on various aspects of Alex's life, including his work and interpersonal relationships. Alex is just beginning to be aware that his orderly approach to many of life's challenges may in itself be causing him some unexpected problems. At this stage of therapy he is not yet ready to take responsibility for acknowledging how this behavior may affect others, as articulated in his comment about his previous girlfriend. As a therapist, I am aware that the theme of control may be a pathway to reaching Alex's portal to emotional depth.

Both Ron and Alex are making discoveries about themselves as we explore their current situations and the patterns of both present and past that seem to intertwine in the unfolding reality of the therapy process. Both have minimized the emotional impact that their relationships have had on them. Both have told us how they defend against being overwhelmed with feeling.

Ron, like many men who have suffered overt trauma at the hands of parents and peers, uses anger and body intimidation as a sure-fire method to regain control of situations he perceives to be out of control (Harway & Evans, 1996). Ron feels the adrenaline surge through his body when he is threatened, and he learned in the male world of childhood and adolescence that this can translate into power. A significant axiom of male acculturation is that one should not show weakness or vulnerability, because this will give others an advantage over you.

Alex, who suffered little overt abuse when growing up, learned how to control his physiological reactions, even as a child. Although it is possible that Alex was biologically predisposed to be less physical in his reactions than Ron, it is more likely that control was modeled and reinforced by his parents and social environment. As an adult, control over one's feelings is a very effective tool to achieving success. Men who can remain calm, cool, and in control often feel like they have a tactical advantage over those who "lose it." Alex has taken to heart the male axiom that one shall always remain in control. He has learned to monitor his body, keep his work environment uncluttered and neat, and use socially acceptable manners in his interpersonal dealings. However, the controlled social facade learned in his family and reinforced by society has left Alex sensitive to what others expect and isolated from what his body is telling him.

SESSION 3: CULTURAL BACKGROUND

It is extremely important for a client's cultural background to be brought into the therapy encounter. In early sessions, probing about the childhood milieu in which a man has been raised offers clues to some of the issues that he may be currently facing. Learning about a man's family, socioeconomic, religious, and ethnic background provide a tapestry of understanding for the therapist of his client's basic values, assumptions, and influences.

Ron

I asked Ron directly whether he had ever acted violently toward his own family members. We had been touching on his relationship with his wife, and I felt that a frank discussion of the issue was important given his history of being beaten as a child by his father. I was mindful of the powerful force that child abuse has on men and how a man might unconsciously transmit this abuse in his own family. I wondered if he would be truthful with me.

Therapist: Have you ever been physical with your wife or children?

Ron: To tell you the truth, this is one area where I did not want to repeat my father's actions. I have felt ready to do it, but I've stopped myself.

Therapist: How did you do that?

Ron: I remember when we were first married and Pam pissed me off. It was about something stupid like not having the right stuff to go with my dinner. I felt myself moving toward her like I was going to kill her right then and there. I saw the terror in her eyes, and I flashed on my own childhood. It scared me so much I just went limp. I don't remember much after that except that I didn't hit her.

Therapist: Wow! That must have been frightening for you.

Ron: It was. If I'd had some sense, I would have gone to therapy right then. As I look back, I was so out of control with myself. But hey, I was

21 years old, and no way would I admit that I had any problems. I was young and strong and had my whole future ahead of me.

Therapist: Like you were invulnerable. How else were you out of control?

Ron: I was partying a lot. Booze and herb. I felt pretty trapped in my life situation. I married when I was 19. We were expecting our first kid, and I was still a kid myself.

Therapist: You had a lot of responsibility for someone just out of high school, huh?

Ron: You're not kidding. I was working construction, up early and then coming home to a whining, pregnant wife. I'm not trying to be disrespectful, but she was pretty needy by the time I got home. I probably drank 12 cans of beer between the time I got home and when I went to bed.

Therapist: Did you share any of your fears with your wife?

Ron: Are you kidding? Like I said, she was the needy one. I was supposed to be the strong, silent type. You know, Clint Eastwood or John Wayne. They were the guys I modeled myself after. My old man was such a loser, I didn't want to use him as a role model.

This is a clear expression of the masculine-specific self-structure Ron had adopted to fit into the traditional male culture of his peers and society at large. When he was a younger man it involved reckless risk taking, a denial of mortality, and an inflated sense of control and power. I am aware that we will have to look at the costs involved in him having taken on this type of identity.

Alex

I was surprised to see Alex at this session. I thought that I might have been a bit too intense for him last session. He was impeccably dressed in a suit and tie, looking very much in control of himself. He took off his suit jacket, lay it neatly on a nearby couch, and spoke superficially about the traffic and weather. I asked him if he was ready to work and waited for him to start. Alex instead asked me if I still had questions of him. Rather than play the "therapist game" of putting it back on him, I addressed our ethnic differences. I knew that for us to begin to bond this would need to be openly acknowledged.

Therapist: How has it been for you being an African American man in this culture?

Alex: I thought you might go for something a little less direct. This leads down a slippery road that I don't want to go down.

Therapist: You've been asked this before?

Alex: When you're a successful Black man every White person who thinks they know you even a little well asks you this question in one form or another. I am tired of it and don't really want to get into it. It really has nothing to do with my current state of affairs.

Therapist: You sound pretty sure of this. I'll back off, but it seems relevant to me in our work.

Alex: Why is that?

Therapist: Because for me, the way you have been raised in your family as well as how you have experienced your culture affects who you are. The intensity of your desire not to speak about this tells me it must be a charged topic for you.

Alex: Sorry about that. I always wonder what people are really thinking about my color, secretly hoping they are not thinking anything about it. I just want to be known as Alex, not Alex the Black guy or Alex the token Black guy.

Therapist: You want to be seen for who you are, not judged by your color or ethnicity.

Alex: Yes, of course. I made it this far on my own merit, not because I was promoted in some racial quota system. That's what I think people are thinking: He's up the corporate ladder because of some affirmative action thing.

Therapist: Alex, I believe you have made it on your own merit. My question was directed to help me understand how your ethnicity has affected you.

Alex: Well, you can see how it has affected me. I'm usually very polite with people, but this issue just frustrates me.

Therapist: The way people perceive you feels out of your control.

Alex: Yes. And you know how I feel about control. It's survival, plain and simple. Let's just say that I have had my run-ins with racism, and it isn't pretty. I'd rather not blame or excuse myself or others based on ethnicity. I was born in the USA, and I have most of those values, if that's what your after. I believe in working hard and getting rewarded for that.

Therapist: But what does it cost you?

Alex: I'm not sure what you're after.

Therapist: What price do you pay for buying into the American hard work ethic?

Alex: I don't know. At least I'm not dragging a wife and kid through my workaholism. Someday my future wife and kids will be grateful that I paid my dues, and have the material comforts, all without ripping them off.

Therapist: Maybe they will be grateful, but what are you doing now to make it so you might someday have a wife and kids?

Alex: Fuck you (smiling).

Our discussion of ethnicity seems to draw Alex out emotionally. He senses his own defensive anger as he responds to my questions. He wants me to know that this part of him is off limits in our relationship at this point. I respect his wishes but still let him know that I have noticed his reaction. Although Alex admits his workaholism and rationalizes that it is acceptable because he has no family, I challenge his thinking, knowing he is not dealing with his relational world. He responds by giving me a mixed message of anger and acknowledgment. I feel a certain sense of connection with him in his defiance and anger and hope that it is the beginning of him sharing some of his inner passion with me.

INFLUENCE OF GENDER ROLE SOCIALIZATION AND CULTURE IN THERAPY

One's family and culture heavily influence gender role identity, the felt sense of maleness or femaleness. Differences in parental interaction styles, expectations of behavior, and even toys given to boys and girls begin the process of gender role socialization early in life. Aside from having some physiological differences, boys are more likely than girls to be encouraged to play aggressively by adults, to be physically punished for wrong actions, and to be discouraged by parents as well as by peers from exhibiting behavior that diverges from prescribed gender norms (Rabinowitz & Cochran, 1994). Crying and expressing feelings are often kept in check by older males, including many fathers, who remind young boys that "only girls cry." As a young boy develops into manhood he is exposed to a plethora of exaggerated male role models who often equate maleness with independence, toughness, competitiveness, control, and dominance. Many males are reinforced by family, peers, media, and social institutions to avoid "feminine" qualities such as dependency, submissiveness, and emotional expressiveness (O'Neil, Good, & Holmes, 1995).

Ethnic and cultural identity also interacts powerfully with gender role influences to shape masculine expectations. Many men of color who grew up outside mainstream European American, heterosexual, middle-class American culture are reminded by their experiences of prejudice and oppression on a personal and institutional level that, although they are men, they are less privileged and more vulnerable to forces outside of their control (see L. D. Caldwell & White, 2001; Majors, 1994; Majors & Billson, 1992; Washington, 1987). Although many men try to maintain a color-blind perspective, America at the turn of the new millennium is still racially divided. It is difficult for White men to comprehend the subtle harassment that men of color experience on a daily basis. Questionable stares; increased scrutiny; and automatic suspicion by peers, strangers, and police are regular occurrences for these men, who work and live in the mainstream culture

(Lazur & Majors, 1995). Not only are they subject to the stresses of traditional masculinity, but they must also cope with the overlay of subtle and not-so-subtle racism. A layer of anger related to this cultural predicament is not uncommon in many men of color, even those who are trying to live by the rules of mainstream society (Franklin, 1998).

Although not as obvious as skin color, there are varieties of "White" identity as well that leave men vulnerable to feelings of alienation. Men who are unemployed, or who work in the blue-collar work sector, may feel alienated from those in white-collar jobs. In many places in America, gay men are fearful of expressing aspects of their sexual orientation in the presence of their straight counterparts. Jewish, Muslim, and Christian men, as well as men from other religious backgrounds, also feel ambivalence about how public they should be in acknowledging their religious identities. Men with physical and psychological disabilities also are subject to unwanted scrutiny and judgment from other men.

Both Ron and Alex have been influenced by not only their families of origin but also by the dominant cultural rules of manhood. Ron followed a typical path for a young man of our culture who did not plan to attend college. He got a well-paying entry-level construction job, married his high school sweetheart, and began a family with a child of his own by the age of 20. Although to some people this might reflect an ideal situation, it was wrought with conflict for Ron, who had very little sense of awareness about his life direction. He was doing what was expected of him, even though it frightened him at the same time. Because of his unconscious adherence to the rules of traditional masculinity, he did not seek help with his fears, choosing instead to drink beer and smoke pot to calm himself and obliterate his nagging doubts about himself. He had to suppress his violent impulses at home and, luckily, tired himself out physically at work to reduce his acting-out potential. It is significant that Ron can now look back at this period of his life and admit that it would have been a good time for him to confront some of his issues about being a man. Coming to therapy now sanctions what he has known for a long time: that his construction of masculinity has a down side to it.

Alex learned early in his life that he would be rewarded for hard work. Following not only the rules of his family, but also society's infatuation with work, he has gotten ahead in his career. Alex has left little time in his day for emotional intimacy. This may be because he is fearful that this will take him off task from being successful, or it might have to do with having to face the contradictions of his upbringing, including the intimacy he shared with his mother and the distance he felt from his father. He has remained goal oriented and does most of his communicating with others in the work environment. Alex has also had to confront his ethnic identity, although he has not done so by choice. Earlier in his life he may have been sheltered by his close family structure and church community. Now he, like most men of color, has had several life experiences that have made him aware that no matter how hard he tries, he is not fully accepted by the majority culture. Alex harbors simmering anger that he is not being judged by others purely on the basis of his output as a worker. It contradicts an internalized belief that he is in full control of his life. The strong defensive reaction he had to my probe tells me that this issue is volatile and is not fully worked through in his life. His reluctance to share with me his wounding in regard to racism is not unusual. Many African American men feel that people from the majority culture won't understand their dilemma, so they are used to denying it in their presence (White & Parham, 1990).

As therapists treating men, we know that it is important that the issue of cultural heritage be approached in a straightforward manner. Whereas some male clients will disavow its importance, others will find it as a broadening and deepening aspect of their therapy. L. D. Caldwell and White (2001) suggested that therapists question their biases toward ethnic groups that are different than their own and expose themselves to strategies for intervention that are not exclusively based on a Eurocentric model of therapy. Interpersonally oriented therapy in which the therapist is genuine, involved, self-disclosing, and committed is integral to working with men of color, especially African American males (Lee, 1999). Culturally responsive psychotherapists may have to show more of themselves and expect longer testing periods before African American clients allow themselves to engage fully in the therapy process.

SESSION 4: OPENING THE VAULT

The early exploration of childhood, family, and cultural background in therapy often brings memories and emotional material to the surface. Forgotten experiences may be recalled, creating ambivalence in the male client about how much to reveal to the therapist. It also confronts the client with a look at the potential depth of his life. This can be frightening and overwhelming. The therapist needs to encourage the client to talk about these memories while maintaining a safe and supportive atmosphere in the therapy session.

Ron

This session brought Ron closer to some of the losses of his childhood. Since our last meeting, he had been thinking more about his entire life, not just his present situation. He reported to me that he had had a job interview and that he thought it went well. When I probed about the experience, I found him answering with superficial statements. I got the sense that that wasn't what was foremost in his mind and asked him what he wanted to talk about today. He said he wanted to try to remember more of his childhood. I perceive this as an important step in Ron's becoming invested in therapy. He was inviting me to accompany him in taking the plunge as he endeavored to look more deeply at himself and his life.

Ron: I don't remember much from my childhood. My mom stayed at home with us until I was old enough to go to school, and my father seemed to always be working. He worked in construction. Mom took a job at the local grocery store as a checker.

Therapist: How did it feel for you when Mom took that job?

Ron: I hated it at first. I ended up having to go to a babysitter's house with a bunch of other little kids, including my little brother. After awhile I got used to the routine. The TV would be blaring with cartoons, there was always cookies, and the lady who ran it seemed nice.

Therapist: It would have been a big adjustment for me to go to school all day and then not see my parents until dinnertime.

Ron: It was even later, sometimes. We were always the last ones to leave the house. It . . . (he pauses for several seconds).

Therapist: It what, Ron?

Ron: It sucked. I hated life back then.

Therapist: You hated life back then? Was there something else happening?

Ron: Yeah. Mom and Dad were always fighting when we got home. Dad was pretty physical with her. (He avoids eye contact and pauses for 10 seconds.) I hate talking about this. Can we talk about something else?

Therapist: These seem like pretty painful memories.

Ron: No shit. What's this have to do with me getting my life back together now?

Therapist: Maybe some of what happened to you still comes back to haunt you when life isn't going the way you want it to?

Ron: I try not to think about this stuff.

Therapist: You've done everything you could to avoid the pain, but since you are feeling lousy anyway, how much worse are you going to feel if we look at what happened and try to make sense of it? (Ron stays silent, looking out the window.) You were the one who wanted to speak about your past today.

Ron: You're the therapist. You really think going over all the shit in my life is going to help?

Therapist: I hope it will, but in the short run it's probably going to be pretty uncomfortable. Are you up for the challenge?

Ron: Oh, man. Doc, I hope you're up for the challenge. This vault hasn't been open in many years.

Ron is intensely frightened of looking at his past, yet he seems to intuitively know that it is important for him. With support from me, he stays with the material during the session despite his flight into defensiveness and what appeared to be dissociation when the material got overwhelming. I have balanced a sensitive yet empathic approach, to keep the intensity turned up and move Ron toward the portal to his emotional depth. A mix of cognitive and interpersonally challenging interventions helps him acknowledge his fear and confront his investment in therapy.

Alex

Alex had been home for a visit between sessions. He directed the conversation in our session to how he felt about his father, reflecting a growing awareness of the significance of this relationship in his life, past and present. Alex also said that he wished that he had known his grandfathers and grandmothers, two of whom had died when he was very young and two before he was born. He sensed from talking to friends and family that maybe he would have had an opportunity to get guidance and mentoring from this generation about his cultural identity as an African American man.

Alex: I wish that I knew my grandparents. My older cousin told me that my Grandpa Joe was a really cool guy. He told me that Grandpa Joe used to live at their house and that it made a big difference when his parents were acting all freaky toward him. It would have been nice to have someone like that to talk to.

Therapist: I can see that you are feeling like you really missed out on a special person. What do you feel like you might have gotten from Grandpa Joe?

Alex: I don't know. Dad was so religious and seemed to not give me much guidance as a Black man. I fantasize that Grandpa could have given me some of his stories and wisdom.

Therapist: Dad didn't do this for you?

Alex: You know, not really. We weren't supposed to question Dad's authority. For a lot of the time growing up, I thought he had a direct line to God since he was a minister. Dad spent a lot of time at the church, and it seemed that from Friday to Sunday we had to stay clear of him 'cause he'd be working on his sermon.

Therapist: So you didn't see him very much. What kind of interaction did you have with him?

Alex: We saw him Sunday after church. He was usually pretty relaxed since his responsibilities were over for the week. There were five of us, so we didn't get a lot of personal time with him. He'd ask me to show him what I'd been doing in religious school, and he would praise my drawings and other projects. Even back then I was pretty meticulous with my schoolwork. We saw him every night at dinner, which was always at 6:00 p.m. on the dot. It was a real formal deal. Everyone had a place at the table, and we even had the same menu from week to week. We took turns saying the thing we were most grateful for from God that day. Otherwise we ate in silence.

Therapist: What about your relationship with your mom? What was that like?

Alex: Mom was very compliant with Dad's wishes, but most of the time she ran the house. She was always home when we got back from school. She made sure we did our chores and our homework.

Therapist: You described your mom, but what about your interactions with her?

Alex: I loved her. She never got mad and always seemed to be smiling, which isn't easy with five kids running around. Since I was the oldest, she would talk to me about how to take care of the other four. I really did a lot of babysitting for my brothers and sisters.

Therapist: So she confided in you when your dad wasn't around?

Alex: I guess you could put it that way. She let me know what she was thinking and feeling. I really liked being around her. I felt special.

Therapist: You're smiling.

Alex: Yeah, I really miss those times. In the afternoons before Dad got home, she and I would have a meeting about what to do with the kids before dinner. We'd talk about our days. It was nice.

Therapist: This was the time when you got a lot of your needs met. She gave you attention and made you feel important.

Alex: Yeah. When Dad was around, I felt pretty generic. I was supposed to be his perfect son, upstanding, polite. You know. But to tell you the truth I can't remember having the kind of personal interactions with him that I did with my mother. It was much more formal and distant.

Therapist: How does your relationship with him feel to your body?

Alex: When I think of Mom I feel really warm and safe. With Dad I don't feel much. Right now my neck aches, and I can feel my jaw tighten.

Therapist: What does that mean to you?

Alex: I feel tense and tight when I think about my dad. I guess that makes sense. I had to live up to his expectations all the time and couldn't let down when I was around him.

Therapist: Sounds to me like you were always onstage with him.

Alex: Yeah, that's what it felt like. Tiring.

Therapist: Even actors need a break sometimes.

Alex: I wish.

This session allowed Alex to acknowledge some of his loss of not having been nurtured by his grandfather during childhood in regard to what it means to be an African American man. Alex also noted how different he felt around each of his parents. The warm, tender emotion he has toward his mother is contrasted with the stiff, anxious feelings he feels toward his father. The image of Alex as an actor is a metaphor that captures his experience around his father. I am pleased that Alex acknowledged that he is tired, because it reflects some of the real costs of trying to stay in control of all aspects of his life. It may represent a chink in his armor that I can use to help him discover his portal to the depth that lies beneath his role playing.

TOUCHING THE LOSS AND INVESTING IN THERAPY

For both Ron and Alex the fourth session has brought to the surface some more serious loss issues. Ron has both an attraction to and a wish to avoid knowing his past. He recalls with vivid detail separating from his parents, attaching to the after-school babysitter, and then witnessing the violence in his household. His childhood is filled with images of fear and a survivalist's denial of basic needs for love, mirroring, and idealizing (Kohut, 1977). This marginal environmental adaptation to Ron's needs as a child caused me to wonder about how we would balance the necessary repair work needed for the damage he had sustained with helping him with his more immediate concerns. Ron became a protector of his younger brother and mother and a sworn enemy of his father. Ron cannot recall a positive interaction with his father and has only a frightened mother from whom to learn. The goodness and safeness of the babysitter is a highlight in a memory chock full of negativity and disappointment. The only set of positive values for Ron to incorporate is one of being the guard and companion of his mother and brother.

Unfortunately, so much fear, hate, and self-doubt are present in his life that Ron must make do with a mere shadow of a full human existence. His anger and sadness are palpable in these sessions, and yet he still feels uncomfortable making them fully known in my presence. Although a part of him strongly desires to trust me, his defensive system will not allow him to be fully seen. I, like most other men, am still a threat to his emotional vulnerability. With my academic and professional credentials, and my projected power to get "inside his head," he feels that I can "shred" him anytime I wish. Yet Ron is overwhelmed by his memories and his current predicament and has no choice but to leak the emotional contents in our encounters. His denial defense has been battered and is on the verge of collapse.

In contrast, Alex recalls an idyllic childhood relationship with his mother, who confided in him and made him feel special. Much of his sense of worth came from her acceptance of him as a person and intimate confidant. As he described his relationship with her it seemed as if he was truly a surrogate for his father in the realm of emotional intimacy and parenting of the younger children. His mother lovingly used him to meet her own unmet emotional needs. In the process, she allowed Alex to feel a certain superiority to his cold, formal, and distant father. Although he got a feeling of specialness from his mother, Alex found that his father treated him as one of his generic children, quite the opposite of specialness. His hurt and anger about his relationship with his father is substantially subverted by the "goodness" he attributes to an idealized father who is a holy man. How could a young boy be hostile or rebellious against a man so aligned with a powerful god? Instead, Alex must trade off his true feelings to hope that his father will someday bestow specialness on him. If he is good enough, and his life is perfect, he might actually get to be acknowledged by his father. The gap between who his father really is in his life—an absent, emotionally distant figure—and the fantasy of him as an important bestower of specialness has left Alex with an indescribable sense that something is missing. His awareness that he also missed out on being mentored by his grandfather adds to this sense of loss.

In our sessions, Alex hopes that I might substitute for his father by praising him for his life choices and mirror his wish for specialness. He also fears, with good reason, that I might burst his bubble of idealism and force him to face his true feelings, which are dark and forbidden. In the meantime, information that does not fit the "good boy" script is ignored consciously but recorded and experienced by his body. Any negative thought or unpleasant emotion must be hidden from public view, a strategy he has honed since childhood. It is not surprising that, at age 33, Alex has isolated himself in his work and found a lifestyle that keeps him from having to expose his private self to friends or family.

For both Ron and Alex, therapy in the early sessions has begun to bring some of their major conflicts into focus. Personal family histories mixed with the adoption of society's expectations for men has left both of them with defenses and "doing" coping styles designed to protect them from pain. Ron is more raw in his self-expression, fresh from the wounding of multiple life traumas. Alex is more subtle, vaguely aware that he has been paying the price of emotional emptiness for his need to be in control, resulting in self-imposed isolation. While the early stages of psychotherapy have exposed some of their defenses, we have empathically supported the coping that each man has done in his life. We have challenged both men to begin to look inward in a process that is unfamiliar and uncomfortable. They have been encouraged to connect their emotions and bodily reactions and to interact relationally with male therapists. Despite their fears about what they might find, Ron and Alex have begun to invest in the deepening therapy process.

5

ENTERING THE WORKING PHASE OF DEEPENING PSYCHOTHERAPY WITH MEN

On the way into the otherworld, bread was enough to pay the price of entering. On the way out, the price was a piece of the man himself. (Meade, 1993, p. 351)

The working phase of therapy with men involves a movement toward greater investment in the therapy relationship. Although often this initially feels like "one step forward and two steps back," the increase in investment makes the therapy process proceed in a more emotionally intensive manner. The therapist becomes more important to the client as a supportive, solid partner in the therapeutic journey. With increased trust in the therapist and the process, a man is likely to encounter aspects of himself that he has only glimpsed before.

To go further and deeper into the roots of some of a man's current life struggles means that there is more emotional risk and often a greater dependency on the therapist for stability and guidance. The therapist's interventions tend to go deeper, because the male client is more open to following the streams of consciousness that take him into his inner world. The further a man descends, however, the more likely he will be faced with his fears of deep emotional connection with the therapist and, ultimately, himself. Often, resistance to going into the emotional and relational world appears even when a man has made the conscious decision to move ahead in this direction.

Men have been socialized since childhood to resist relational intimacy and, by implication, psychotherapy (Brooks, 1996; Pollack, 1995b). Even a man who has taken the first steps to enter the psychotherapy relationship does so with ambivalence. As the therapist uses his interpersonal communication skills to encourage a male client to reveal himself, the client is at the same time unleashing a counterforce to block the attachment (Scher, 1990). This struggle is to be expected, because most men in this culture have been taught to solve their problems on their own. For a man, not being able to take care of himself is equivalent to failing the exam on life. The shame of seeking psychological help can even eclipse the original reasons for coming to therapy (Osherson & Krugman, 1990).

Bergman (1995) suggested that men's troubles are not due to some sort of deficit in the self but rather to a "disconnection from others, isolation, violation, and dominance in relationships that are not mutually empowering" (p. 72). This theoretical perspective rejects the more static model of male development as an unfolding of an increasingly independent self (e.g., Erikson, 1963; Kernberg, 1985b). Bergman argued that male identity is based on an ongoing relational process with others that for many men has been stymied by cultural factors that make manhood equivalent to "turning away from the whole relational mode."

Pollack (1995a, 1998) has explained this turning away from relational processes as an unconscious reaction to early trauma that has been delivered in the separation a young boy makes from his mother. Partially fueled by Western culture's emphasis on independence for boys as well as a growing awareness by the boy that his mother is not like him, boys begin to identify with their fathers and others outside of the maternal relational orbit, starting around the age of 3 years. Unless a father is connection oriented in his relationship with his son, the little boy identifies with a male gender role norm that emphasizes separateness, individuality, and competition. To be valued as a man, a boy learns to make comparisons to other males, seeking his "specialness" from winning or achieving rather than through relationships (Bergman, 1995).

In the psychotherapy relationship this translates into seeing the interpersonal situation as an arena to show off, dazzle, or be better than the other person in the room: the therapist. This dynamic is especially pertinent for male therapists who, through their own cultural upbringing, are predisposed to respond to this type of male display with their own competitive impulses. It is not uncommon in the initial stages of therapy for a male client to wrestle for control of the session with the male therapist (Scher, 1990).

A male who is in therapy with a female therapist may feel trepidation and shame for heading back into the feminine–maternal relational orbit that he had to escape earlier in his life. A man may feel pulled toward the relationship but also unconsciously fight against it to protect himself from the potential pain of separation. He may do this by sexualizing the relationship or keeping his emotional distance in response to the female therapist's openness to emotional sharing (Potash, 1998). The female therapist must be aware of a potential tendency to ask for too much emotional sharing or to be angry at the man for withholding connection.

The psychotherapy relationship is vulnerable to sabotage by a male client who is feeling threatened by its intense interpersonal nature. This sabotage can include amnesia and a devaluing of what has occurred in previous sessions. For example, he may forget appointments, have difficulty with spontaneous self-expression, not be able to transfer from the consulting room to real life his new perceptions and behaviors, and refuse to give up control within therapy sessions. If a therapist does not gently address these resistances through humor, self-disclosure (i.e., "If I were in your shoes I'd be feeling pretty betrayed"), patience, mild confrontation, or encouraging the exaggeration of the resistance, the therapy hour can regress into emotionless intellectual storytelling void of any type of authentic client self-expression (Rabinowitz, 1998).

It has been our experience that many men, in a state of resistance to their therapy, will retell parts of their story and treat each therapy session as if the previous one did not occur. This isolation of therapy from the "real world" is common. It seems to correlate with the shameful nature of having to seek help for life issues and verbally acknowledge that one is not in control of his own life (Osherson & Krugman, 1990).

It is important for the therapist to monitor his or her countertransference reactions to being devalued as a part of a secret, shameful relationship. Although it might feel frustrating and nonproductive to the therapist to have to pry information from a hesitant client or go over similar ground from session to session while not feeling especially valued, the client's defense system is actually using these interactions to detect rejection and verification of his worthlessness. The client may even be overtly asking for a cure to his life problems to see how hard the therapist will work to help him. These initial sessions are unconscious tests by the client to see if the therapist will really be there in a caring and consistent way (Goldstein, 1991).

MONTH 2: FEAR OF FLYING

As therapy enters the working phase, new challenges arise. A man who has lasted through the initial sessions of history taking and relationship building faces the reality that he has issues he must confront. Like a skydiver on his first flight, anxiety is palpable even before the issues are encountered. It is not uncommon for there to be defensive reactions to unconscious material that has been stirred by interactions with the therapist.

Ron

Ron came to this session ready to work. His pupils were dilated, and he had a nervous kind of energy, barely able to sit in his chair without squirming and changing positions. He had had flashbacks from childhood and seemed to need to describe them and flush them out of his consciousness. Therapy was probably the only place he could do this.

Therapist: How have things been for you this week?

Ron: I've been having a lot more memories of my parents, like little-kid memories.

Therapist: Tell me about what you are remembering.

Ron: There would be blood on the walls, broken dishes, and lots of screaming. I used to take my brother with me back into our room, and I'd hold him tight. I would put my hands over his ears so he didn't have to hear so much of it. (Ron holds his arms folded across his chest as he speaks, almost hugging himself.)

Therapist: You protected him.

Ron: Yeah, I guess that helped me deal with being scared.

Therapist: What usually happened next?

Ron: Mom would be crying. Dad would call her a "fucking bitch" and then get in his truck and leave the house and go down to the local bar to drink with his friends. I would then come out of my room and help Mom get cleaned up and help her clean up the house. We were all real quiet, like we knew something intense just happened, but we had to live with it. We just cleaned, and then had a normal night watching TV while sitting close to each other.

Therapist: Sounds to me like you comforted each other after the emotional storm was over.

Ron: Yeah. I would let Mom hold me then, and my little brother would sit between my legs. That part has warm memories attached to it.

Therapist: That does seem nurturing.

Ron: I just remembered as I was telling you this story that me and my brother both wet our beds as kids.

Therapist: What do you think that was about?

Ron: I don't know. It probably had something to do with being scared and nervous around my dad. He used to wake us up in the middle of the night and beat us if he found out our beds were wet. What an asshole!

Therapist: Before you called him an asshole you said you were scared around him. Where did you feel that in your body?

Ron: In my stomach. It's like having butterflies before a big game.

Therapist: I know you said your dad was an asshole, but try to stay with your fear.

Ron: Why do you want me to do that?

Therapist: Because your fear seems like it is a big part of you that you deny.

Ron: I'm losing it.

Therapist: That's OK, Ron. We'll get back to it.

Ron: Anger is a hell of a lot easier to feel than fear.

Therapist: Yeah, it seems that anger has been your companion most of your life, and fear has never been allowed to sit in the front seat.

Ron: You're not kidding.

Ron begins to uncover intense emotions about his childhood and then backs off in this session. It seems that his fear of his father may be his portal, but it also is the trigger that activates his anger. His anger takes him away from the range of his deeper emotional life. Although I try to reassure Ron that it is acceptable to feel fear, he quickly moves to anger, a more familiar emotional state for him. He seems to feel some shame for first exposing his fear and then for not being able to sustain the intensity of his earlier bodily and emotional reaction to his childhood memories. It is not uncommon for a man to have an approach–avoidance reaction to this kind of frightening material.

Alex

Alex had not shown up for three of his last four sessions but was right on time for this one. I had been concerned that the material from the earlier sessions was overwhelming him, especially after he had been "exposed" as a "mama's boy" and "actor" in the session before he started missing appointments. I had already begun to prepare for a late cancellation again. I feared that Alex was not quite ready to tackle the big issues in his life and was finding a smooth way to bail out of therapy. Surprisingly, Alex was very chipper and alert, speaking in quick bursts. It almost seemed as if he was trying to convince me that his session cancellations were no big deal. He was here now, and that was all that mattered.

Alex: Sorry I missed the last couple of meetings. The company has really been pushing me in this last part of the quarter to catch up on all of our accounts. I've been working late every night, and then when I realize what time it is, it's too late. You did get my phone calls, didn't you? Anyway, I'm ready to go this week.

Therapist: Do you think there might be some meaning to missing the last few sessions?

Alex: Like I told you, the time got away from me. (He looks down, and when his eyes meet mine again, he continues.) You think that maybe I unconsciously didn't want to see you?

Therapist: Is that a possibility?

Alex: I really liked talking with you the last few times we met. So I don't see the connection.

Therapist: Do you remember what we talked about?

Alex: Sort of. It had to do with my need to be in control. I remember I told you about my work and some of my family background.

Therapist: Was there anything about your work or family background that felt uncomfortable to you?

Alex: No, not really. I didn't think too much about our previous meetings until I got back here tonight.

Alex was admitting to himself and to me that he was avoiding taking in what he had been processing in the sessions. I was aware of a negative countertransference reaction to his devaluing of the therapy. I knew that he was defending himself against being emotionally overwhelmed in a manner that was typical for him. The fact that he was defending himself told me that there had been a significant charge to our few hours of therapy.

Therapist: Would you be willing to shut your eyes for a minute, relax, and when you are ready try to recall some of what we discussed?

Alex: OK. (He sits quietly for about 2 minutes.) I talked about my relationship with my mom and dad, and I kept telling you how important control was for me.

Therapist: Good. Keeping your eyes closed, are there any feelings that come up for you about any of these topics?

Alex: I'm not sure how I feel.

Therapist: Let's check in with your body on this. Do you notice any tension or discomfort in any part of your body when you imagine your family?

Alex: (He is quiet for a minute before responding.) My stomach feels like it is churning. My head feels hot. My eyes feel tense.

Therapist: Good work! You are feeling something.

Alex: I don't know what to call it.

Therapist: I'm not so sure that that's so important right now. It's just good to let yourself be in touch with your body's reaction to the image.

Alex: What does it mean? (He opens his eyes.)

Therapist: What do you think it means, Alex?

Alex: I must be kinda scared of my family. But that doesn't make sense. They've been so good to me. This is really confusing.

Therapist: Confusing or scary?

Alex: Both. I'm not sure I like this.

Therapist: This?

Alex: This probing around in my psyche. It seems dangerous.

(Alex looks and sounds like a parachute-jumping student who is looking out of the window of the plane and realizing that he might be asked
to jump out. His eyes are shifting, and he is squirming in his seat.)

Therapist: What seems so dangerous about it, Alex?

Alex: I feel like I'm going to find something out that I don't want to
know.

Therapist: Yes, there is a strong possibility you will find out things your
head hasn't been conscious of, but it won't be news to your body.

Alex: I'm not sure I want to go in this direction. (His arms are folded
across the front of his chest.)

Therapist: That's up to you. You came to me to get help with feelings of
being frustrated with your life. I believe that connecting with your body
will help you deal with some of the emptiness you've been talking
about.

Alex: I wish I could fully believe you, but this stuff makes me feel out of
control again.

Therapist: I can see that. We won't go faster than you can handle. I
trust that you'll let me know if we move too quickly, and I will listen to
you.

Alex: That's a relief. I want to let go of some of my control, but not all
of it.

Therapist: Understood. We'll take it at your pace.

By having Alex shut his eyes, I am hoping he can take a break from
trying to read my face for what he should be saying. This seems to work but
also throws him into a frightening body state that he has trouble cognitively
identifying. I reassure him that it is not new information he is finding out
but rather that he is letting information in that his body has already
received. The idea that his body and mind are not fully connected is disturbing and throws Alex into an out-of-control feeling again. As he starts to
retreat, I try to give him some cognitive reason for why it is important to
move forward in his awareness. I am hoping that he will start to identify
with his body as also being a part of him. When he hears that we will proceed at his speed, Alex seems to regain his equilibrium. This is a significant
compromise that Alex can make, because it gives him the sense that he is in
control of the process and that he has a choice regarding how fast and how
deep we go.

The resistances exhibited by both Ron and Alex provide us with a
challenge. Although they reluctantly verbalize memories and difficult emotional situations, they nonverbally show their ambivalence through silences,
closed body language, and hesitation to share. Ron is a bit more naive about
where his verbalizations are taking him. He found himself telling me about

memories of emotional intensity with his parents that he did not expect to be so overwhelming. The separation from his mother as a young boy and the witnessing of his parents' fights were traumatic experiences for him.

The therapist must walk the line between empathy and challenge. It would be too easy for Ron or Alex to sweep their emotional heaviness aside if the therapist accepted their minimized versions of how they felt. On the other hand, the therapist must be empathic to the shame they carry about that which is not working in their lives. In both sessions we are forced to confront them with why they are in therapy when they avoid verbalizing and feeling something significant. We let them know that the harm of looking at what they have swept under the rug will be no worse than how they have handled it up to this point. Both are seeking some reassurance that therapy will help them feel better. We are reluctant to give them a pat "everything will be all right" response but are willing to say there is at least hope in approaching their lives from a different, more emotionally honest angle.

By the 10th week of therapy there seem to be some cracks in the "fortress walls" of each man. Ron is having flashbacks of his childhood that he cannot control. He drops them into the session not knowing why they are there or what they mean. He has not shared them with anyone and has begun to use therapy as the dumping ground for his uncomfortable feelings. Beginning to trust the therapy session as his refuge is a big step for him. He is still resisting going toward his fear, but he is acknowledging that it is there. Ron is still testing the therapy relationship to see how far he can go in divulging his inner pain. He wonders if I will be able to handle the abuse and ugliness that he feels inside. At this point, anger diverts his movement toward fear and terror, which appear to be his emotional portal to a deeper connection to himself. When he is afraid, he shifts into an adrenaline-based anger that, in warriorlike fashion, will attack and defend his being.

Despite his missed sessions, Alex is also defending, although with less vigor. He is beginning to see the link between having to perform for his father and needing to be nurtured and validated by his mother in his role as her son. To his father, he must uphold the pure and righteous standards of a biblical reality. Dad is like a symbolic god whom Alex must not disappoint. He must always be on guard and do the right thing or risk the wrath of his internal "father judge," a harsher critic than his real-life father. Alex can relax and enjoy himself more with his mother. He felt her warmth and received praise and love for helping her with the other children.

Alex is slowly letting me see the complexity of his emotional life. He has been trained to obey authority and simultaneously has a simmering anger toward it. I keep him off guard by being both a male authority as well as an empathic therapist. It is as if the crack in his armor shows when he shifts from dutiful son to mama's sensitive boy. He tests me with his emotional ambivalence. He is not sure if he wants to buy into the psychological probing, for he knows intuitively that it will lead to some deeper, unknown parts of himself.

There is a difference in how we as therapists respond to the life-damaged masculine style exhibited by Ron and the social chameleon style of Alex. With Ron, I am more blunt and direct in my interventions. The life-damaged man's resistance comes more directly. He has an outer toughness from his life experiences and has been battered harder than a therapist will ever come at him. This allows me more freedom to confront him while still searching for the scared "little boy" inside. It is important to help Ron discover this little boy, who had to hide in order to survive the traumatizing environment of his childhood. Although Ron's lack of conscious access to this sensitive inner boy has led him into dangerous and unstable pathways as an adult, his rigid defenses of denial and minimization have protected him from free falling into a deep abyss.

Alex continues to try to manipulate me, to butter me up, and to circumvent my coming at him with a direct challenge. He senses that he can be seen through his chameleonlike defense and, instead of giving in, finds himself relying on it more. I know his style, because I was once a social chameleon myself, a master at reading others' emotional reactions and former confidant of my mother. It is no secret that being a skilled psychotherapist involves being able to read a variety of clients, and stay empathic to their pain, while at the same time remaining a safe and reliable parental figure. Our confrontation at the end of the third session in which Alex said "fuck you" with a smile let me know that we were making some headway. Alex then used the social chameleon's ultimate trump card of resistance: not showing up for scheduled appointments. Whereas Ron "no showed" at the start of the process, once he began therapy he did not miss a session. Alex may be saying he is not yet ready to make therapy more important than his work and the status quo of his life. Alex is a more difficult client, because he has so many ways to distract himself from inner reflection. That is why I used the shut-your-eyes technique. It gave him an opportunity to stop his outer vigilance and connect to something of substance existing internally. Alex's fear is that he will find something important there that will force him to make changes in his life. Superficially he buys the concept of change as good, but at his core he is afraid of exposing too much of his anger, sadness, and frustration. He is afraid that his tenuous grip on control will be demolished by waves of molten emotional lava.

Each of the men is projecting different images onto us that allow them to both resist us and let us in. A female therapist would encounter other projections such as the abandoning mother or the all-good mother (Carlson, 1987; Johnson, 2001; Meyers, 1986). Ron would likely be a bit tentative, believing that a female therapist might somehow abandon him. After all, his wife is threatening to do that now, and his mother seemed to pull away when he needed her.

Alex still idealizes his mother and believes that others need to be more like her. He might at first have high expectations of a female therapist. He might anticipate that she would be more likely to bestow on him the specialness he craves. On the other hand, he might be extremely disappointed when she doesn't deliver the way his mother did. All of these projections are grist for the mill in therapy. Whether male or female, the therapist must adequately use the projections to help the male client become aware of his expectations in relationships and how these projections can influence the way he lives his life around others.

MONTH 3: SLOGGING THROUGH THE RESISTANCE

Resistance is to be expected when dealing with emotionally difficult concerns. As a man deals with his issues in therapy, his dependence on the therapist brings up shame and vulnerability. He may feel worse as his psychological defenses become less effective in defending him against emotional pain. Successful therapy at this stage involves the therapist showing empathy for his client's shame and vulnerability while continuing to challenge his resistance to awareness and change.

Ron

Ron came to this session looking ragged. He had bags under his eyes, a runny nose, and a look of desperation in his wide pupils. We had spent two previous sessions continuing to discuss his childhood and the trauma he encountered as a boy. I could feel a strong connection developing with Ron as he shared some of this material with another person for the first time.

Ron: I haven't been able to sleep very well.

Therapist: Tell me what's been happening.

Ron: I think this therapy isn't working.

Therapist: What do you mean?

Ron: I haven't gotten any better since I've been seeing you. I sleep worse, I worry more, and I keep having memories of things that aren't pleasant. In fact, I feel like I'm getting worse.

Therapist: You had expected to be solving the problems of your life in here by now?

Ron: Yes. I haven't been very motivated to look for a new job. My wife and I seem to be arguing more. And I just feel nervous.

Therapist: What would you like to do about this?

Ron: Well, I thought maybe we should focus on this stuff and set up a plan of action.

Therapist: OK. Let's do it.

It seemed to me that all the initial exploration had begun to tatter Ron's defenses and that he needed some containment. The structure was his way of instituting some kind of safety mechanism in the therapy relationship. I was fine with this and was happy that he had initiated the idea. It was like he was taking some ownership of the therapy and taking me off the "doctor" pedestal. The therapy relationship was developing, but we needed a more practical project to work on together to balance the "being" aspect of therapy with the more familiar "doing" mode.

Therapist: Which issue do you want to tackle first, Ron?

Ron: I'd like to stop feeling so anxious all the time. I think this is why I can't sleep or stay focused long enough to job hunt.

Therapist: Tell me where in your body you feel the nervousness.

Ron: It's in my throat and my stomach mainly. I also get lightheaded.

Therapist: Are you feeling it right now?

Ron: A little bit.

Therapist: Take some deep breaths. (I demonstrate breathing from the diaphragm, and Ron copies my in-and-out breath movements. I also suggest that Ron relax in his chair as he breathes and that he closes his eyes.)

Therapist: How does that feel?

Ron: I feel more comfortable having my eyes shut.

Therapist: Fine. Keep breathing. Leaving your eyes shut, talk to me about what's making you anxious. There aren't any right or wrong answers. I just want to hear what is true for you.

Ron: (There is a minute of silence.) I feel like I have screwed up my life. I can see all the stupid things I've done and all the people I have hurt and disappointed. It overwhelms me. (His eyes moisten, but no tears flow.)

Therapist: I can see you're overwhelmed. It's OK to just feel your pain right now.

Ron: It hurts in my stomach and my head. I don't know if I can take this.

Therapist: You been carrying a lot of pain inside for a long time. It's all right to let it out some.

Ron: It feels like I'm going to die.

Therapist: I know it's frightening, Ron. I'll be here with you.

This is an important session for Ron. Whereas at first he is ready to quit therapy because of the turmoil it has unleashed, he begins to take ownership of his fears. He wants to manage his anxiety more effectively. Ron lets me join him in this even as his affect is overwhelming him. Bravely, he verbalizes his fear of dying if he expresses all of the pain that has accumulated over his lifetime. Feeling more connected, Ron trusts me to help him face his pain, fear, and loss.

Alex

Alex pulled out a small journal at the beginning of the session and began reading a list that he had made. The journal interested me. He was showing some tangible investment in the therapy process and, possibly, a willingness to begin a more introspective approach to his life. Alex was certainly asserting his stamp on the session, with the journal and his own structure for how we would proceed. I decided to not fight him on this but challenge him on the emotional level during the session.

Alex: I'm not sure what I should talk about. So much is going on for me. I asked out a woman on a date who I met on an Internet dating service. I also found out that we're going to merge with another hospital, and my father is coming to visit me while he's in town for some church function.

Therapist: Wow! There's a lot going on for you. How are you feeling about these events?

Alex: I knew you would ask me that. I thought about preparing my answer but decided that it's probably not a good idea. (He grins playfully.)

Therapist: So what do you want to talk about first?

Alex: I don't know. I think I want to save the father visit for the last part of the session. Maybe we could spend the first 20 minutes or so talking about dating and things related to that. I realized in the last few sessions that I have been really avoiding intimacy in my life. Since I was on the Internet a lot anyway, I decided to check out the classifieds. There are a lot of lonely people out there.

Therapist: How about you? How are you feeling about making a connection?

Alex: I think I'm ready. Don't you?

Therapist: I don't want to make that judgment, Alex. I was just wondering how you were feeling in your body as you anticipate dating again.

Alex: Oh. I guess a little anxious, but I need to get over that if I'm going to break out of this shell I've created.

Therapist: Tell me more about the shell you've created.

Alex: I've told you how I have pretty much shut out others from my life. I don't think I've done it on purpose, but I don't really have anyone who I really make a full connection with. I don't even have a pet goldfish (laughs).

Therapist: What does it feel like in your body to not feel connected to anyone?

Alex: (Shuts his eyes on his own.) I feel nothing. A big empty space in my chest, like I'm floating around in space with no solid ground. Just a lot of space.

Therapist: How do you feel in that big empty space?

Alex: Lost, scared. (He suddenly opens his eyes, drinks me in with his gaze, and looks down.)

Therapist: What's happening, Alex?

Alex: I just got a glimpse of what I think I've been running from. I haven't felt that sensation except in a falling dream.

Therapist: Say more about it.

Alex: I felt what it was like to lose control, to let go for a minute. I felt all alone with no one there to reach out to. I thought I was going to die for a minute.

Therapist: Yes, you touched something real. You let yourself feel your loneliness and isolation.

Alex: That was scary. How did we get here?

Therapist: You allowed yourself to go here, and you survived it. I appreciate you trusting me enough to let me be there with you.

This interaction is significant for Alex. Not only does he take initiative in the encounter, but he also shows a willingness to go further in his inner exploration. The moments when he felt like he let himself feel the emptiness and lose control need to be built on. He tends to grip tightly onto control, because it feels like his way to stay alive and avoid a sense of an inner void. It seems that the emotional portal is likely to be accessed when control is loosened. For Alex to really make internal changes in his life, he will have to visit this place in himself again and again.

According to Scher (1990), a major conflict for a man is acknowledging to himself and the therapist that he is afraid and, by implication, weak. So even as progress is made in working through his resistance, a man may find another layer of shame he must confront in order to remain in therapy. Sometimes therapy moves at a quick pace only to be interrupted by absences or a surprise termination. For some men, the vulnerability of being exposed too quickly can be overwhelming. Especially in initial sessions with male clients new to therapy, a slow pace is preferable to a fast one. A therapist should not underestimate the shame that comes from self-exposure and emotional connection in male clients.

Attachment shame may be rooted in the dynamics of the early mother–son relationship or identification with a father who is absent, rejecting, inadequate, or disinterested (Osherson & Krugman, 1990). Shame may also be elicited by seeing one's life through the eyes of another, a process that occurs in therapy as the therapist provides challenge and feedback. The projection of a critical parent onto the therapist despite the therapist's warmth and empathy is common in the early phases of therapy. The male client may be disgusted with himself and imagine that the therapist also feels this way.

Even if a man obtains gratification from unloading some of the emotional burden he has carried alone, he may find himself doubting its value in between sessions. Each session in the early phases of therapy is a test of ambivalence. On the one hand, the client believes that he should be able to take care of these problems himself. On the other hand, he can see that the therapist seems to know how to get him to move farther and more quickly than when he goes at it alone.

Male clients struggle to resist the tug of dependency, which unconsciously resembles the maternal orbit. Women, who typically are more comfortable with a wide range of emotion, are more comfortable with the depressive position, a feeling state that accompanies interpersonal loss. In contrast, men, who are used to less intense emotional relationships, have not had practice tolerating the feelings of the depressive position that accompany the loss of deep interpersonal connection. Such relatively infrequent exposure makes them reluctant to establish a strong bond with a therapist (Gomez, 1997). Feelings of engulfment, fear, and terror often precede the relational attachment to the therapist. It is important for the therapist to be sensitive to these feelings, because their power can overshadow the building of the therapeutic relationship.

SESSION 13: APPROACHING THE PORTAL

Therapy proceeds at the client's pace. At times the therapist supports the client in order to make the process feel safe. At other times, the therapist pushes and challenges the client to express his underlying emotions. This delicate balance of support and challenge nudges the client toward the portal, the opening to his rich inner life and core psychological issues.

Ron

After canceling our last session, Ron arrived at this one with a haircut, wearing a tie, and appearing less emotional and more alert than he had in his previous session. He had nearly broken down in tears the last time we were together, and I wondered if this was his way of feeling more put together.

Ron: I wanted to apologize for missing last week. That cold really zonked me out. I also want to say I'm sorry for my whining the last time I was here. I was sick, and I guess things felt really hopeless. I didn't want you to think I was such a basket case.

Therapist: I didn't have that perception, Ron. I felt trusted by you when you let me into your pain.

Ron: Well—I have some good news for you. (His face breaks into a warm smile.) I have a new job working as an insurance appraiser for damaged buildings. I go into buildings that have had structural damage and estimate how much it would take to do the repairs. I can use my knowledge as a contractor without the heavy physical labor.

Therapist: Good for you, Ron!

Ron: I've only been on the job this week, but I like being able to move around and not be stuck on one site or at a desk. There is a lot of paperwork, though, and I have to get better at using the computer.

Therapist: You must be relieved to find something you like.

Ron: I am relieved. But I'm also worried that it might be too late.

Therapist: What do you mean? Too late for what?

Ron: (His pupils get smaller, and there is no emotion in his voice.) Pam left over the weekend. She said she was needing some time away from me and my problems. She is staying with her sister, about 100 miles away. I called her and told her about my job, and she seemed happy for me.

Therapist: But she didn't say "I'll be right home."

Ron: No, she didn't. (He is silent for about 30 seconds.) I still got up each morning and went to work. I'm not going to give up on me even if she has.

Therapist: Ron, I'm genuinely pleased that you're taking care of yourself and keeping up with your work obligations. But I also am OK with you having strong feelings about the situation with Pam.

Ron: I told myself I'd be strong. I've been such a wimp in the past. I'm tired of feeling sorry for myself. If Pam wants to leave, let her. I've been able to handle worse situations than this.

Therapist: Ron, I am really in awe of your strength. I also know that in the past you have denied your needs in order to appear strong and tough. What needs are you pushing away in order to be strong through this crisis?

Ron: (Looks at me with a dark intensity. His carotid artery pulses in his neck.) I don't know. I have no friggin' idea what I'm denying.

(I quickly pull a small towel out of my desk, twist it, and hand it to Ron.)

Therapist: Ron, take this towel and twist it as hard as you can, one hand in one direction and the other in the opposite direction. Stand up as you do this, look me in the eye, and tell me what you're feeling.

(Ron stands up, takes the towel and, with all the intensity he can muster, lets out a loud growling sound as he turns beet red with the force of his twisting.)

Therapist: Go ahead and let the growl get louder.

(Ron continues with determination, and a deeper sound comes from his throat.)

Therapist: If you can, put some words to your growl.

Ron: I hate you, asshole. Get out of my face, you fucker.

Therapist: Stay with it Ron. Keep going.

Ron: I'm so tired of you messing with me, asshole. Enoughhhh!

Ron screams, hanging onto the "enough" for a good 20 seconds of vocalization. He is now sweating, the towel so tight it seems like it's going to rip. I throw down some pillows on the floor from the couch and tell Ron to let himself collapse onto them. He falls to the floor and begins to heave dry tears. He cries into the pillows, muffled. This "doing" technique with the towel allowed him to move into deeper and more intensely primitive material. For many men, an active "push" as they near the emotional portal facilitates deepening and intensity in the therapy process.

When Ron announced that he had found a new job, I was genuinely happy for him. It seemed that a huge weight had been lifted off of his shoulders. As Maslow (1968) suggested, if one's basic needs are not met, it is difficult to strive for personal growth. I was also struck by how symbolic Ron's job seemed in light of the "structural damage" he had sustained as a child and the repairs he was currently engaged in through therapy. I am so used to dealing with bad news in therapy, it is sometimes difficult to reinforce the positive events that do happen. Because one of his major stresses has been alleviated, I wondered if Ron would still be motivated to continue the therapy process.

I also had a strong protective countertransference feeling toward him. He was letting me "father" him in a positive way, praising his achievement and staying with him emotionally as he faced potential devastation. I felt uneasy that he might be setting himself up for a bigger fall with this commitment to not let Pam's abandonment affect him. His situation reminded me of my own painful experiences of loss. Ron's willingness to express his pain in my presence was a huge step of trust. Not only did he seem to sense my support, but also he let himself follow the movement in his body. Like a wounded bear, he vocalized the depth of his pain without inhibition.

Alex

I was aware from reading my notes from our last session that Alex had said he was going to speak about his father, but he never got to this in the session. I figured that he was both fearful of opening that door but at the same time moving perilously close to it by even mentioning it as a possible topic in his therapy. Alex arrived at this session with a concerned look on his face.

Therapist: What's going on for you, Alex?

Alex: I just came from work and was told that I need to improve my work as a supervisor. Some of my employees must have gone over my head to my boss with complaints. I can't believe it. (Alex looks stunned. He shows very little emotion. His facial features have tightened, and his body looks stiff in the chair.)

Therapist: This must be quite a shock.

Alex: I don't know what to think.

Therapist: Rather than think, let's check in with your body. What do you feel?

Alex: I feel numb. I don't know what I feel. I just can't believe they would go behind my back and criticize me. Why didn't they just come to me if they had a problem? Am I that unapproachable?

Therapist: Are you?

Alex: (His eyes began to water. His body convulses with sobs. Almost a minute passes.) I'm sorry, I'm really sorry.

Therapist: It's OK to feel, Alex. You were hurt by what they said about you at work.

Alex: I should be stronger. I held it together at work, but when I walked into your office I knew I wasn't going to be able to hold on. I've never really had a place to go like this in my life. I always would have to just suck it up in front of people, pretending that their disapproval didn't bother me. Then I would get to my room and cry into my pillow, face down so I couldn't be heard. This is the first time I ever showed it to anyone.

Therapist: How does it feel to let me see you like this?

Alex: It feels scary and good at the same time. There's a part of me that wants to run out that door and never come back here. You've seen my vulnerability. But there's some other part that is strangely familiar that's keeping me here talking to you.

Therapist: Tell me about those parts, Alex. They seem to be important aspects of your emotional self.

Alex: The good part is like a feeling of relief. I don't have to hang onto the burden of life all by myself. I can share it with you. The other part is disgusted with that soft side. It feels ashamed and dishonored. No one is supposed to get by the gates. Appear strong. Don't give in.

Therapist: How would you feel about talking from each of these parts in the first person?

Alex: I'm not sure I can do this.

(I give Alex two separate chairs to sit in for each part and encourage him to speak in the first person. Although reluctant, he lets himself go with the suggestion to speak personally without explaining himself.)

Alex: You are such a little baby. You are a pussy, a mama's boy. (I encourage him to switch to the other chair and speak back from that position.) You are a prick. You don't know shit about what you feel. All you know how to do is work and bullshit people. (Switching chairs again) I am smarter than you think. Who do you think got you your job and got you out of the house? If I was like you, you'd still be living at home with Mommy. (Switching chairs again) You think you're so tough. How come we don't have any relationships? How come we're so damn lonely? Because you don't think we have time for that emotional stuff. Well, I think you are wrong. (Switching again) You are just a cry-baby. The weak don't inherit the earth. The tough do. I can make you a success. Those assholes at work were afraid of me. That's why they had to go over my head. Nothing wrong with causing some intimidation. (Switching again) You dumb shit. You may want power, but what is power when you have no one to share with?

Therapist: How are you feeling now, Alex?

Alex: I actually feel better. I've never isolated those voices inside me. I felt powerful and yet OK with my emotional needs. I liked what I was saying, both parts.

Alex sounded more integrated and real than I had ever heard him in his therapy with me. The facade and calculated responses had disappeared during the dialogue. Alex had a smile on his face, and his body was more relaxed. In his gestaltlike self-dialogue, Alex seemed to have his introjected parents battle with each other: the softer, more interpersonally sensitive voice of his mother with the harder, more controlling and powerful voice of his father. The result was a realization that both parts were significant aspects of himself that could not be denied.

Although resistance to change re-emerges again and again in the therapy process, it is a significant event for a man to feel in his body that which he has been unconsciously fearful of knowing. The process of moving through resistance at both the psychological level and the body level is a cornerstone of deepening psychotherapy. The initial stages of deep personality change involve the cathartic release of emotion accompanied by meaningful understanding of the issues being worked through.

Active, experiential therapy methods encourage a man to value the emotions he feels pumping through his body as he struggles with perceiving his psychological world in a different way. Deepening psychotherapy breaks familiar patterns of defense, releasing both excitement and fear. One such breakthrough does not change a man forever, but it does open him up to the possibility of experiencing the world in a fresh manner. Repeated visits to the more vulnerable aspects of the self reacquaint him with his disowned inner parts. With the supportive guidance of the therapist, the male client can begin to incorporate these pieces into his conscious awareness. Instead of spending energy constantly defending against feeling, he can instead be in touch with the full range of his emotional spectrum. This allows him to experience not only his pain and vulnerability but also his feelings of joy, pleasure, and satisfaction.

For Ron, who has spent much of his life limited by the socialized male role, the breakthrough into his emotional depth came when he felt permission in the therapy relationship to feel his pain. This occurred despite his learned tendency to defend against its emergence. The impact of the body-oriented interventions was enhanced by the developing trust he had in me. He began to sense it was safe to share more of his deeper emotional material over time, leading him to respond affirmatively to the challenge to go further than he had before in expressing and understanding his past and present experiences. As Ron's defensive structure ruptured, he was inundated with anxiety. This helped motivate him to work through his concerns rather than deny or medicate them. He began to feel greater gradations and contrasts in his emotional world, at both the high and low ends. Instead of acting out in his real life, he found that the therapy relationship provided both a place for release of emotion as well as a container for it. This trust in the process of therapy allowed him to move forward into the unknown territory of his own unexamined emotional history and experience.

For Alex, therapy has been an odyssey from lack of awareness about his issues at both the physiological level and the psychological level to one of heightened exposure to where he has come in his life and who he is right now. Moving from distrust to trust in the therapeutic relationship has been reflected in his willingness to share and take responsibility for his actions. In therapy he has become less fearful of giving up some of his control and more able to respond honestly to my probes and interventions. He is more in touch with varying aspects of himself. Alex is better able to accept not only his coping defenses, which have made him successful in his career, but also the insecurity and emptiness that he has felt compelled to hide for many years. At this point, by making therapy a priority in his life, Alex has begun to integrate his work and personal life.

The initial breakthrough to the portal of emotional depth for each man provides a marker for the more intensive, deepening phase of the therapy process. It signals Ron's and Alex's trust in the process and a willingness to go beyond what was consciously known before. We now have more permission to remind our clients that they have allowed themselves to feel intensely and that it is a worthy endeavor. In future sessions, therapist and client can move more quickly in sessions to this trusting psychological space, allowing for more experimentation and risk, including the use of the transference relationship as a vehicle for self-understanding.

6

WORKING PHASE THROUGH TERMINATION OF DEEPENING PSYCHOTHERAPY WITH MEN

At that moment, when the world around him melted away, when he stood alone like a star in the heavens, he was overwhelmed with a feeling of icy despair, but he was more firmly himself than ever. That was the last shudder of his awakening, the last pains of birth. Immediately he moved on again and began to walk quickly and impatiently, no longer homewards, no longer to his father, no longer looking backwards.
—Herman Hesse, *Siddhartha*, 1929/1951, p. 34

The working phase of therapy cannot be delineated as an exact time period; rather, it is a stage of the process in which the therapeutic alliance has been firmly established (Wolberg, 1954). The client and therapist have weathered the storms of conflict that make the relationship tenuous, especially for men, who are not used to the give and take of intimate relationships (Cochran & Rabinowitz, 1996). If the shame of relationship dependency has been empathically worked through in the initial stages of therapy, the client is able to continue the process with an enhanced sense of trust, safety, and challenge (Krugman, 1998). Shame will still be a major issue in the therapy process, but it will be more easily addressed within sessions.

The working stage of therapy will also move beyond the immediate life crises and psychological symptoms that brought the man to therapy. The initial resolution of situational problems and the alleviation of presenting symptoms that often occur in the first part of the therapy process give a man a sense that there are some tangible rewards to being in the relationship. The connection to the therapist is associated with a greater sense of self-awareness and perceived control. This is also a time when a man may decide that he wishes to terminate therapy.

EARLY TERMINATION

Some male clients decide to terminate therapy early in the working phase. It may be clear that a man has made some progress but not as much as the therapist knows could occur in extended treatment. However, the initial symptoms that brought the man to therapy are not as pervasive or bothersome. It may be that many of the goals that he brought to psychotherapy have been attained. Often, the sense of being understood by another person is enough to bolster a man's defenses. He may feel less anxious about life, more self-aware, and not willing to alter too many of the relationships or situations in his life at this time. It is as if therapy allowed him to confess his sins, his failures, and his pain. He now feels supported and less critical of himself. The new insights may have led to some behavior changes, such as being more assertive, more self-disciplined, or less overtly needy in his relationships.

Forces outside the therapy room may have also shifted. For instance, a man may have gotten into a new relationship or found a new job. Both of these events often mark a sense of starting over for many men. There is an optimism that suggests that he will not repeat his old mistakes. This time life will work out for him. By turning over a new leaf and getting the support he needs in a new relationship, a man is likely to feel less of a need for the therapy relationship. In fact, the questioning, the digging into the past, the increased awareness of his motives and actions, are now seen as threatening again. "I feel good. I don't want to mess it up with something I dredge up in therapy" is a common message the therapist hears when his male client has found an outside source of hope and gratification.

Other situations, such as an impending move or money concerns, may also prompt a male client to end therapy at this point. It is important for the therapist to be willing to reflect and listen to his male client's rationale for leaving therapy. No matter how much more a man has to work on from the therapist's point of view, it is the client who should dictate the movement in the therapy process. The therapist can show him how much he trusts the client's process by graciously supporting his decision.

Confrontation of a wish to terminate treatment at this point may be serving the needs of the therapist more than those of the client. The therapist must deal with his own feelings of being devalued or abandoned to be clear with what he might perceive as a premature termination. If the therapy relationship has been effectively established, the client will be open to the suggestion of reinitiating contact if life circumstances change. The nonjudgmental therapist should offer to be available if the client decides to return to treatment. This gesture in itself will help the client by providing him with a place he knows he can go if things don't work out or if he feels desperate again.

If therapy is to end at this point, it is important to help the client consolidate his gains and to help him understand what he has done to reach this point of feeling better about himself. In an optimal situation the client would not leave immediately but would spend a few sessions processing his decision and what it means. This time of reflection can help him review where he started and what he has accomplished. It also gives him time to mourn the loss of therapy even if it feels right to leave. This in itself gives a man a chance to deal with some of his loss issues in a direct way. Although it is not necessary to draw this out indefinitely, the extra few sessions to say goodbye allow for the relationship to end on good terms. The therapist can share some of what he has gotten from the client, and vice versa. These verbalizations make the leaving process bittersweet for both. The honesty that is expressed may be more direct than in previous sessions.

We have also seen clients reconsider their decisions about termination at this point. A man who had come to therapy after his wife left him was ready to leave therapy when he hooked up with a new woman. He found that the honesty in saying goodbye to the therapist made him reconsider his decision. He realized that he had not fully grieved the loss of his wife, especially after he had a strong emotional reaction to leaving the therapist. He cried for the first time in therapy and made his own insight that he always felt like people were leaving him too soon. He then worked on significant grief issues in therapy about his father, who left the family when the client was 7 years old.

ADDRESSING MASCULINE ISSUES

Men seem to fare no differently than women once they have committed to psychotherapy. What is different for men is that the salient issues of the psychotherapy process often reflect masculine developmental and gender-based conflicts. The working phase of psychotherapy permits the therapist to address the issues of masculinity that often underpin male distress. These include the early developmental separation from one's mother; the initiation into the autonomous and shame-based world of boys and men; the valuing of a "doing" orientation as opposed to a "being" one; and the emotional minimization of multiple disappointments and losses. These foundations are likely to be manifested in therapy as masculine shame about weakness, vulnerability, and imperfection (Osherson & Krugman, 1990); coming to grips with competition with one's father and difficulty in separating from one's mother (Freud, 1917/1961); emotional dependency on women and defensive autonomy (Pollack, 1998); ambivalence about expressing emotion (Levant, 1998); questioning the function of the intellect as the sole guide for life decisions (Jung, 1968); connecting the armoring of the body to past trauma (Lowen, 1975); exploring abusive past relationships with men and women (Lisak, 1998); acknowledging and working through failures of parental mirroring and support (Kohut, 1977); dealing with trauma and loss (Cochran & Rabinowitz, 1996); and confronting the existential realities of death, freedom, isolation, and meaning (Yalom, 1980).

SIX MONTHS: INVESTMENT IN THE PROCESS

As the client trusts the relationship and acknowledges tangible results in his life, he becomes even more invested in the therapy process. At this stage he is more open and more willing to confront and work on issues that would have been repressed or avoided early in the process. Therapy is now seen as an integral and helpful part of his life rather than a shameful admission of weakness.

Ron

Ron's wife had still not returned home. She had taken up residence at her sister's house and had found a job nearby. Ron continued to work but was finding it harder to remain optimistic about his marriage. He was purposely putting in long hours on his job. He had gotten into the habit of stopping at a local tavern on the way home. After drinking a beer or two, he would fall asleep in front of the television set, emotionally sidestepping the emptiness he felt in the house by himself. Nonetheless, he faithfully kept his therapy appointments and seemed to be fully invested in the process. His brutal honesty in therapy about how he was coping contrasted with the avoidance of interpersonal depth in his outside life.

Ron: I think I'm in a rut.

Therapist: What do you mean, a rut?

Ron: I don't know. It's like I save everything I'm really thinking and feeling for our meetings. In real life I just go through the motions. (Ron has a faraway look in his eyes as he gazes out of the window.)

Therapist: Something must be happening in real life that is making it so emotionally flat. Nickel for your thoughts.

Ron: Oh. I was just daydreaming there. Sorry.

Therapist: Ron, there's no need to apologize. I'm curious about what you were daydreaming about.

Ron: I just remembered a dream I had last night. Vivid as hell. You want me to tell you the dream?

Therapist: I'm listening.

Ron: It was like a time warp. I was in high school, on my way to football practice, when I realized that my father was waiting for me out on the field. He had this smile on his face, which is pretty unusual. I tried to ignore him, but I couldn't. He told me to come over to him. I was so used to him punching me, I put on my football helmet just in case. As I got closer, he started to get this devilish look on his face and for an instant he looked like the devil, horns, everything. Then I felt really scared, so I put my head down and tried to hit him with full force. I felt the impact, and it was a solid hit. Then the dream switched to the funeral of my son. I saw Ronny at his own funeral. I hugged him, and he looked at me lovingly, not saying anything. I told him I loved him. He said, "Dad, I love you, too." I kept saying, "I want you to come and live with me." He started to cry and so did I and then I woke up.

Ron had tears in his eyes. I stayed close to Ron and let him sob for several minutes before addressing him verbally.

Therapist: It's OK to cry. You've been holding onto so much grief.

Ron: (Cries harder. His whole body shakes and rocks.) I can't believe he's dead. Why is he gone? Why am I feeling this now?

Therapist: A big part of you died with him.

Ron: I know. It hurts so much.

Therapist: Your pain means you're no longer numb. You're starting to come back to life.

Alex

Alex had been looking much more relaxed during our sessions. He had gotten into the habit of changing out of his work clothes and into jeans before our appointments. His attendance had been perfect over the last months. In his outside life, he had started to date. He had been contemplating changing jobs but was very ambivalent about giving up all that he had worked for at the hospital. Alex was not working the long hours he had in the past and had committed himself to other nonwork activities. Therapy had been dominated by his focus on his relationship with his father, including a strong transference relationship with me.

Alex: I wanted to tell you about my visit to my parents last weekend. Instead of my usual tactic of talking to Mom and avoiding Dad, I actually sought him out.

Therapist: How did that feel?

Alex: At first I felt some guilt that I didn't have the same desire to hang out with Mom. I could tell she seemed disappointed that I didn't spend any special one-on-one time with her.

Therapist: How did you know she was disappointed?

Alex: I could just tell. She didn't smile as much, and I felt like she was keeping me from going to Dad. It wasn't what she said, but more like her body language.

Therapist: This is a change for you.

Alex: Yeah. Normally I'd go and seek comfort from her, but it just didn't seem the same this time. I even felt a little repulsed by her.

Therapist: What do you mean, repulsed?

Alex: Did I say that? I guess I felt like I didn't want that kind of connection with her. I could see her neediness, and I didn't feel comfortable playing the good boy.

Therapist: The good-boy role isn't quite what it was for you before.

Alex: You said it. I'm beginning to realize how limiting and fake it is. Not that I don't want to be a good person, but to always try to act good seems inauthentic.

Therapist: It's easier to be real than fake?

Alex: Yeah. I never realized how much Mom and I played this game. I guess I am changing.

In the working phase of therapy both Ron and Alex, each on his own trajectory, are now facing the limitations of their character structures. Ron can no longer hold back the grief he feels for his son, who died more than 2 years ago, or the emotional betrayal he feels about his father. The cold storage of his emotions is defrosting and manifesting itself in his dreams. He is thawing slowly at a pace that allows him to confront what he has repressed. He has found permission in the therapeutic relationship to reveal his private thoughts, feelings, fantasies, and dreams. In his life outside of therapy he is containing the intensity of his feelings so that he can function. When he arrives in the consulting room, however, his defenses relax. He softens physically and psychologically and uses the therapeutic encounter to risk saying what has been before unthinkable and unfeelable.

Alex is experiencing a similar process. He is no longer comfortable with his inauthentic role playing. Over time, he has grown used to feeling and has enjoyed the emotional energy that has accompanied this freedom. Alex now has extra energy to spend on relationships that had been previously channeled solely into work and the avoidance of intimacy. At this point in the therapy process Alex is actively trying out his new-found "real self" with me in sessions and cautiously bringing it into his relationships with each of his parents and the women he is dating.

Although both men are more self-aware and comfortable with their feelings as the feelings arise, both still depend on therapy to help them interpret their new experiences. Therapy is an essential feature of their lives, even though it is occurring only 1 hour, and occasionally 2 hours, a week. The centrality of the treatment is a hallmark of the working stage. It is as if life is being lived through the prism of the values of the therapy process. Risk, growth, change, and awareness are new ways to look at the world, but the sessions themselves act as containers of the intensity being unleashed in the process.

Later in the same session, Ron discussed his dream some more.

Ron: So, do you want to help me interpret the dream?

Therapist: Well, what do you think it means?

Ron: The first part of the dream with my dad was strange. He really seemed like the devil.

Therapist: Why don't you imagine him sitting in that empty couch over there and talk to him as if he was the devil.

Ron: I'm not sure I can do that, but I'll try. (Ron hesitates for 10 seconds, and then his voice booms.) So you think you're so powerful. You are full of crap. You're a wimp asshole, Dad. I kicked your butt. What do you have to say about that, old man?

Therapist: Ron, go over to that couch, sit there, and respond as the devil-father.

Ron: Don't be so damn proud of yourself, son. You are the son of the devil. That means you carry my sword of destruction with you. You can't get rid of me.

Therapist: Ron, let yourself laugh like the devil would. Open your eyes wide and really put on a sinister laugh.

Ron: Ha ha ha ha. You think you're free. Ha ha ha. (Ron has an intense, devilish-looking expression on his face, with eyes wide open and a mischievous laugh.)

Therapist: Keep going with the dialogue, Ron.

Ron: I have the power to kill you if I want, you pathetic creature.

Ron was stunned by his last words and stopped. Perhaps it was the unconscious connection to his own son's death that hit him, for in a way, his son had been killed partially out of Ron's neglect as a father. While Ron had been drinking and not attending to his family, Ron Jr. had become involved in drinking and drugs. Ron had not intervened in his son's destructive behavior and felt guilty after the fatal car accident. I told him to go back into his original chair and respond but first to check in with what he was feeling.

Ron: I feel small. I can't take on that kind of force.

Therapist: Ron, stay with your feelings. There is no right or wrong response here. Your dad terrorized you. Anyone in that situation would have a reaction of fear.

Ron: But I couldn't show it to him. He would have picked on me more.

Therapist: See if you can show the terror now. He can't hurt you here.

Ron: I can't.

Therapist: Ron, open your eyes and mouth wide. Put your hands up, open, and let yourself experience your terror. I'm here to make sure nothing bad will happen to you.

I showed Ron how to put his body into a terror position. Using his body musculature to elicit the emotion, Ron began to shake. For several minutes, Ron shook with fear. I then encouraged him to collapse onto the couch. He crawled into a fetal position, and I covered him with an afghan. Ron sobbed to himself for several minutes. When he was ready, he sat up, quiet, his eyes bloodshot and his face softened.

Ron: I feel relieved. I've never let myself go there.

Therapist: It takes more courage to feel your fear than just your defensive anger. Just let this sink into your body.

Ron stayed wrapped in the afghan until the end of the session. We would tackle this dream again in another session. What was significant was that Ron had faced his introjected abusive father, his greatest internal nemesis. He had tapped his dark power and felt his own childlike vulnerability. A door that hadn't been open in many years had been opened. His grief about his son's death had powerfully and temporarily disintegrated the strong, multilayered psychological walls protecting his fragile, childlike ego. Remnants of the session would be felt in Ron's body and psyche for several days. We would encounter his overwhelming grief regularly in our sessions from now on.

Later in his session, Alex continued his recollection of his weekend with his parents. The role he played in siding with his mother and alienating his father was a new insight for him. Alex remained in the special role of his mother's little man while his father worked outside the house, building his career in the ministry. Alex identified more with his mother than his father, and his mother unconsciously did nothing to encourage the father–son bond, because she enjoyed the emotional support Alex could provide. Now it was time for Alex to begin his separation process from his mother and identify with the deeper aspects of masculinity, beyond the superficial gender role norms.

Alex: I realized during the weekend that I didn't really know my father very well. He was always occupied with church business. At the time I sort of admired him from afar. I thought that he must be real important, but I felt like I didn't mean much to him.

Therapist: How does that make you feel, Alex? To not mean much to him.

Alex: You mean what do I feel right now, or then?

Therapist: What do you feel right now.

Alex: (He responds in a soft voice.) I feel kind of hollow. It's like there's something missing in me. It makes me sad, I guess.

Therapist: Yes. It is sad to not be noticed by your father.

Alex: I guess that's what is propelling me toward him right now. I used to think he would notice if I got a good job and showed him how hard I could work. But he didn't really notice.

Therapist: Stay with the feelings, Alex.

Alex: I feel like giving up. Nothing I do can please him or make him notice me.

Therapist: So what stops you from giving up and not trying?

Alex: I don't know. It's become a habit. Maybe someone will notice if I work my ass off.

Therapist: If this is not the way to get your father's attention, what is?

Alex: Don't give me these damn riddles. You know and you just won't tell me.

Therapist: You sound angry at me.

Alex: I am angry at you. You are always holding out on me. You probably think I'm really lame being a mama's boy.

Therapist: You feel like I don't really let you in and that I judge you.

Alex: Damn right.

Therapist: Would you be willing to say that with a lot of force to my face?

(Alex hesitates and puts his head down.)

Therapist: What's stopping you from telling me, Alex?

Alex: I don't want to hurt you. I don't want you to abandon me. I know that sounds stupid, but it is holding me back.

Therapist: Alex, I won't abandon you. I can take it.

I then handed Alex a tennis racquet I keep in the office for releasing emotion. I set up some pillows on the couch, stood behind it, and asked Alex to start pounding the pillows with the racquet. As he started, I told him to go faster and harder. Once he was hitting rhythmically and solidly, I told him to verbalize "Let me in."

Alex: Let me in. Let me in. Let me in, asshole. (The verbalizations start to get louder and more powerful with his blows with the tennis racquet.) Let me in, Dad!

Therapist: How do you feel now?

Alex: Like I'm worth something. Like you and my dad ought to let me in. I haven't done anything wrong to deserve this.

Therapist: Damn right.

Alex: I never thought of being direct about my needs.

Therapist: It never seemed safe, I bet.

Alex: Well, I'm a grown up. I make money. I have a job. I can ask for my needs to be met. Let me put it this way: I'm tired of not asking.

Therapist: You never get what you don't ask for.

Alex has made a breakthrough in terms of his relationship with his father. By using me as the object of his angry projections he is able to access deeper feelings about his father and what he feels like he missed. He also realizes in the process that he shares blame in not asking or being direct about his needs. This is a crucial discovery for Alex in that it will be able to be applied to other relationships in his life.

The working stage of therapy allows for the dynamic issues that have been raised throughout the process to be addressed directly. Earlier in treatment, uncovering the same issues would have elicited more defensiveness or avoidance. Both Ron and Alex had approached strong emotions earlier in therapy and were only partially successful in experiencing and understanding the issues associated with them. The incremental trust in the therapist over time facilitates the client's willingness to go deeper. Men are especially in need of knowing that their perceived weaknesses will not be used against them, especially because they are prone to shame-based defensiveness (Krugman, 1998).

Successfully working through more conscious concerns first lays the groundwork for the more intensive psychological work of this stage. This work often resonates with themes of loss and grief (Cochran & Rabinowitz, 1996). Ron and Alex are invested enough in the process and in the therapeutic alliance to take the extra step needed to tap into strong affect and gain insight at both a psychological level and a body level. For Ron, grief about his son's death and his father's abuse and emotional absence generates a consistently strong affective response. For Alex, intense emotion is found as he explores the truth about his family dynamics and especially how hard he has tried to engage an emotionally absent father.

NINE MONTHS: GRIEF AND LONGING

The deepening therapy process involves acknowledging a man's grief for what has been lost and longing for what could have been. As men continue in therapy, much of the process centers on these themes. By revisiting grief and longing, a man's narcissistic defenses are replaced by a realistic acceptance of his vulnerability and humanness.

Ron

Ron has spent the last several sessions working with his grief. In an ironic twist of fate, his father is on his death bed and has requested that Ron stop by every day to be with him. Ron is more strongly feeling the loss of his son and of his wife. He is in touch with his own tragic circumstances, yet he continues to go to work. His job provides him with structure so that his emotional energy is not diffuse and chaotic. Therapy provides him with a safe container in which to release and explore his feelings. Ron is more open with his feelings and has made gestures to reconcile with his brother Jack. Much of the therapeutic conversation revolves around accepting these losses as a part of life and continuing on a day-to-day basis. The issue of acceptance of loss permeates the therapy, ranging from the loss of Ron's innocence as a child to his awareness of his own mortality. In therapy, Ron has continued to face his inner demons, using physical exercises when necessary to jump start the expression of feelings. In this session, Ron has been talking about visiting his son's grave and his father's deathbed in the same afternoon.

Ron: I can't hardly describe the feelings I have been having. I had avoided seeing Ronny's grave since we buried him. Last week I was there every day. On top of that, I have also been seeing my father every day. He doesn't have much longer to live. He actually has asked me to come as much as I can.

Therapist: What feelings are you having, Ron? What happens in your body when you visit your son's grave?

Ron: When I first went, I had to force myself to get out of my car. It took me 2 hours to make it from the car to his site. Once I got there, I just looked and it felt like my heart had a huge hole in it. The last few times I've gone up there, I can imagine him. I have conversations with him. I can almost sense him responding to me. I look forward to going there.

Therapist: Sounds like it's bittersweet.

Ron: Yeah. I would give anything to have him back alive. Yet, once I settle into the fact that he is really dead, I sort of enjoy being close to him at the cemetery. Is that morbid, or what?

Therapist: Sounds like love to me. Maybe you have so much love that wasn't able to be expressed when he was alive that it is pouring out now.

Ron: (His eyes begin to tear.) But I should be loving those who are alive. My brother and my father.

Therapist: What stops you?

Ron: I have hated my father and felt angry at my brother for leaving me. I can't remember the last time I felt anything really positive toward them. Except yesterday at the hospital. I actually felt something affectionate toward my father. He asked me to shave him. As I was lathering his beard, I felt the kind of feeling I had for Ronny when he was a baby. All the hate drained out of me for those minutes. Then he said something derogatory to piss me off again.

Therapist: It seems significant that you're experiencing some love with the hate that usually comes up with your father.

Ron: He's still an asshole, but he's so weak right now, it's hard to be scared of him. He seems really needy.

Therapist: Very different from the monstrous devil he has been.

Ron: I feel sorry for him these days. He knows he's close to death, and maybe that changes things.

Therapist: Maybe you know he is close to death, and it changes things for you.

Ron: Well, it does make me realize that time is limited. I don't really want him to die alone. I guess I'm making an effort to see something in him that's good.

Therapist: What do you see?

Ron: He's just a guy. He's a lot of bluff. I knew that intellectually, but now it is real. He'll say stuff to me like, "You little fucker, you're just waiting to inherit that money from me, aren't you?"

Therapist: What is your reaction?

Ron: I want to pummel him, to be honest. Then I look at him, and he's so pathetic I just have to laugh to myself.

Therapist: What are you laughing about, Ron?

Ron: I'm laughing at how lame he really is and how much I truly believed his stories and threats.

Therapist: Laughing or crying?

Ron: You mean my laughter is really about being sad?

Therapist: Is it funny to be threatened constantly?

Ron: Well, when you say it that way, I guess I have learned to laugh so the tears won't come. He was an asshole. I know that, but he's also a hurting human being.

Therapist: It takes one to know one.

Ron: No shit.

Alex

Alex has been expressing more of his feelings toward his father in therapy, especially his longing to be connected to him. Although Alex has yet to have a direct talk about his feelings with his father, he has gone out of his way to spend time with him. Somehow just sharing physical space has intensified Alex's desire to have some resolution in their relationship. He studies his father's gestures, movements, and words but has yet to talk about his mixed feelings toward him. In this session, he has noticed his hesitancy and wants to deal with it.

Alex: I just look at him. I have so many thoughts going through my head, and nothing of substance comes out.

Therapist: Tell me some of your thoughts.

Alex: I want to grab him and hit him, and then I also want to hug him. I want to tell him how much I've missed him being in my life. Then I want to tell him what a sorry ass he is. I want to say "you've screwed up your life living for God and not for your family." I then think that it is so noble to give your life to God. I can't say anything because I have such mixed-up feelings. It's like I hate him and love him. I want to be close to him, and yet I am repulsed by him.

Therapist: It's hard to live with having mixed feelings. It would almost be better to just feel one way or the other.

Alex: Yes, it would. So I'm stuck. Help!

Therapist: What does your body tell you?

Alex: I have my hand in a fist, which tells me I am really frustrated. My stomach is churning, and I am feeling incredibly hot. I guess that means I want to hit something.

I handed Alex a pair of old boxing gloves. There is a punching bag hanging in the corner of the office for occasions like this. He seemed to know what to do and began pounding the bag. I asked him to verbalize his feelings each time he lands a blow.

Alex: I am so damn frustrated with you. If I tell you how I feel, you won't understand. If I don't tell you, you are clueless. I hate you for not understanding me, for not paying attention to me. (He then pummels the bag for 5 minutes. Breathing heavily, he then sits on the couch.)

Therapist: So what did you find out?

Alex: It doesn't matter.

Therapist: What doesn't matter?

Alex: It's not about him. It's about me. I have to deal with the fact that he wasn't there; that he wasn't paying attention and that he doesn't understand.

Therapist: What does that feel like?

Alex: It's deflating. Like I puffed up a balloon and it has a hole in it.

Therapist: What do you mean?

Alex: I have to accept the fact that he doesn't get who I am and may never will. I have to get comfortable with that. I don't like it, but that's the way it is. I have to live with it.

Therapist: You seem sad.

Alex: I am sad. What's strange is that I feel OK with this sadness. My body is relaxed. The tightness is gone.

Therapist: Maybe you can live with yourself now.

Alex: Maybe I can.

As a man in therapy stays honest to his feelings, not knowing where they are taking him, he finds that eventually there is some reason for his reactions. It may be not the rational reality he has learned since childhood to embrace but rather a nonlinear mode that takes into account emotion and body reactions as well as imagery and thought. The simultaneous awareness of how his usual character style works and how he might experience the world differently if he focused on feelings rather than rationality means that the deepening therapy process is working.

The physical exercises that are used to get through impasses of logic and rationality make the therapy process at this stage a true exploration. The working phase means that thoughts, feelings, and behaviors have no prescribed direction. All that a man knows is that he will be safe and his emotions contained in the room with the therapist. New behaviors may emerge spontaneously in reaction to new ways of thinking and feeling. When risk in the sessions begins to feel like the norm, rather than a special event, the deepening process is in full motion.

Ron has begun to heal significant male relationships in his life. He has found that he can trust his subjective reality in ways he never could before. His emotional wounds, although at first painful, now provide him with a freedom to feel and act, transcending the traditional male gender role. The wounds have exposed his mortality, his ordinariness, and his honest feelings. No longer is it necessary to defend against pain to such a degree that he feels nothing. He can still contain his inner world enough to hold a job, but no longer does he have to be blinded by the stoic, emotional impairment of his abusive upbringing.

Ron is working through his splitting defenses, which were erected to deal with his traumatic past. He now sees both himself and his father as real, vulnerable men who have suffered and done the best that they could. His authenticity in sessions and his willingness to be open to his emotional reactions at his son's grave and his father's bedside make it clear that Ron is fully invested in this important reparative stage of his therapy.

Alex has trusted therapy enough to follow the thread of his longing, his desire to be noticed by his father. In the process, he has become more genuine and less of an actor. Although he still can perform the essence of his work, he no longer feels obsessively driven by his career ambition. The sought-after reward of narcissistic admiration—a defense against covert, interpersonal trauma—no longer shines as a beacon for him. Instead, he has learned from his narcissism that he wants true connection and that he hurts when he doesn't have it. He longs to be loved, to be accepted for who he is, and he grieves the fact that his father has been unable to give him this mirroring. Instead, Alex is learning to live with his disappointment and loss. Rather than trying to hide his needs or manipulate others to obtain love, he can now be himself, acknowledging his human imperfection and accepting it in others in his life.

TERMINATION

Psychotherapy is an ongoing process. As such, it is probably arbitrary to try to delineate when it should end. For most men, dependency on a therapist triggers an unconscious pull toward an all-encompassing, nurturing mother from whom a man has had to separate in order to be indoctrinated into manhood (Pollack, 1998). Traces of this loss of a primal relationship still manifest themselves unconsciously in the psyche of men, affecting the way they respond to intimate relationships.

Deepening psychotherapy by its nature encourages a man to work through his fears and shame about dependency in order to attach to the therapist. Despite the emphasis in treatment on dealing with life's losses, the impending end of therapy brings up a recapitulation of a man's primal abandonment. This sense of abandonment is often the residual emotion from a male's premature exodus from the mother–child orbit into the world of boys and men. This means that the last phase of therapy is bound to be fraught with conflict.

At the mention of termination, some men seem to relapse, experiencing the symptoms of anxiety and depression that first brought them to treatment. The relapse, if interpreted in the therapy as connected to the upcoming termination, is an important part of the therapeutic process. Rank (1947) maintained that learning to deal with separation from the therapist in a healthy, non-neurotic way is the core of good psychotherapy and the true test of successful learning from the transference relationship.

Other men pull away emotionally, distancing themselves from the process to avoid feeling the pain of separation. A man may refit himself in the traditional masculine role of stoicism, toughness, and autonomy to prepare to separate without the emotional intensity. This may manifest itself as a return to an "I'm all right" attitude and a withdrawal from deep interaction with the therapist that belies the male client's underlying separation anxiety. Although this defensive posture is familiar to most men, it is a significant part of the therapeutic process to confront and work through. A therapist would be remiss in not using a man's emotional withdrawal as a way to point out the consequences of this style, including how it has affected his relationships, as well as his mental health.

ONE YEAR: TO LET GO OR NOT TO LET GO

The therapy relationship is powerful. Thoughts of ending the relationship bring up emotional ambivalence. While it is healthy to use therapy as a way to ensure emotional support and to facilitate change in one's life, it also raises issues for men of emotional dependence. It is important to discuss these feelings openly to know when and how to let go of the therapy relationship.

Ron

It has been about a year since Ron started his therapy. His life looks quite different than it did when he began. His wife has filed for divorce, his father has died, and he has a new job. Ron has made a strong effort to keep in contact with his brother Jack. He has also gotten involved in a support group for parents who have lost their children. He still comes to therapy on a regular, weekly basis.

Ron: I think I could stay in therapy forever. Maybe not, but it sure seems like it would be hard to leave.

Therapist: Are you thinking about leaving?

Ron: To be honest, I feel pretty good. I know I haven't dealt with all my issues, but I feel a lot clearer on who I am and what I need.

Therapist: Sounds like a solid way to feel. What issues do you feel like you haven't dealt with?

Ron: I guess I'm still worried about actually meeting someone to spend my life with. Since Pam filed for divorce, I've realized that I am alone. No more fantasies of her coming back.

Therapist: I can't help you with that one. But maybe knowing yourself better will leave you open to a woman who can appreciate you.

Ron: Well, I hope so. I just feel the void, and it makes me wonder.

Therapist: I wonder if you are also worried about filling the void of therapy?

Ron: To tell you the truth, I really like you and how you have stuck by me through all of my craziness. I'm not sure I can let you go from my life. You and this room have become so much a part of who I am. I'm not sure how I'd actually wean myself from it.

Therapist: How does it feel to be so tied in that you can't imagine not being here?

Ron: It feels scary just talking about leaving. I can remember the day my mother first went to work. I got left at that sitter's. It reminds me of that. It makes me want to throw up, my stomach is so nervous.

Therapist: What would you have wanted to say to your mother if you could?

Ron: Help. Don't leave me. I'm not ready. Wait. I'm not ready to leave here yet.

Therapist: No one said you had to, Ron.

Ron: I hate this feeling. I don't think I've let myself feel this kind of neediness before.

Therapist: Not since you were a child and Mom left you before you were ready.

Ron: I didn't know I could be this needy. I really don't like it.

Therapist: I'm not leaving you until you're ready.

This response is what Ron needed from his mother. He needed to have his needs, rather than hers, be primary. I am hoping that we can work together to end therapy on his terms, not mine. This would be an ideal corrective emotional experience for him, helping to repair the sense that he was not that important and that he is worth being valued.

Alex

A year into his therapy, Alex came into his session curious about the men's group that I run with two of my colleagues. It was the time of the year that we recruit new members and begin the process of screening. I had thought about the men's group for Alex but wasn't sure if he was ready to give up the sole attention he was receiving from me, because he seemed to be working well individually. His curiosity allowed the issue to be explored directly.

Alex: I've seen that sign you have next to the desk about the men's group. Can you tell me something about it?

Therapist: Have you been thinking about it for a while?

Alex: To tell you the truth, I noticed it last year in the first session, but I forgot about it. It was pretty threatening, the idea of hanging out with other men. I noticed a few weeks ago that you had a new sign for this year's group up. I'm anxious at the thought of joining, but definitely curious.

Therapist: Before I tell you about it, I wonder if you'd tell me what your fantasies are about it.

Alex: Well... I imagine that these guys will be older, more experienced in life. I wonder if they would accept me. I probably would seem like a young kid to them who hasn't lived long enough to know what life is really about. I guess that's the part that intrigues me. Maybe they would be able to show me the ropes, what it's like on the road ahead.

Therapist: Sounds like you are looking for some older mentors.

Alex: Yeah. I've given up on my father being the one to show me. His choices and limitations make it hard for me to imagine getting much mentoring from him. But these guys are at least thinking about their lives and issues. That's more attractive to me.

Therapist: I wonder if you're considering ending individual therapy?

Alex: Well, the thought has crossed my mind. I like coming here, but lately it seems that most of the stuff in my life I can handle. It doesn't have the charge it had before. It just seems a bit redundant. I hope you don't take this personally.

Therapist: You seem like you're ready for a new challenge.

Alex: That's a good way to put it. I don't want to stop the growth, but find some new ways to stimulate it. I'd still be able to see you every week, but in the group. If I wanted to still see you individually, I could. Right?

Therapist: Let me tell you about the group. If you're still interested, we can arrange a meeting with me and my colleagues to interview you for the group. If it doesn't seem right, we can talk about what other options there are for you. I don't want you to feel like you need to rush out of individual therapy. In fact, it would be OK if you did both for a while.

Alex was feeling strong and independent but still a little nervous about leaving the comfort of the individual therapy nest. I did feel a bit like his father and mother, and I know that he was relating to me like a teenage son who was ready for some action on his own. I thought it was healthy for him to want to join a group of older men, to be indoctrinated in a deeper way to the masculine world. As his "male mother" I knew it was time for him to leave the "special" individual relationship orbit that recapitulated much of what Alex had experienced with his real mother.

Although Alex's intentions seem healthy, a part of the rush to be in the group may be his attempt to avoid dealing with some conflict he has toward me in our individual work. His interest suggests that he may be trying to find a way to let go of individual therapy but still have contact with me. That's not a bad compromise to soften the anxiety of separation, but we still need time to talk about where our relationship is before he moves on to a new mode of therapeutic interaction. It would be unfair to him to enter the new situation with unresolved feelings toward me that could inhibit his work in a men's group.

It is important for the therapist and client to work through their honest feelings toward each other before termination. The transference relationship must in some way be demystified. The therapist needs to be seen by the client as a real person, not only as the idealized parent whom he or she is often projected to be. Even therapists who have been self-disclosing and open as opposed to formal and distant may be the victim of parataxic distortion (Sullivan, 1953). *Parataxic distortion* is the need for the client to see the therapist in a way that best meets his unconscious needs, even if that means distorting the nature of the relationship. Although not all distortions can or need to be corrected, it is a noble goal to make the therapeutic relationship one that represents genuineness and honesty. In the end, the client must take away from the relationship values that he can apply to his life.

Before the final session, the client and therapist need time to review the process they shared together, high points as well as low ones. It is important for the client to consolidate and consciously recall all the work that he has done to make changes in the way he thinks, feels, and acts. By reducing the transference distortion and taking responsibility for his own changes, the client is more psychologically ready to lead an empowered life of healthy, independent decision making.

In practice, the therapist should still leave the door open for the client to return to therapy if necessary. This means that the therapist should overtly tell the client that he or she will be available in the future if more issues arise in his life on which he wants to work. Some therapists scale back therapy gradually from weekly or twice-weekly sessions to every other week, once a month, or irregular check-in periods. This weaning allows the client to experience his life with less of a therapeutic safety net. Some clients find this an ideal way to reduce their dependency but still maintain some contact.

Some men might be ready for a new therapeutic experience that builds on the work they have done individually. A men's group (see Andronico, 1996; Rabinowitz, 2001), a mixed group (see Corey & Corey, 1997; Yalom, 1985), couples counseling (see Philpot, Brooks, Lusterman, & Nutt, 1997), or family therapy (see Goldenberg & Goldenberg, 2000; Philpot, 2001) may be the next step for a man, depending on his issues and relationship needs. The therapist needs to make sure that a man knows what is asked for in these modalities and should use trustworthy referral sources. Transitioning to another form of therapy may require a period of time when a man is still being seen in individual therapy until he feels secure with the new therapeutic situation. Sometimes the new therapist is invited into the individual therapy hour to be introduced and associated with the relationship with the original therapist. This can also be done if the therapist must terminate therapy because of his own life circumstances (e.g., moving, sickness, or retirement).

Ideally, a man who is ready to leave therapy does so because he has accomplished his goals. In deepening therapy this means having freer access to the spectrum of his feelings, from sadness to joy, while still being able to function and defend himself in a social world that is at times unhealthy.

A major goal to accomplish is the acceptance of the male client's own humanness, which is made up of both fragility and strength. It means that he is ready to seek relationships out in the real world that approximate what he knows is possible based on his therapeutic relationship. Like a child who has been loved and nurtured, he must eventually seek his fortune outside the family and create in his own life the intimacy he has found in the therapy environment. He must take the lessons he has learned and apply them to the challenges of relating to people in his interpersonal world. This will not be easy, because few individuals he will encounter will act as supportively and unconditionally as a therapist. This means that he will have to internalize the empathy and unconditional support that he received from the therapist. In the absence of such a positive mirror, the man will need to find the strength within himself to sustain a positive sense of self (Kohut, 1977).

Just because a male client is ready to leave therapy doesn't mean that leaving won't be painful: It is another loss in a long series of losses that have occurred over his life span. So many of the issues a man has worked through in therapy gravitate around the themes of grief and loss regardless of whether they are manifest concretely, in the loss of an intimate relationship or the death of a parent or child, or symbolically, in the loss of status and prestige associated with employment limitations, loss of one's physical prowess over time, or loss of childhood vulnerability and playfulness due to adherence to the traditional masculine gender role. Ultimately, a man's acceptance of the beauty and tragedy of life will be his savior. It will allow him to know at a deep level that living life openly and fully is worth the risk of being hurt or left behind.

7

DEEPENING GROUP PSYCHOTHERAPY FOR MEN

Think of the wretches who in your experience have borne the heaviest load of sorrow, and I will match my griefs with theirs. Indeed I think that I could tell an even longer tale of woe, if I gave you a full account of what I have been fated to endure.

—Homer, *The Odyssey*

Men's groups are able to deepen a man's experience in several ways. A men's group recapitulates the trajectory a man experienced when he was thrust into the world of men from his mother's orbit. Instead of entering a hardened and competitive male world, however, a men's group participant enters one that is interpersonally receptive. The men's group is supportive of feeling rather than rejecting of it. The men of the group nurture each other in a uniquely male way through words and gestures.

The men's group deepens a man's psychotherapy experience by helping him confront his disappointments and losses. Instead of denying past hurt, shame, and wounding, the men's group asks its members to bring these feelings out into the open, where they can be healed by the supportive actions of the group. It is safe to get angry, to cry, or to express one's frustrations and grief.

The men's group also deepens a man's experience of himself by challenging the gender role norms of culture. Instead of maintaining rigid patterns of behavior that result in the avoidance of intimacy, addiction, and privately experienced distress, the group encourages warmth, support, and trust so that conflict can be dealt with in a straightforward fashion. Men are free to engage in confrontation because they trust that they will gain personally from the interaction. Affection, rather than being avoided, can be used to show caring among men.

Men learn also how to take their "doing" orientation to life's problems into the "being" world with each other. Rather than trying to solve problems, men are given a chance to express feelings, empathize and support each other, and learn to stay with uncomfortable feelings. Although "fixing" is not a part of the men's group, making use of the male tendency toward action is. Through exercises and activities men learn to be with themselves and their feelings.

Finally, men's groups encourage men to approach and enter the emotional portal of depth. Men are asked to give up some of their control and vulnerability in order to explore beneath their social roles and facades. Men support each other in taking on this challenge.

INGREDIENTS FOR SUCCESSFUL MEN'S GROUPS

The attractiveness and success of group therapy for men is built on the premise that the group situation is often a better fit for many men, especially those with traditional gender role orientations, than individual psychotherapy (Brooks, 1998a, 1998b). Even though many men who participate in a men's group have also been in individual therapy, they freely acknowledge that the multiple relationships that are developed in a well-run group are often better able to push them to deal with conflict, emotion, and interpersonal connection than an individual therapy approach that involves only one relationship, between therapist and client (Rabinowitz, 1998, 2001).

Men's therapy groups build on the support that men can uniquely give each other. Sharing similar physical bodies, similar socialization, and similar relational perspectives, men often feel a different kind of support than what they receive from women in their lives. One man in a weekly therapy men's group put it this way:

> I have always gone to women for emotional support to my tender and expressive side. With my male friends, I tended to relate about sports, school, and work and not burden them with the stuff I would tell my mother or girlfriend. I felt like I couldn't be completely real with either women or men. In the men's group I have found out that most men feel this way. It has been such a feeling of a burden lifted to realize I can be totally myself here; gentle, aggressive, compassionate, wild, or competitive, and still be accepted by these guys, who I initially thought were going to judge and reject me.

Men's groups help men trust other men again. In our competitive culture it is not uncommon for men to be pitted against each other at work and even at play. The buddies one might have had growing up are more difficult to find in the adult world. Many men find that the pressures of work and family take most of their energy and time. It is easy to lose touch with one's emotional self by trying to obey the social rules in each aspect of one's life. In a men's group it is expected that each man will talk about who he really is, not just his work or social persona. Because of rules of confidentiality and through honest sharing, men learn they are not alone and in the process build trust with each other at a personal level.

Men's groups are action oriented rather than purely conversational. Much male friendship is built around activities rather than interpersonal sharing (Caldwell & Peplau, 1982). Shared activity can help men feel more comfortable and trusting in group and can lay the groundwork for later interpersonal risk taking. These exercises and activities can change the social role-bound consciousness of the men entering a group session from the outside world to one of reflection, honesty, and emotional self-awareness (McDargh, 1994).

Men's groups give hope and rebuild confidence in members. In very few settings do men actually verbalize and show each other support, respect, and care. The men who initially come to a group are often emotionally isolated and discouraged, receiving very little positive support from relationships or work (Rabinowitz, 1998). Often they are in the midst of a personal crisis, such as a divorce or other significant loss, or they are in a situation in which they must change to avoid family dissolution or incarceration. Some are recovering from addictions to drugs, sex, gambling, or work. What is common is that they feel like their lives are out of control and that they see little hope in turning their lives back around. Self-disclosure of feelings of impotence, as well as expressions of anger, frustration, and sadness, are usually met by supportive comments, sharing of similar experiences, and even supportive physical touch in certain cases (Rabinowitz, 1991). A man may begin to feel less alone and find hope from the camaraderie found in the group.

Many men who are dependent on women for initiating interpersonal conversation and giving them social validation find an all-male group challenging. Although some men's groups have female leaders, the group situation brings up a different set of dynamics for men than a group made up of both men and women. Competition centers not around the need to posture for female attention, as is common in mixed groups, but more around personal insecurity and inadequacy (Wallach, 1994). Without women, men are forced to deal with their discomfort with each other, including learned homophobia (Rabinowitz & Cochran, 1987). Introjected anger toward other men may also be a source of discomfort, stemming from unexpressed resentment toward one's father (Osherson, 1986) and socialized distrust of other men (Pleck, 1995). The men's group can potentially provide a corrective emotional experience for men who have been culturally alienated from each other (Brooks, 1996).

Men's groups challenge men to constructively deal with interpersonal conflict. Many men have been socialized to avoid conflict through distracting activities, intellectual rationalization, rage, or silence (Philpot, Brooks, Lusterman, & Nutt, 1997). It is not uncommon for heated exchanges to arise in a men's group. Depending on the stage of the group, men will respond to these interpersonal challenges with varying degrees of effectiveness. In the early stages of a group, conflict is typically ignored to focus on commonalities among members. Although this allows for early trust building, it also sets the stage for conflict later in the group process.

Once initial trust has been established through mutual sharing and self-disclosure, group members will begin to tire of being nice to each other.

Niceness, if allowed to go on for too long, will become a group norm that supports safety but provides no challenge. For a men's group to work, it must provide a challenging psychological atmosphere (Brooks, 1998b). Group leaders must encourage and model interpersonal confrontation of as well as support for men. Learning to deal with confrontation can help participants acknowledge their own feelings, value interpersonal feedback, and understand the projective nature of many confrontational remarks. These interpersonal skills can be used in relationships in the world outside of the group to facilitate intimacy and connection.

Men's groups allow for the safe expression and containment of strong emotion (Brooks, 1996). Many men have been taught that to express strong feeling exposes too much personal vulnerability. Many men, having been socialized to keep their feelings to themselves, find that even under safe conditions, such as a confidential group, they are unable to speak. Some men have unlearned how to identify their feelings, whereas others have very few distinctions among emotional states. For men who are detached, unassertive, or depressed, anger-releasing exercises may encourage openness to feeling in the body, leading to more emotional honesty. In domestic violence groups it may be more important for men to learn strategies to control their anger and identify other emotions, such as fear, sadness, and hurt, that often have been overridden by expressions of rage.

Men's groups encourage men to re-explore their family-of-origin roots. Through the process of storytelling, interpersonal encounter, and strong emotional expression the story of one's earlier life often emerges. Memories about one's mother, father, siblings, friends, and others who had a significant impact in one's life, are often rekindled. It is not unusual for a man to recall something his father said or did when he was a boy or to reflect on interactions with siblings that helped shape his views on trust, masculinity, or his sense of self. The past unlocks some of the mystery of current interpersonal problems and allows for a reframing of current emotions, reactions, and behaviors (Yalom, 1985). Although it is useful to know from where one's life has emerged, the past is not to be used as an excuse to rationalize behavior. Once a member becomes aware of his behavior, he is encouraged by group leaders and other members to deal with the emotional core but not use it to avoid dealing with current life issues.

A men's group also deepens a man's experience of himself by addressing the existential predicaments of life. In the presence of his peers, a man can face his fears of the unknown. Often group discussion centers around the willingness to take risks. Ultimately this is based on the assumption that life is finite and that if one is to make the most of his time here he must be willing to risk leaving the safety of the familiar and move toward the potential unknown (Yalom, 1980).

Men may come to the group intellectually ready to leave a job or let go of a dysfunctional relationship but are often deeply frightened of risking life change. The group uniquely encourages men to take the risk. The voices from a well-functioning group often counter internalized messages from society, family, and work that say "don't change" or "just be a man and suck it up." Although it is up to each man to decide what, when, and how to risk, he knows that the group will accept him no matter what choice he makes. This knowledge gives him the impetus to leap and to trust that if all else fails his comrades in the group will be there with him in his failure or triumph.

ALEX: NOTES FROM A MEN'S GROUP

These case notes represent selected entries from Fred's and his two cotherapists' observations of their men's psychotherapy group across a 9-month period. We have chosen to focus on Alex, one of the men whose individual therapy we have detailed in this book. The exact nature of the events that are described here have been altered slightly, and the names have been changed to protect the identity of former and current group members.

Session 1: Beginnings

The first men's group of the year always raises some therapist performance expectations and brings on neurotic anxiety about what we are doing as well as a curiosity, knowing the various personalities who signed on for the group, about how the group members will interact. The coleaders spend the hour before the group processing what is happening in their own lives, sharing feelings, dreams, and private thoughts with each other about their own experiences as men. This leads to a planning session about what to anticipate and how to structure the night's activities.

I had dreamed of the first group meeting the night before. In my dream, several people I know in personal relationships had decided to join the group. We were doing some ritualistic mythopoetic exercises in the group that were obviously making several of the men uncomfortable. Three of my friends got up and walked out. "Fred, this is interesting stuff, but I'm not sure its right for me," one of them said. I replied, "Wait, don't leave. This isn't the whole group. We also talk and make real sense of what's going on in life, too." My desperation turned to fear that we were "too far out."

Tom, a 50-year-old psychologist and one of the other group leaders, recalled a dream about a group of naked, balding, fat, middle-aged men beating drums showing up at his doorway. Tom felt that the dream reflected his own feelings about being middle aged and not playing by society's rules any longer. It also suggested his anticipation for this year's group.

Jim, a 46-year-old substance abuse counselor and administrator and the third leader, had spontaneous images of the group as several huge, wild-eyed men with no shirts on, pounding drums with passion. The beat was deafening and the feeling exhilarating. Jim, too, was energized about the beginning of the men's group.

We had interviewed in individual sessions prior to the first group meeting the four men who were interested in joining the group for this year. Each man was given an opportunity to tell his story, explain why he was contemplating being part of the group, and encouraged to ask us questions about the group and ourselves. We described the group process to give the men a framework for what to anticipate. If there seemed to be a match between a man's goals and our vision and knowledge about the group's process, he was welcomed into the group. We encouraged the men to make at least an 8-week commitment before deciding whether they wanted to stay with the group or leave it. This seems to be the minimum amount of time for the men to get through their initial fears and see if the group holds some benefit for them. Typically, 80% of the men stay for the entire 9-month schedule, and 60% sign up again for the following year's group.

As has been typical with our groups over the last 12 years, on the first night the newest members all show up early or on time, and the older members wander in 5–10 minutes late. In our pregroup preparation meeting Tom, Jim, and I decided on a three-part introductory exercise that would not be too frightening for new members but at the same time bring up something unexpected for the old members and even the playing field for new and old members. Our goal was to make sure every man's voice was heard, especially those of the new members, who were almost guaranteed to be questioning why they had made a commitment to come.

The old members entered the large, rectangular room, which was strewn with large, soft pillows, greeting each other warmly after the summer hiatus. They exchanged hugs, joked, and then took seats on the floor next to each other. The new members sat clumped uncomfortably across the room, quiet, glancing with wariness at the display of affection among the men. Some of the old members tentatively asked the four new men their names and shared their own. The room was already divided into the "old guys" and "new guys" subgroups.

We went around the room with each man saying something about himself. The old members praised the group as if they were talking the new guys into staying, and the new guys revealed basic facts about themselves. As the relatively superficial disclosures ended, I asked the men to reveal just one word that described how they were feeling tonight. There was a slow and fairly conservative response from each member, "excited," "curious," "lost," "searching," "scared," "whole," "grumpy," "tense." This seemed to deepen the atmosphere a bit, because the one-word revelations were more present than rehearsed life stories. The third part of the warmup exercise on this first night might have been a stretch, especially for the new guys. They each answered the question "How have you impacted another man in your life?" Our expectation was that there would be some discussion of fathering, children, or friends.

After some tentative disclosures from a few of the old members, Alex, now a new group member, took his turn. Alex was the youngest man in the room, just as he had envisioned it. He was also the only person of color in the room. Alex briefly made eye contact with me. I nodded for him to go ahead.

"I don't feel like I have really had too much of an impact on any other men in my life, except maybe my two younger brothers," he said, his voice quivering. Alex was more overtly anxious than I had ever seen him in our individual therapy sessions together.

"Tell us about your brothers," requested one of the old-time group members in a concerned and caring way.

"They are twins, about 5 years younger than me. When we were kids, they always were put into my charge by my mother, who was busy with my younger sisters. How I impacted them, I'm not sure. We only see each other a few times a year these days."

"I know I really looked up to my older brother," interrupted another of the experienced members, Ned, age 55, who was in his fifth year of the group.

The interruption took Alex off the hook. I imagined that he was already feeling some support from the old timers in the group with their initial comments. Soon the conversation was off onto brothers and fathers. Other men contributed, and although he had left his disclosure unfinished, Alex seemed to have broken the ice by talking in this group of male strangers. He seemed to be mostly in the observing mode for the rest of the first session.

The initial stage of a long-term men's group is often marked by emotional ambivalence. Despite assurances by group leaders of confidentiality and safety, group members question whether the group and its leaders can be trusted. For many men, the world outside of therapy has included few situations in which confidences have been kept or vulnerability not exploited. Sharing of personal information in this stage is often superficial and tentative. Early disclosures, regardless of their quality or relevance, are often met with verbal acceptance but nonverbal neutrality by the group. The group leaders' task is to help men feel included by encouraging each member to speak. Through empathic verbalizations, the leaders model support and show the members that they will be trustworthy and not exploitive of their vulnerability.

Session 10: Boot Camp

I felt energized coming to the group tonight. I had had a mentally and physically active day. I had taught my college classes, had had time for some reading on object relations theory, played basketball at lunchtime, and spoke to Jim over the telephone about some interpersonal conflict we were having. Tom and Jim both arrived at similar emotional places. The freed-up energy we all had was shared during dinner as we continued to understand and accept our differences in how we see ourselves as men and at the same time feeling a love for each other. When I am with Tom and Jim I feel high, strong, and full. I realized that I want that feeling more, and when Jim hadn't gone to a group therapy conference in San Francisco with Tom and me 2 weeks earlier, I had missed his presence. Last week, Jim had been angry with me for telling him that I wished he had been with us.

We discussed beginning tonight's group with something physical, and what eventually transpired was a three part "boot camp" exercise. After nine sessions and no dropout of members, we were fairly certain that the group was ready to start taking some more risks. I was aware that I needed to back down some of my expectations for the progress of the group. After 11 years of leading this group, I may have grown a bit impatient for the "working phase" of the group to arrive.

As lightning lit up the night sky, the group members gathered together in the room for the 2-hour session. Tom introduced the boot camp exercise we had created in the pregroup meeting. The first part of boot camp for each man was using a tennis racquet to whack a pile of pillows several times with full force, with the encouragement to verbalize a grunt or words that helped make the aggressive action relevant. This was intended to loosen the muscular and psychological defenses. Then each man was directed to lean backward over a stool to open up his chest. Each member was then shown how to do a reverse stretch on the floor in front of the mirror. The next move was to open one's eyes wide and make a noise at his own image in the mirror. The men lined up on one side of the room and watched each other go. After all the men went, each was asked to make eye contact with the others before sitting down on the pillows. The energy in the room was high, and when we sat down I felt an almost surreal, altered state of consciousness, as did many of the participants.

Tonight, Alex was the first to speak in the group. I had watched Alex do the exercise with particular vigor and was not surprised. Something seemed to be up with him, and the boot camp workout let him express some of his anger in a nonverbal way. Alex seemed to be adjusting to and bonding with the group fairly well. A good indicator we have found is how long a man lingers after group sessions, talking with the other men in the hallway or outside. After the fifth session, Alex had become a "regular" with those men, who seemed to be processing what had happened, talking about their lives, and just bull-shitting to bask in the aftergroup glow of intimacy.

"I'm having a hard time dealing with something, and I've wanted to bring it up before but it just didn't seem right," began Alex.

"What's made it right tonight?" asked Jim.

"When I was hitting that pillow and then growling in the mirror, I saw my father's face. He was telling me to calm down, be rational, and not get so worked up. It pissed me off."

"What's your father like?" asked one of the other new group members, a man in his early 50s, dealing with his own ambivalence about his aging father, who had abused him as a child.

"My father is a minister. He is totally devoted to God, and he has such high moral values that I usually feel like a sinner when I'm around him."

"My father was a pastor. I think I know what you're going through," said Gary, a 42-year-old second-year group member. "Sometimes I wish my dad had just been some normal guy rather than everyone's holy role model. I felt like our family came second to the congregation a lot of the time."

"Exactly!" replied Alex, excited that someone in the group knew what he was talking about.

"Anyone in the group remind you of your father?" I asked Alex. He looked around. "You mean physically?"

"No, I mean does anyone strike you as having some of the same characteristics of your dad? Maybe the way he says things, or how you feel when he speaks?" I added.

"Well, Brian does a little."

"How does Brian remind you of your dad?" asked Tom.

"He seems kind of judgmental to me, like he disapproves of me in some way."

"Can you say this directly to Brian?" I asked, trying to make the interaction personal and not like we were talking in the third person about Brian, a tall, slightly built man, who was sitting across the group circle from Alex.

"Brian, you seem judgmental to me. You seem like you don't like me for some reason," stammered Alex, struggling to make eye contact.

Brian, a 54-year-old, successful, workaholic medical researcher, looked genuinely surprised to be chosen. He was one of the new members in the group and had tended to keep quiet. He had yet to reveal too much about his past and seemed to best respond in group when he was called on, rarely initiating conversation.

"I'm not judgmental of you, Alex," he said quickly and defensively.

"Not so quickly, Brian," I intervened. "You'll get your chance to respond. It might be good feedback to you to see how Alex is perceiving you."

"Well, you don't say much, and when you do, it is usually about lame employees or bosses that don't understand you. When I say I'm tired of working so hard or that there is more to life than work, I imagine you are thinking I'm one of those people you can't stand," replied Alex.

"Yeah. I see you that way, too," said Stan, another group member, jumping in on the discussion.

"Stan, you'll get your chance to address Brian, but right now Alex is in the middle of an interaction with Brian. Hold onto your thoughts," said Jim, aware that Stan had a tendency to "pile on" when another member was getting feedback. He had been confronted about this last year in group, but he still had a tendency to get worked up by confrontation. One of Stan's goals was to initiate interaction without using another group members' words or reactions.

"Can I respond now?" asked Brian.

"Sure," I said.

"To tell you the truth, I admire you, Alex. When I was your age I was so caught up in having to do everything perfectly that it cost me a lot."

"What do you mean?" asked Alex.

"I mean I nearly had a nervous breakdown. I was trying to be a father to two little kids, a good husband, and the best researcher the university had ever known. Guess what happened? My wife had an affair, my kids barely knew me, and it didn't seem to matter how much I worked, I always felt like I wasn't doing enough," he said with resignation.

"I don't know what to say," answered Alex.

"Well, I can tell you that you're doing the right thing by being in this group at your age. I could have saved myself a lot of grief. The reason I'm in this group is to deal with my workaholism. I can barely make it through a Sunday without going into the office. I still work most of the day on Saturday. Alex, you have a lot to teach me." Brian reached over to Alex awkwardly, looking like he was going to shake hands, but then gave him a hug. Alex responded to the hug and replied, "I don't know about that, but I do feel like I know you a little better. You're a lot different than my father. He would have never admitted what you just did."

"I feel like I know you both better. That is beautiful." bellowed Ned, the eldest member of the group, from across the room.

Although Alex didn't quite work as he would individually with the issue of his father, he got support from one of the men who also had a father in the clergy. His interaction with Brian turned from projection to intimacy. Alex's feedback to Brian allowed both of them to appreciate unknown aspects of each other in a manner unique to group. Alex found that his feelings toward his father could also affect his perceptions of other men. The deepening at the interpersonal level he experienced with Brian was directly related to the work he was doing in understanding the relationship he has with his father. Over time, the interpersonal and experiential men's group environment will allow Alex to revisit his father issues in various incarnations.

Some authors (e.g., Crews & Melnick, 1976; Heppner, 1983; Washington, 1979) have suggested that men's groups should use a structured format to reduce the interpersonal discomfort among men and to build trust in this anxiety-producing arena. Others (e.g., Lieberman, Yalom, & Miles, 1973; Rabinowitz & Cochran, 1987) have found that structure may lead to member passivity and excessive reliance on the leaders for direction. The type of structure provided is a significant element related to encouraging active participation and readying men for deep emotional work. Leaders can facilitate men's reconnection with their emotions by introducing exercises in the early stages of group that focus on the body. These exercises soften ego defenses and increase access to emotion stored in muscle memory while engaging men in an ambiguity-reducing structured activity. Techniques that encourage men to become aware of their breathing and body rigidity and that promote physical movement and vocal expression seem to result in more integration of feelings and verbal content during the group sessions (Rabinowitz, 1998).

Once group members have become comfortable with the group's structure, format, and membership they can start being more open to the content and implied messages of member disclosures. A successful group will be characterized in the early stage by members who feel secure and safe. This stage will then be replaced by a period of restlessness and a return of ambivalence as the men are faced with the reality that they must deal with the conflicting emotional material being raised by increased disclosure. For instance, some members may find it uncomfortable to continue to give unconditional support to someone in the group who is annoying or negative. If the group members are not challenged to take risks to speak honestly about their feelings about others and themselves, there is a high potential for some to drop out.

A man in one of our groups said during this stage, "I came here to learn about myself and be challenged. Right now I feel like we are just sitting around being supportive and safe, and it's boring. I don't really want to confront anyone in particular, though, because I don't want to single anyone out or get attacked." These words are an indication that the leadership needs to personalize the process by encouraging group members to verbalize feelings about specific people in the group. The leaders might also open themselves up to any negative feelings about the group or their leadership, demonstrating a willingness to handle criticism and modeling an openness to conflict.

Session 18: In the Shadows

My friend Frank's sudden death on Thursday kept me from writing up the group notes until Tuesday of the following week. His death hit me hard, because he had been like a father to me in Redlands, having welcomed me to the university and been a coteacher in several classes, a lunch friend, and a golfing buddy. Frank was also an artist who illustrated the cover of our first book with a colorful painting called "Man Alive." He was a man who embraced the idea of living life fully. I will always remember his emotionality, enthusiasm, and gestures. Sometimes he was quick to judge a person or situation, and his confrontational style sometimes pissed me off. Images of him rumbled inside me all week. It was comforting to go to Frank's house, visit with his wife and children, and be at the memorial service with Jim. Confronting and feeling our own grief, Jim and I pushed for a session that would allow us to explore some of the darker, less acceptable aspects of being a man.

Jim wanted for the group tonight to somehow have some exposure of the members' real selves, and I had brought in my slide projector for "shadow work." We combined our ideas and developed an agenda for the evening in which we would ask each man to show what was going on inside of him. With the projector making a shadow, each man would go up and act out the inner struggle with the rest of us watching him and his giant shadow image on the wall.

Bill, a large man in his mid-30s, went first. He had been early to arrive at group and seemed agitated about something. His shadow image showed anger. He gave the group "the finger" and roared a loud growl. He had felt betrayed and unsupported by the group last week. He stood up, walked around the group, and chose Jim and Tom toward whom to vent his anger. I instructed the rest of the group to physically hold Bill back while he expressed fully his anger, trying to move toward them as if to actually hurt them. This holding acts as a psychological container so a man can fully embrace his emotion without worrying that he is going to hurt someone.

"I hate you guys for being condescending to me," he raged at Jim and Tom. "I just want to fucking belong." After a few minutes of struggling to get out of the hold of several of the other men, Bill quit struggling. He had an insight in his rage. "I want you guys to challenge me more in this group. All of you." As he said this he made eye contact with Tom and Jim as well as the rest of the group.

"I don't want to have to challenge you. Why don't you challenge your-self?" said Hugh.

"I don't care what you want to do. I said what I wanted. You don't have to do it. I just want you not to hold back on me if you have something to say. I can take it." Bill said this with a kind of assertiveness I had rarely heard.

"I hear you, and I will," said Hugh in a huff.

"What's going on with you, Hugh?" I asked.

"I'm just tired of feeling like I have to take care of everyone else's shit."

"You sound pissed about that."

"I understand what Hugh is saying. Why should he be responsible for Bill's issues?" piped up Alex.

"Alex, what's your investment in this conflict?" asked Tom.

"I don't know. I just feel like Hugh should get some support here for his anger."

"Do you have an issue with Bill also?" asked Pete, a 45-year-old new member in the group.

"I guess I do. I have been in this group for about 4 months and Bill, you have seemed to have not noticed me or responded to me in any way. Does it have to do with me being a new guy? Being Black?" questioned Alex, his tension mounting notably.

"What? Of course not," replied Bill.

"Then what is it?" asked Alex, making direct eye contact.

"Has anything changed for you since Alex joined the group this year, Bill?" asked Jim.

"Well. Last year the group was real tight, and this year it doesn't seem to have the same flavor. I don't know if it has anything to do with Alex," Bill responded.

"Bill, you're not the baby of the group anymore," blurted out Gary, a third-year group member who was also a social worker. This was an insightful observation of the group dynamics. It was true that Alex was now the youngest member, supplanting Bill, who had had this role the last 2 years.

"That's bullshit!" cried out Bill.

"Maybe it is, but I was just pointing it out," continued Gary.

"Bill, stop for a minute and let in the possibility that Alex has been getting some of the attention you had in the past," I intervened.

"Bill, I don't necessarily want to be the 'baby' of the group. I'm just trying to fit in," said Alex in a conciliatory tone. The baby-of-the-group interpretation must have connected with Alex on some level. He was much less defensive.

"Yeah. Gary, you're right on some level. I never even thought about it before, but I have been agitated this year. I'm the oldest of three brothers in my family, and I really did enjoy being the young one here. It's like having a lot of older brothers." Bill was more calm.

"I'm also the oldest of five. I like being the youngest for once, too," stated Alex, looking directly at Bill.

"Maybe you can both be the little brothers in here," interjected Gary. Heads nodded in the group when Gary said this. Alex and Bill gave each other a hug and seemed to have worked through the emotional block by acknowledging their parts in the dynamics of the situation.

The conflict stage of group is often both exciting and frightening. Dynamic issues include challenges to leadership, resistance to exercises, disagreements about interpretations of interpersonal behavior, confrontation of quieter or more talkative members, and the formation of norms about risk taking. Group members often thrive on the emotional charge of trying to be honest but are also fearful that what they say will be taken the wrong way.

When all group members feel accepted, they begin to loosen their censorship on honest reactions and engage in some blaming or criticism of other members as well as of leaders. Leaders should encourage honesty but help members interpret their actions. Both the projector and recipient of a critical comment will benefit by expressing their immediate reactions and then processing their feelings. This can be done in the context of what the comment has stirred up from a man's past or current life situations. In the process, the projector is encouraged to reown his projection, realizing that the man he has confronted probably characterizes an aspect of himself he has depreciated. The one being confronted often learns about how others are seeing him and can practice differentiating the feedback from his own insecurities and fears about himself.

Session 27: Deepening Sadness

I had been reading Terrance Real's (1997) book *I Don't Want to Talk About It: Overcoming the Secret Legacy of Male Depression* in the last few days before group and was resonating with some of his ideas about covert male depression. It seemed to me that many of us geared our outer lives toward holding off feeling our deeper senses of loss and grief. As Jim pointed out, the way to a man's feeling mode is through grief. Tom shared his feelings about his recent trip with his parents and how his father seemed empty and lost in the midst of his mother's criticisms of his behaviors. When he was younger, Tom's father seemed bolstered by his involvement and prestige in the outer world, but as he has aged he has seemed hollow.

We decided that in relation to where the group had been in the last several weeks we would plan an exercise to access some of the grief, especially that related to our fathers. It seems that the men had begun a process of breaking down their shells and needed a push to go inside of themselves.

The exercise involved each man, one at a time, hugging the large green futon mattress in its rolled-up vertical position. Four men would stand behind the mattress to provide resistance. The man would then hug the mattress and try to push it as hard as he could for as long as he could.

We introduced the exercise by asking everyone to imagine their fathers at a time when the fathers were being all-powerful in their lives and then to recall a time when their fathers had abused their power or lost the men's respect. After a few minutes, each man took a turn at trying to "push his father off the pedestal." Although Jim asked the men to limit the pushing to 1 minute, most gave up in breathless frustration within 20 seconds. The mattress barely moved, and each man was left panting and frustrated, but the effect was that each of us sank into a strong feeling zone that could be labeled depression or grief.

The next part of the exercise involved putting one's father, in an imaginary form, on the empty center pillow and telling him what you didn't get from him what you needed. After each man had a turn he was then asked to sit on the pillow, imagine himself as the father, and admit to the transgressions as his father.

For Alex, this exercise was exceptionally powerful. As he looked at his imaginary father sitting on the pillow, his eyes watered.

"Dad, where were you? I so much wanted you to see me for who I am beyond being just your son. I wish you knew me better. I bet you didn't know that I prayed at night that you would say something to me like 'Let's you and I go fishing or to a baseball game, just the two of us.'"

"What are you feeling as you say this?" asked Tom.

"I feel like I'm going to cry if I let myself do it."

"What's stopping you from crying in here?"

"I don't want everyone here to see me bawl. I know we've said its OK to cry, and some guys have, but I don't feel that comfortable."

"I would see you as strong if you cried," said Hugh, age 52 and in his fifth year of the group.

"Go back to talking to your dad and go with what you feel," I instructed.

"Dad, I feel sorry for you. You have no idea what it means to feel something deeply about another person. I realize that your obsession with God and the 'flock' is about keeping your distance from the real people who should matter in your life."

"Alex, switch to the other pillow and be your father talking to his son," I guided. He moved to the other pillow he had been talking to.

"Son, I have been preoccupied with my work. I see that I missed out on seeing you grow up. I don't know you very well. I wish I did." The tears were back in Alex's eyes. Other men in the group were also clearly moved by his dialogue. There was rapt attention, along with some watery eyes. What Alex was saying and feeling could have been said by many of the sons in the room. When Alex was finished, he looked spent, as he began to release his tears. His sadness permeated the room. Ned, who was sitting next to him, reached out with his large bearlike body and let Alex cry into his shoulder.

The father–son scene was repeated several times during the evening. The exercise was powerful and revealed much of what we as men were sad about in regard to our fathers. Owning the legacy of our fathers and admitting it to our children was a significant piece of the exercise, because it let us acknowledge that we also exhibit some of the same behaviors and attitudes as our fathers, even if we are conscious of trying to do better.

The felt sense of despair in the room was freeing to me personally. I felt like I had gotten rid of my role as therapist for a few minutes and was just a "feeling" being, a comrade in grief. A couple of the men, uncomfortable with the emotion, tried to rationalize their way out of the feeling, but they were confronted by others in the group. I suggested that the group drink in this feeling state, because most of us tried to avoid it at all costs. This communion of intimacy around our fathers and grief stayed with me for several days. I even wrote my dad a letter after the group to tell him how I had felt about him during his last visit. It was very clear to me, and although the letter was not easy to write, it felt honest and truthful.

Session 36: Endings

In our pregroup meeting Jim, Tom, and I spoke of what had been going on in our lives. I spoke with a passionate energy about going to my 20-year college reunion the past weekend, which was better than I had expected. Tom spoke in depressed tones about wanting to switch his day job, which was doing psychological evaluations, and do something that had more soul. His recent work involved more paperwork than therapy or supervision. Jim had found out that for now his current job is safe and the company with which he had interviewed is not hiring. Going through the motions did help him realize that he could leave his current employment of 28 years if he wished. In regard to the group, we decided that a good way to kick off the final month would be by having the men give and receive honest feedback from each other about what they had been working on this year.

After some warmup stretching exercises, we explained the evening's format. It involved each man going to the center of the room and listening to the other group members comment on their relationships with him and his progress in the group, as well as aspects of his behavior on which he still might want to work. We also asked each man to give some thought to his own issues before it was his turn to receive feedback.

After several men received feedback, Alex took his turn in the center of the circle. He looked anxious. He started his piece by saying a few words about the issues on which he had been working.

"Before you guys say things to me, I just want you to know that I have been honored to be a part of this group. You have accepted me unconditionally. I had hoped you would, but had my doubts that first night I came."

"Well, I'm surprised we didn't scare you off right away," laughed Hugh. Joking with Alex seemed to be easy for many of the men, and Alex seemed to appreciate the sarcasm and humor.

"Seriously, Alex, I want to tell you that I have been extremely proud of you this year. You came into the group knowing no one, except for Fred, who was your therapist, and right now you seem like you are really one of the guys," continued Hugh.

"I've seen you go from being really intimidated by us older guys to being comfortable around us, especially me. I'll always remember the night you cried on my shoulder. That was special. It's one of my best memories of the group," said Ned.

"If there is one thing I wish for you this summer, it is to find someone to share your life with. You are a cool guy, and I can't believe there isn't someone out there for you," he continued.

"Alex, I feel like you have earned some 'warriorship' status in my mind. You have held your own in this group and made your presence known. You haven't backed down from confrontations in here. I like your intensity, the way you take all the exercises and stuff full on, 100 percent," said Gary, giving Alex the thumbs-up sign.

"I guess you have earned my respect, too. That time when we agreed to be the 'babies' of the group was a highlight for me too. You didn't back down. I even liked it when you got intense and thought I was 'dissing' you because you were Black." Bill said this with affection.

"You still need to take yourself a little less seriously," remarked Brian. "I relate to your intensity, but just like I've had to learn to laugh at myself more this year, so do you. You're a wonderful young man, and I feel privileged to know you. Maybe we'll be able to meet sometime this summer and hang out," he continued.

"I really look up to you in here. I've been in this group for a couple of years and was impressed by the way you got into the flow of things. I remember my first year in group, I could hardly say anything. I was tongue tied. This year I made some progress. You helped show me the way. You really did. I said to myself, if this guy is getting out there and taking risks, then maybe I can, too," said Stan effusively.

"Your passion for this group was great. You seemed to be ready for the experience and never let up," said Tom. "I was especially impressed with the way you took to the physical exercises with a lot of energy. If I could give you something to work on for the future, it would be to let more of your negativity out. When you get angry, you are powerful. I had a sense during the year that you held back some on your anger. Maybe that is something to look at."

"I just like you as a person. You make good eye contact. You express your feelings well. I sometimes think, though, that you are trying to please me," began Jim. "You sometimes are too good. You do exactly what you're asked. Perhaps a little more defiance is needed. Maybe it goes with what Tom said about anger. I sometimes see a flash across your face when someone says something in group that upsets you, but then it is gone and forgiven fairly quickly."

"I hope you're not getting too overwhelmed by all this feedback," I said.

"I am a bit overwhelmed, but it feels good to hear what everyone has to say," Alex replied, beaming.

"I've known you longer than the other guys," I began. "I too have been impressed by your willingness to risk and try new things. I remember when you asked me about this group. It seems like a long time ago. I've enjoyed seeing you become more of yourself, less of an actor. I agree with what Jim said that you still try to please, but you have definitely made progress in that area. I hope that you continue to stay in touch with what you are feeling and not be afraid of the powerful or negative emotions that you feel. I also have been very impressed with how you have dealt with your father in this group. In some ways, you had a room full of fathers to work with, and that could have been incredibly intimidating. Good work!"

Alex was clearly moved by the feedback. He thanked the men in the group for being there for him and seemed to drink in the feeling of validation he had received. In this group, he had gotten more supportive praise for being himself than he had ever gotten in his life. He was able to deepen his understanding of himself and how he was perceived by others. He had experienced very powerful emotions in the supportive company of other men. By using the interactions to get feedback and to practice expressing himself in an honest way, Alex had grown immensely in the group.

As the men's group comes to a close for the year, it is important to review progress, give feedback, and get closure on interpersonal issues. For many men, the group has become a stable, consistent part of their lives in which being genuine and honest has been valued, a quality that often feels lacking in work and outside relationships. Expressions of apprehension and frustration that the group is ending are common. The final group sessions often center around reviewing and celebrating the year's work. It is important for the men to give each other feedback about what they value and what they could continue to address in their lives. The ending rituals in the final sessions help to ensure closure.

THEMES AND ISSUES IN MEN'S PSYCHOTHERAPY GROUPS

In our men's group many themes and issues were recycled in gradually deepening ways throughout the year. Whereas in earlier stages themes might have been spoken about in a more intellectual manner, in later group stages the themes had a more personally relevant quality. Themes and issues that emerged included trust, vulnerability, fear, shame, pride, rage, strength, weakness, the dark shadow self, warrior, father, fathering, male–male relationships, competition, mother, male–female relationships, boundaries, family of origin, friendship, sexuality, tenderness, disappointment, dominance, submissiveness, desire, love, hatred, dreams, pleasure, pain, grief, secrets, passion, will paralysis, obsessions, work, and death. Many of these themes were stimulated by exercises and teachings introduced by the leaders and were facilitated as they arose from a member's personal experience.

On the basis of a research questionnaire administered at three different occasions to the group members, the following themes and exercises were considered the most impactful: shame (i.e., a man sharing past trauma that had happened to him); anger release (i.e., being able to hit pillows with tennis racquet to work on release of frustration and rage); grief, especially in regard to one's father (i.e., using guided imagery to encounter one's father in fantasy); trust and interpersonal doubts (i.e., creating a sociogram of how close to and trusting of group members a man feels); masculine and feminine differences (i.e., ritual exercises to explore what has been traditionally considered masculine and feminine ways of being in the world); the dark side of one's personality (i.e., feeling one's more aggressive and sinister self through towel twisting and speaking to one's shadow); and sharing honest feelings (i.e., interpersonal confrontation).

The research questionnaires also asked the members for the most impactful events in the group. We translated these findings into Yalom's (1985) curative factors of group therapy in order of importance, with actual examples from the men of what had occurred in the group.

1. *Catharsis* (e.g., taking the therapists on in confrontation, not holding back on negative feelings I was having in the session, breaking through to real emotion and letting go of control, projection and working through my authority issues toward the leaders, growling and releasing my aggression, towel twisting, forced self-expression)

2. *Interpersonal learning input* (e.g., the group's feedback that I am a decent person worthy of being loved, finding out that another member would be willing to socialize with me outside of the group, getting feedback about how others really see me)

3. *Interpersonal learning output* (e.g., standing my ground when confronted, trusting myself to stand firm with my feelings more often, confronting others in the group about "reporting events without emotional expression," asking for and receiving acknowledgment in the group from the other guys)

4. *Family re-enactment* (e.g., realizing my current baggage is due to childhood wounding; confronting my father first in the group and then in real life; symbolically "killing" my mother in a psychodrama, knowing the group was a safe place to work)

5. *Existential issues* (e.g., knowing I can't take responsibility for everyone else's actions; no one can fix my life except me; realizing that life is worth living fully, not in a half-assed manner; I need to make tough choices, knowing there are consequences for not choosing also)

6. *Universality/group cohesion* (e.g., realizing I'm not alone in my struggles, how similar we all feel, a willingness for us all to explore the dark side, relating and identifying with the stories of other group members, being able to help another man in the group with my sharing)

SUGGESTIONS FOR THERAPISTS WORKING WITH MEN'S GROUPS

Men's group therapists are encouraged to be creative in their intervention strategies. Emotional risk taking can become an expected outcome when framing the men's group experience as an adventure or journey, appealing to the more "doing"-oriented masculine perspective. Because men tend to relate better in action situations, each session, especially in the beginning of a group, should have some activities that facilitate interpersonal interaction as well as body-oriented emotional awareness.

The group leader must be vigilant in his observations in the group. Much of what happens occurs at the nonverbal level. For instance, a man who is speaking without much energy or passion may elicit bored looks from other members. Although he may not verbally acknowledge feeling hurt or rejected, it is important for the leader to make note of both his reaction and the group's so that he can effectively intervene at the appropriate time. It is important for the leader to have time to review what has happened in the previous session to anticipate themes and note the psychological progress of each man.

Regardless of the techniques used to elicit interaction or emotional honesty, the leader must respect each man's defenses while facilitating each member's movement beyond these barriers. Self-disclosure by the therapist in terms of relevant, here-and-now emotional reactions is also an excellent way to model verbalization of feelings and give permission for men to take risks (Rabinowitz, 1998).

To deepen therapy with men it is important to have empathy for their life experiences. Before working with them therapeutically one must deal with his or her own psychological issues and introjections about masculinity. Much typical male behavior and emotional expression push psychological buttons for therapists. Many traditionally socialized men show sexist and homophobic attitudes, have engaged in vulgar and degrading behavior toward men and women, and have very little emotional repertoire beyond anger in many cases (Brooks, 1998a). Working with this population demands that the therapist deal with his or her countertransference feelings. To identify with many men's issues, the potential group leader must be willing, in his or her own therapy and supervision, to explore the darker aspects of the self, including tendencies toward addiction, anger toward women, and resentment toward significant males in one's life.

As a modality for deepening, the men's group offers men an interpersonally inviting atmosphere. It often acts as a supportive male "family" for men, who in their own childhoods were thrust into some of the harsh realities of the masculine world without much assistance. The group provides modeling for how to be intimate and how to trust others and oneself. It also is a powerful force in counteracting the negative side of male gender role socialization, with its emphasis on control, competition, and stoicism in the face of pain. Finally, men's groups encourage men to feel alive again by rewarding and appreciating the connection each man makes to himself and his fellow members.

8

A QUESTION-AND-ANSWER
SESSION WITH THE AUTHORS:
SOME FINAL WORDS

Reason was only a way of trying to make the incoherent coherent, and it never did all the job. It washed over grief, but it left grief intact. It shrunk grief into a tiny matted lump in the belly, but it left the shame and grief where they lay. (Gold, 1966, p. 152)

HOW DID YOU ARRIVE AT THIS THERAPEUTIC APPROACH?

With a combined experience of more than 40 years devoted to working with men in psychotherapy, this approach is the result of many hours spent discussing, debating, refining, and attempting to understand this experience. We have read many of the works of the great psychotherapy masters and tried to apply their insights to our work with our male clients. We have struggled with how to engage men in therapy, how to provide a unique and challenging environment in which men may choose to become more authentic and emotionally vibrant. In addition to our clinical work and academic research, our own personal therapeutic experiences and explorations have freed us to challenge the insidious impact of our culture on our own masculinities. By feeling free to take risks emotionally, we have been able to develop ideas and directions for therapeutic understanding and intervention that might not have come to us otherwise.

We also have our doubts. A part of embracing our depth is understanding that our ideas and perceptions carry some distortion with them. We do not wish for our readers to walk away from this book saying "those arrogant psychologists think they know how to treat men better than I do." Instead, we wish only to share our ideas and experiences so that readers might be stimulated in their own thinking about how to work therapeutically with the men they see.

Our goal has been to articulate a coherent approach that serves men by extending the boundaries of how a man might be seen and understood by therapists. We believe that in this era of "efficiency" and "quick results" it is important that men not be shortchanged. We hope that our vision of helping male clients rediscover their emotional depth is a step toward men as a group reclaiming their wholeness, vibrancy, and wisdom.

SO, IN A NUTSHELL, WHAT IS DEEPENING PSYCHOTHERAPY WITH MEN ALL ABOUT?

This approach, which we call *deepening psychotherapy*, integrates a psychodynamic developmental perspective with a gender role strain perspective. The distinct features of combining these two points of view include a recognition of the emotional depth of men, an approach to opening up or uncovering this depth, and a "mapping" of the masculine-specific conflicts that have been encouraged and reinforced by our cultural attitudes toward masculinity. The most significant of these masculine-specific conflicts are in the realms of interpersonal dependence, the management of grief and loss experiences, the shaping of masculine-specific self-structures, and men's comfort with and preference for "doing" as opposed to "being."

Deepening refers to a process of uncovering and elucidating masculine-specific conflicts many men experience on an emotional level. Of course, a big emphasis in our culture is the denial or avoidance of emotion in men. Hence, the deepening approach directly addresses this element of masculinity by encouraging therapists to look beneath the surface and to help men embrace in a more holistic manner the emotional aspects of their lives.

Often, a traumatic experience or wounding event that has led a man to come to psychotherapy serves as a catalyst for deepening. This wound, which has pierced a man's psychological armor, is usually the result of an immediate loss experience, such as the end of an intimate relationship, the loss of a job, a death of a friend or loved one, or a perceived failure.

The pain from the wound awakens a man to his inner emotional life. Like a beacon, it points the client and his therapist toward a portal to the man's emotional world. The portal, a psychological window into his deeper, genuine, true self, can be identified through empathic listening and is made up of a constellation of images, words, thematic elements, emotional associations, and bodily sensations that reflect the core themes of his emotional existence. This portal is illuminated most brightly by pain caused from a wounding experience.

The deepening therapy process allows the client and therapist to enter a portal and conjointly navigate the fears, defenses, and cultural gender role obstacles that have kept the inner emotional landscape from being owned and understood. The result of this exploration is a reconnection with the emotional world, outwardly manifested by increased vitality and emotional expressivity.

WHY DO YOU THINK DEEPENING IS IMPORTANT IN PSYCHOTHERAPY WITH MEN?

As noted, we have discovered that men's conflicts go beyond the surface. Because men are taught from boyhood to disavow emotional experience and be strong and in control, a psychotherapeutic approach that engages men on the level at which these cultural values shape and interact with emotional dynamics is essential. Anything short of this will fail to capture the full range of men's emotional depth and will result in an oversimplified, politically correct approach to men's problems that in fact alienates most men who come to a therapist for help with their emotional problems.

We have had many male clients who have been in previous therapies that focus on only pieces of the emotional puzzle. For instance, a client who had been in a more behaviorally oriented therapy spoke of having learned to speak up more and be less shy in his interactions with others. This was wonderful, except that he still felt that something important was missing in his life. When he explored this sense of something missing in deepening therapy, he found that a great deal of his tendency toward shyness and avoidance was connected to early betrayals by his parents in the emotional realm. By re-experiencing his fear, his anger, and his internal self-rejection through empathic exploration and body-oriented interventions, this male client regained his connection to the emotional world from which he had disengaged out of self-preservation earlier in his life.

We believe that for men to become whole they must have a strong partnership with their emotions. Deepening therapy focuses men on finding this connection to an emotional life from which they have learned to disengage. By following, with the help of a therapist, the "leads" from their words, body reactions, and recurring life themes, men can find their portal and rediscover the hidden communication conduits to their emotional world.

We have found that connections made through the deepening approach for men can have positive impact at both the conscious and unconscious levels. Consciously, a man becomes more aware of what he is feeling, labeling this affective state, and accepting it as true in the moment. It allows him to use this information in the choices he is making. We have noticed that many men unconsciously look less to the external world for validation and reinforcement. They seem to be more directed by an inner source of energy that has been freed up by facing and breaking through introjected fears, barriers, and prohibitions on their emotional lives. The result is a man who is more whole and functions with greater emotional and behavioral potency.

CAN YOU SAY MORE ABOUT HOW YOU ASSESS MASCULINE-SPECIFIC CONFLICTS WHEN YOU WORK WITH MEN IN DEEPENING THERAPY?

Assessment is done as a part of the development of the therapeutic relationship. We believe that men must be listened to, respected, and welcomed into therapy. This involves being able to empathically hear a man's "underground stream" of pain, loss, vulnerability, and disappointment beneath the words and gestures he uses to describe his experience. A great deal of the assessment process involves listening for core themes and veins of emotional depth that arise out of the therapeutic encounter.

We have learned to use a combination of masculine-specific conflicts as our map or guide. Each man is unique, but each must navigate the four main conflictual themes we have mentioned before: relationships, loss, self-structure, and the doing-versus-being orientation.

As an integral aspect of our listening we notice how a man describes his relationships with the people close to him. What words, gestures, and emotions arise when he tells of his intimate relationships in the present and past? How does he relate to the therapist in session? Are there discrepancies between his relationship stories and his in-session behavior toward the therapist? How and when did he emerge into male culture? How long did he stay in his mother's orbit? What kind of relationship did he have with his father? What effect did familial, ethnic, sociocultural, religious, or geographical influences have on his construction of relationships? How has the client dealt with disappointment, loss, and grief? What emotions have been taboo to express, and which have been more acceptable? What is the nature of the current trauma or wound that brought him into therapy now? How has this individual encountered the cultural notions of masculinity? What were the values of his family, friends, and cultural environment regarding what it means to be a boy or man? How does this man express his sexuality in terms of attitudes toward women or other men? How much does he judge himself by society's standards, and in what ways? How comfortable is this man with "being"? How much has his orientation been aligned with action and doing? These are some of the questions whose answers we try to find as we make an emotional connection with our clients in the therapy process.

CAN YOU ELABORATE ON THE CONCEPT OF THE PORTAL AND HOW YOU USE THAT IN YOUR SESSIONS?

The portal can be envisioned as the door or entry to deeper levels of processing. It is often an event or trigger around which a man's core issues may be organized. For example, a man who has just lost his job because of his drinking and whose spouse has just moved out on him may have core issues surrounding adequacy, competence, and success activated. When he says "I just feel like I have failed at everything" he is indicating to the therapist the portal to his emotional world. This key phrase, and the emotional intensity that lies behind it, represents the entry, the key, to a deeper level of processing on which his core issues are given emotional meaning. The therapist should be alert to comments such as this, for they are the openings, the cracks in the armor through which greater depth will be found.

Once the portal has been breached, a man will have an easier time accessing it again. Although there is often initial resistance to exploring the emotional realm, over time it becomes the focus of therapy. With repeated exposure, men become less fearful and more curious and interested in what they find through the portal. Although the emotional working-through process can be painful and make the man feel out of control, the positive results are tangible. These include more energy for life activities, less role restriction, more interpersonal honesty, and more emotional expressivity.

HOW DO YOU KNOW WHEN TO USE A BODY-ORIENTED TECHNIQUE AND WHICH ONE?

Many body-oriented techniques can be used to facilitate a specific goal or process in the therapy. For example, if a man is struggling with feelings of sadness or grief, but cannot get in touch with these feelings on an emotional or physical level, a body-oriented technique may facilitate this. In addition, body-oriented techniques may be used to work with male resistances to emotional exploration that frequently arise in deepening therapy. For example, a man might be encouraged to externalize his negative, internalized self-talk by speaking to himself in an empty chair. Or, in a group setting, some group members could play the role of the man's resistance by actually restraining or holding back the man as he attempts to reach one of the group members who might represent a relationship connection or a desired goal with which he has struggled.

In general, there are no cut-and-dried rules for when to use a particular body-oriented technique. Consider them when dealing with resistance to the deepening process or when exploration of an issue on a deeper level is desired. A body-oriented technique can be used to enhance or exaggerate awareness of an emotional state already being experienced, or it can be used to help elicit an emotional reaction that a man is having difficulty accessing. These techniques always result in a nonverbal approach that tends to side-step the often-intellectualized or rational approach many men enlist in dealing with their emotional lives. In group situations, physical techniques are especially effective, where the context is clear and the group members can assist each other in the guided activities.

Of course, any intervention that involves the body should be used carefully and its purpose explicitly verbalized to the client. If a therapist has not had training in this realm, then he or she should not use these techniques. It is imperative to respect client boundaries when touch or physical activity is involved. We have our clients sign an informed consent and liability form that gives us permission to use body-oriented techniques, and the client always has the option of declining participation.

For further information and rationale for body-oriented interventions, we suggest reading some of the writings of Reich (1942/1973, 1949/1976), Lowen (1975, 1984), Keleman (1971), and Feldenkrais (1972).

CAN THERAPISTS REALLY LEARN THE DEEPENING THERAPY APPROACH, OR IS IT TOO PERSONAL AND INDIVIDUALIZED?

This approach is personal and individualized, for both the therapist and the male client. However, that does not mean that therapists cannot learn from this model. For instance, it is possible to use our conceptualization of male clients by looking at the masculine-specific conflicts we delineated, including how a man deals with dependence in relationships, how he manages his grief and loss experiences, how much he has culturally defined himself from a traditional masculine gender role perspective, and his "doing" versus "being" preferences. By following empathically how a man has been wounded in his life experience, a therapist can differentially approach the portals in a wide variety of male clients.

By being creative, fully engaged, and genuine in implementing interventions, each therapist can find strategies that fit his or her style and resonate with male clients in the emotional realm. Deepening therapy will look somewhat different for each therapist–client dyad or group but have the same goal of connecting a man with his inner emotional life.

HOW DOES RESPECT FOR THE RELATIONAL BONDS ESTABLISHED THROUGH PRODUCTIVE "DOING" GET INCORPORATED INTO THE THERAPEUTIC RELATIONSHIP?

This is an important question, because it suggests that therapists should acknowledge the positive elements of male-oriented "doing" relationships. We agree that the key to connecting with men in therapy is using the more natural "doing" orientation to establish a shared, familiar relationship with a male client. Having too much expectation of a "being" relationship, in which a man sits and talks without active therapist input, can be frightening.

As part of the initial therapeutic interaction the therapist should ask about friendship and how a man relates to the people he calls his friends. It is not uncommon for a man to have a variety of friends with whom he shares various parts of his life. For example, a man might have a friend with whom he talks sports, a different person with whom he plays racquetball or golf, and another with whom he relates at work. These activity-oriented relationships, often with other men, may be strong in terms of liking and loyalty but not necessarily emotionally deep.

If the therapist can show a male client that he or she understands and can relate to him on this activity-oriented level, the client will be more at ease in the relationship. We advocate a therapeutic approach that uses activity-oriented interventions with "being"-oriented processing of the emotional outcomes of these interventions. A man can thus learn through doing and being within therapy. The working alliance builds on familiar ways of relating that can then be expanded and deepened.

THIS APPROACH DOESN'T SEEM TO FIT WITH THE SHORT-TERM MANAGED-CARE MODEL, DOES IT?

It may be true that this approach doesn't "fit" with managed care. It does not encourage a quick fix for most men. It recognizes that most men in our culture have grown up with much negative programming about their masculinity and how to manage the emotional aspects of their lives. Layer upon layer of contradictory, unhealthy, and maladaptive proscriptions have been laid down, and this learning is not easily or quickly undone.

On the other hand, though, there are several insights and strategies that we believe could be applied with men that would assist them in resolving a current crisis or could be incorporated into some of the more short-term approaches to psychotherapy. These include being able to listen for the core themes in a man's verbalizations and taking an empathic approach to a man's pain, even if it is not being overtly verbalized or affectively demonstrated in his verbal expression.

Deepening psychotherapy with men is not a manualized approach to be used like a cookbook. It is a way of viewing men's emotional development and how our culture shapes and distorts much of this experience in men's lives. Such understanding can certainly be applied within the narrow confines of most managed care limits on service.

We have found, however, that once a man begins the journey of self-discovery and recovery he often prefers to carry this journey forward beyond the four or eight sessions that many insurance policies and managed care plans will support. This is one reason why we have included a detailed description of how a group setting can be used in this approach. Often, a group setting will allow a man to continue in his journey, share some of the costs with other group members, and not be confined by session limits or impairment requirements.

WHAT IS THE DIFFERENCE IN HOW INDIVIDUAL AND GROUP APPROACHES PROMOTE DEEPENING?

Because the individual therapy process relies on dyadic interaction to promote deepening, it is both facilitated and limited by this structure. It is facilitated by the reality of an intimate, personal, one-to-one relationship between the client and therapist. This promotes the deepening process in a significant way. This is especially true if the male client has not had much experience with this kind of interpersonal relationship. It is limited by the fact that there are only two persons involved in the deepening process, whereas in a group setting a number of men join together to support one another in the process.

In the group setting, male hesitation to share with other men, competitiveness, and issues of homophobia may present substantial impediments initially to the deepening process. However, these potential blocks to deepening are prime grist for the mill in the group setting and, when addressed in a timely manner, frequently result in greater levels of trust and respect among the men in the group, which in turn enhances the deepening potential of the group.

Groups also have many benefits for men that seem to be missing from modern life. Men's groups are often activity oriented, giving men some familiar relationship structure from which to begin the deepening process. Male tendencies toward isolation, avoidance of intimacy, and disengagement from the emotional lives of each other are counteracted in a well-functioning group environment. Once trust has been established, men seem to be able to move more quickly toward their depth. By observing other men struggle with issues that cut across most men's lives, an individual in a men's group is encouraged in his own quest toward emotional wholeness. Men are able to give each other both supportive and confrontational feedback. Emotional risk taking is often a valued activity that receives support, whereas intellectualizing about significant life issues is often confronted. More senior group members often act as role models for newer members in the realm of interpersonal honesty and genuineness. It is an environment that encourages and rewards men for being connected to the emotional part of themselves.

HOW MIGHT DEEPENING THERAPY BE APPLIED TO COUPLES WORK OR FAMILY THERAPY?

Men who are in therapy with a partner or with their family may benefit from some of the principles of the deepening approach. A man who appears to be resistant, uninvolved, or uncomfortable should be seen through the lenses of how he might be trying to navigate the therapy situation given his masculine-specific conflicts. Rather than assuming that he can't somehow share his feelings because he is male, it is better to try to understand what might be causing him to feel conflict, shame, and discomfort in this situation. Often face-to-face, talk-it-out therapy will immediately bring up ambivalence in many men, even if it involves speaking to his partner or children.

Discomfort with the therapy situation may have to do with any of the four identified masculine conflictual themes that emerge from a convergence of a man's personal and cultural history. The sharing of personal emotional information may trigger unconscious issues related to relational abandonment, especially if there is a threat that the primary relationship is in danger of failing. This emerges from the possible trauma of early separation from the maternal orbit in childhood and other relational trauma that may have occurred in a man's life. The unresolved losses in a man's life may make him seem distant or fearful of immersing himself in the therapy when the relationship is on the line. The male self-structure that has been formed over a lifetime of what is acceptable for a man to feel, say, or do may also limit his repertoire for immersing himself in the therapeutic encounter with a therapist and partner and family. A man's doing orientation may also make the therapeutic environment unfamiliar and alien, especially if it involves sitting around and talking only.

A couples or family therapist might use these male-specific conflicts to enhance his or her understanding of the man and address these concerns through empathic comments, praise for being at the sessions, and a gentle and nonjudgmental approach. Creative, action-oriented interventions and assignments might also work well with a man who is having trouble generating material about himself in sessions. A focus on male and female gender role socialization might also be a fruitful topic for male–female dyads and families, with the hope of reducing blame and providing an intellectual framework for how some of the disturbing patterns in the relationships might have been formed and maintained. Finally, guiding interventions toward a man's portal to emotional depth can be achieved through couples and family work, especially if the reason for the therapy has exposed a man's vulnerability and sense of self. A therapist's empathy to the male-specific conflicts many men bring to the therapeutic situation and sensitivity to a man's core personal issues are the keys to promoting male deepening in the couple's or family therapy process. For further reading on gender-sensitive couples and family therapy we recommend Philpot (2001) and Philpot, Brooks, Lusterman, and Nutt (1997).

DOES DEEPENING THERAPY WORK WITH MEN OF DIFFERENT ETHNIC BACKGROUNDS, OR IS THIS A WHITE, MIDDLE-CLASS MEN'S THERAPY?

This approach was developed on the basis of experiences with men of various ethnic backgrounds. We do not believe that it is applicable only to White, middle-class, heterosexual men. The beauty of this approach is that it requires therapist and client to examine the intersection of personal emotional life with culture. Therefore, men of different cultural backgrounds are encouraged to give meaning to their own, individual, cultural experience in a very personal, psychological way. We have not found any approach to working with men in psychotherapy that makes such an explicit invitation.

The empathic approach that we advocate allows each man to be understood individually, taking into account family history, cultural upbringing, and the impact of one's ethnicity and sexual orientation, as well as his adherence to his culture's model for masculinity. Sensitivity to a man's history of victimization is an important part of the process of navigating him toward the portal. Techniques that are used to deepen should be tailored to what works best with this particular man at this particular stage of the therapy process.

For further reading on special issues that ethnicity and sexual identity bring to psychotherapy, we recommend L. D. Caldwell and White (2001) and Franklin (1998) for perspectives on African American men and therapy; Casas, Turner, and Ruiz de Esparza (2001) on counseling Hispanic men; Sue (2001) for working with Asian men; and Haldeman (2001) and Schwartzberg and Rosenberg (1998) for working with gay and bisexual men.

WOULD THE DEEPENING PROCESS BE DIFFERENT FOR WOMEN?

To the extent that men and women receive different socialization experiences in our culture, the deepening process would be different. Many men struggle with culturally derived prohibitions on sadness and grief. It has been our experience that many men access their emotional selves through their anger. Anger, for men in our culture, is an acceptable channel for a wide range of emotion. In deepening therapy men learn to differentiate the emotional spectrum by first expressing their anger. When encouraged to stay with their feelings following the anger, they can be guided toward their sadness, grief, and other emotions.

In our culture, some women struggle with internalized prohibitions on feelings of anger. For them, sadness and tears are the way they access their emotional selves. By first experiencing sadness and then being encouraged to stay with other feelings that arise, a woman can find strength in feelings of anger and defiance. To this extent, some elements of the deepening process would probably be different. However, to the extent that deepening psychotherapy acknowledges the culturally derived influence on psychological processes and how these influences are given individual meaning as men and women grow up, the process is likely to be very similar.

WHAT QUALITIES SHOULD A THERAPIST HAVE WHO ASPIRES TO DEEPENING THERAPY? WHAT DIFFERENCES WOULD THERE BE BETWEEN MALE AND FEMALE THERAPISTS DOING THIS KIND OF THERAPY?

A therapist should be willing to explore in depth his or her male clients' emotional lives. We have found that in order to do this a therapist should also be willing to explore his or her own emotional issues in depth. The deepening therapy process itself is thus best facilitated by a therapist who is also on a journey toward emotional wholeness and connection. For a therapist with this orientation to his or her work, the therapeutic process will not only enlighten and deepen the client but also will be a catalyst for the therapist's own personal growth.

A therapist should possess a high level of tolerance for men's emotional conflicts. Men's anger, sadness, hopelessness, depression, joy, fears, and men's dreams should all be actively and directly embraced by the therapist. Unacknowledged countertransference issues around the psychology of men should be examined directly. These might include, for female therapists, unconscious hostility toward men, fear of men, or mistrust of men. For male therapists, parallel countertransference issues might include unconscious competitiveness with men, overriding needs for control, or homophobia.

Certain kinds of transference issues would be activated in most men in therapy depending on whether they are working with a male or female therapist. For example, a heterosexual male client may tend to sexualize his relationship with a female therapist, especially when he has learned from our culture that intimacy and sexuality are often confused and intertwined. A male client may feel competitive in his sessions with his male therapist, because of what he has learned about interacting with other men in our culture. Of course, the advantage to the deepening approach to psychotherapy with men is that these issues are grist for the mill and are actively discussed in the treatment process when they arise.

Most important, a therapist who would use this approach should have a respect for the positive and adaptive aspects of the male gender role. He or she should see men's ability to focus and solve a problem as an asset and be able to appreciate a man's hard work as devotion to and provisioning for those whom he loves. A therapist who has negative biases toward his or her male clientele, who is resistant to exploring his or her own countertransference reactions to men, or who has rigidity in his or her therapeutic approach will not create the conditions needed for deepening therapy to work.

For further reading about the gender of the therapist and psychotherapy with men, we recommend for female therapists the writings of Johnson (2001), Potash (1998), and Carlson (1987); and for male therapists the writings of Scher (1990, 2001), Brooks (1998a), and Heppner and Gonzales (1987).

DO YOU THINK THERE ARE MEN THIS WOULDN'T HELP?

There may be. Obviously, a male client would benefit most from this kind of treatment if he were interested in examining his emotional life and how his feelings influence his behavior. In addition, for men who are interested in examining their gender role socialization and how this has influenced them, this approach is ideal. There are men, though, who may merely want a rather quick fix to their problems and who are not motivated to explore in depth their emotional and psychological lives. We have found, though, that most men, when approached with sensitivity, empathy, and respect, are quite amenable to this kind of exploration, because they have little sanction to engage in this kind of introspection and emotional exploration in other areas of their lives.

Unfortunately, some men are "written off" by therapists because of their character style. Men who have difficulty verbalizing what they are thinking or feeling, men who challenge the therapist's authority, men who show prejudice and insensitivity toward others, and men who have difficulty making a commitment to the therapy process are often seen as poor risks for therapeutic success. We have found that the acceptance of a man and his initial style are the first steps in establishing trust. Often a man will use his characteristic defenses as a way to test the therapist to see if he or she will really be committed and available. Many men have had such painful experiences with trust in relationships that they are unconsciously compelled to test this relationship, fully expecting that the therapist will reject them. When this doesn't occur, we have witnessed many men, who are in emotional distress beneath their defensive character structure, "collapse" into the therapy relationship and use the process to make important life changes.

HOW WOULD YOU HANDLE A MAN WHO WAS HIGHLY RESISTANT TO SELF-EXPLORATION?

In general, we have not found many men who are resistant to self-exploration when it is seen as an important part of their therapy. Mostly, we have found that resistance in a man to self exploration is based on mistrust or some other specific reaction to the therapist. The therapist may be conveying an attitude of disrespect or lack of empathy for the male client, and what is perceived as resistance is simply a reaction to this attitude. In this instance, the therapist needs to step back and examine his or her own contribution to this resistance.

Other men may manifest distancing defenses when they are fearful or conflicted about investing in an intimate relationship. Rather than interpret this as resistance, it might be better to acknowledge the conflicting emotional reaction to potential dependency. Early childhood separation and gender role conditioning make this a difficult issue for many men. It might be better to err on the side of believing that a man wants to be invested but is emotionally fearful because of past experience. Male clients whose cultural and ethnic backgrounds differ from that of the therapist may also appear to be resistant but in actuality are usually testing the therapist's commitment and trustworthiness.

At other times, there may be some men who are genuinely "resistant" to the notion of getting more in touch with their feelings or exploring their feelings and reactions in depth. These men will probably not perceive much benefit from a deepening approach to psychotherapy and will probably terminate their therapy before it goes too far. It is always important to be respectful of this self-imposed containment and to make sure that the male client leaves his encounter with his therapist with a clear invitation to return at any time should the need arise.

WHAT IF A MAN HASN'T EXPERIENCED MUCH LOSS IN HIS LIFE? WHAT EFFECT WILL THAT HAVE ON THE DEEPENING PROCESS?

The deepening approach emphasizes confronting the cultural conditioning that inhibits men from experiencing and working through experiences of loss regardless of the amount or kinds of losses a man has experienced. Our approach encourages the therapist to attend to a man's experiences with loss and the emotional impact of these experiences on his sense of self.

A man who finds his way to therapy often has experienced a wounding event against which he can not fully defend himself. The working through of this pain often involves the emotional uncapping of other losses or wounds that have occurred during a man's life. The grieving of these other losses is an integral part of the therapy process.

We find that therapy works best if we direct our attention to the man's emotional reactions to loss across the life span. Because in our culture loss, sadness, grief, and tears are generally not associated with masculinity, many men will have truncated or aborted loss experiences. Deepening implies an exploration of not only the current loss experience, but also the full emotional impact of many previously denied loss experiences, allowing for their full integration into a man's life.

IS THERE ANY RESEARCH TO BACK UP THIS APPROACH?

Not yet. Research on psychotherapy has verified that the common, empirically supported treatments such as interpersonal psychotherapy and cognitive–behavioral psychotherapy are effective with men. We believe that by adding a masculine-specific element to these therapies they would demonstrate even greater efficacy with men or would be perceived by men to be more inviting and appealing. The research on how this approach will help men, and with which kinds of problems, remains to be conducted. For the most up-to-date compilations of research on working with men in psychotherapy we recommend books edited by Brooks and Good (2001) and Pollack and Levant (1998).

IS THERE ANYTHING THAT PARENTS CAN DO TO HELP THEIR BOYS KEEP THEIR EMOTIONAL WHOLENESS INTO ADULTHOOD?

This is an interesting question. In our model it is apparent that parental sensitivity and support at important junctures of a boy's experience can circumvent some potential problems. For instance, a mother and father can show sensitivity to their son's movement out of the maternal orbit and into his identification with his masculinity. This is typically a very frightening and stressful period for a boy that goes almost unnoticed by our culture. The loss of the mother's warmth and support needs to be picked up by the father or adult male figure in a boy's life. This softens the intensity of the loss and allows the boy to stay connected to his feelings as he enters the masculine world. The father or adult male figure can then introduce him to the male world in a relational way.

What often happens, unfortunately, is that the adult male has already disavowed relational intimacy to "survive" in the male world of competition and toughness. It is tempting for a father to try to instill this toughness into a boy before he has fully grieved the loss of the maternal connection. What often happens is that the boy represses his feelings or truncates emotional expression in order to take on the male gender role identity. He is shamed by peers and adults if he cries or expresses sensitive emotions and is reinforced for his ability to contain emotions. By the time he reaches adulthood he has lost the connection to his inner emotional world.

If a father figure is not present, it is important for the mother to help her son identify with his masculinity by supporting his involvement in male-oriented activities. Often a coach or male teacher can act as a significant role model for masculine identification. The mother can still act as a source of emotional support but should not shield her son from the realities of the masculine environment. She needs to be careful not to bash men in the presence of her son, because he will unconsciously adopt this attitude and potentially find himself hating his own manhood and resenting his male peers.

For the latest research on the developmental issues of boys and the impact of culturally defined masculinity, we recommend Pollack (1999, 2000), and for up-to-date interventions for counseling boys and adolescents we recommend Horne and Kiselica (1999).

DEEPENING THERAPY SOUNDS LIKE AN INNER ODYSSEY THAT GOES BEYOND THE NORMAL PARAMETERS OF PSYCHOTHERAPY. IS THIS TRUE?

In many ways, our vision of therapy is one that often moves beyond what words can actually describe. The advantage of the deepening approach with men is that it emphasizes a holistic, complete, and inwardly expansive orientation, as opposed to one that focuses on pieces of the male experience. Any true, authentic engagement with a male client will almost always result in a careful look at existential and spiritual concerns, that is, issues around meaning and purpose in life, isolation and connection, personal values, and so forth. These issues are the real grist for the deepening mill, and it is in the arena of these values that men's emotional lives come alive and are given deeper meaning.

Once a man gets on the path to finding his wholeness, he cannot help but to see his world in a different way. It is very difficult to go back to his previous vision when he has experienced a more enlightened life. Living a life that feels authentic does become a kind of soul journey. To be able to stay true to one's values and feelings is difficult in a world that emphasizes greed, superficiality, and manipulation. Deepening therapy helps men find an inner core that can function as an internal center or grounding.

We believe that men's groups are wonderful vehicles for men to gain support for continuing the deepening journey. The transcendent power of a group of men engaged in supportive personal growth is difficult to fathom if one has not had the experience. When men tell their stories there is an archetypal connection to mythology and history that goes beyond what can be described in words. The honest sharing and support that occurs often resembles a rite of passage for many men into a more enlightened and deeper vision of themselves and who they are as men.

REFERENCES

Alexander, F. (1932). *The medical value of psychoanalysis.* New York: Norton.

American Psychiatric Association. (1994). *Diagnostic and statistical manual of mental disorders* (4th ed.). Washington, DC: Author.

Andronico, M. P. (1996). *Men in groups: Insights, interventions, and psychoeducational work.* Washington, DC: American Psychological Association.

Asay, T. P., & Lambert, M. J. (1999). The empirical case for the common factors in therapy: Quantitative findings. In M. A. Hubble, B. L. Duncan, & S. D. Miller (Eds.), *The heart and soul of change* (pp. 33–55). Washington, DC: American Psychological Association.

Aston, J. (1987). Counseling men in prison. In M. Scher, M. Stevens, G. Good, & G. Eichenfield (Eds.), *Handbook of counseling and psychotherapy with men* (pp. 305–320). Beverly Hills, CA: Sage.

Bergman, S. J. (1995). Men's psychological development: A relational perspective. In R. F. Levant & W. S. Pollack (Eds.), *A new psychology of men* (pp. 68–90). New York: Basic Books.

Betcher, R. W., & Pollack, W. S. (1993). *In a time of fallen heroes: The re-creation of masculinity.* New York: Guilford Press.

Black, D., Baumgard, C., & Bell, S. (1996). A 16- to 45-year follow-up of 71 men with antisocial personality disorder. *Comprehensive Psychiatry, 36,* 130–140.

Blatner, A. (1988). *Foundations of psychodrama: History, theory, and practice.* New York: Springer.

Bly, R. (1990). *Iron John: A book about men.* New York: Addison-Wesley.

Bohart, A. C. (1993). Experiencing: The basis of psychotherapy. *Journal of Psychotherapy Integration, 3,* 51–67.

Bowlby, J. (1988). *A secure base: Parent-child attachment and healthy human behavior.* New York: Basic Books.

Brooks, G. R. (1996). Treatment for therapy resistant men. In M. Andronico (Ed.), *Men in groups* (pp. 7–19). Washington, DC: American Psychological Association.

Brooks, G. R. (1998a). *A new psychotherapy for traditional men.* San Francisco: Jossey-Bass.

Brooks, G. R. (1998b). Group therapy for traditional men. In W. S. Pollack & R. F. Levant (Eds.), *New psychotherapy for men* (pp. 83–96). New York: Wiley.

Brooks, G. R., & Good, G. E. (Eds.). (2001). *The new handbook of psychotherapy and counseling with men.* San Francisco: Jossey-Bass.

Brooks, G., & Silverstein, L. (1995). Understanding the dark side of masculinity: An interactive systems model. In R. Levant & W. Pollack (Eds.), *A new psychology of men* (pp. 280–333). New York: Basic Books.

Burstein, A., Loucks, S., Rasco, S., & Green, P. (1993). Presenting complaints of applicants for psychological services. *Professional Psychology, 24,* 370–373.

Caldwell, L. D., & White, J. L. (2001). African-centered therapeutic and counseling interventions for African American males. In G. R. Brooks & G. E. Good (Eds.), *The new handbook of psychotherapy and counseling with men* (pp. 737–753). San Francisco: Jossey Bass.

Caldwell, M., & Peplau, L. (1982). Sex differences in same-sex friendship. *Sex Roles, 8,* 721–732.

Campbell, J. (1976). *The hero with a thousand faces.* Princeton, NJ: Princeton University Press.

Carlson, N. L. (1987). Woman therapist: Male client. In M. Scher, M. Stevens, G. Good, & G. Eichenfield (Eds.), *Handbook of counseling and psychotherapy with men* (pp. 39–50). Newbury Park, CA: Sage.

Casas, J. M., Turner, J. A., & Ruiz de Esparza, C. A. (2001). Machismo revisited in a time of crisis: Implications for understanding and counseling Hispanic men. In G. R. Brooks & G. E. Good (Eds.), *The new handbook of psychotherapy and counseling with men* (pp. 754–779). San Francisco: Jossey Bass.

Chodorow, N. (1978). *The reproduction of mothering.* Berkeley: University of California Press.

Chodorow, N. (1999). *The power of feelings.* New Haven, CT: Yale University Press.

Cochran, S. V. (2001). Assessing and treating depression in men. In G. Brooks & G. Good (Eds.), *The new handbook of psychotherapy and counseling with men* (pp. 229–245). San Francisco: Jossey-Bass.

Cochran, S. V., & Rabinowitz, F. E. (1996). Men, loss and psychotherapy. *Psychotherapy, 33,* 593–600.

Cochran, S. V., & Rabinowitz, F. E. (2000). *Men and depression: Clinical and empirical perspectives.* San Diego, CA: Academic Press.

Corey, M. S., & Corey, G. (1997). *Groups: Process and practice* (5th ed.). Pacific Grove, CA: Brooks/Cole.

Crews, C. Y., & Melnick, J. (1976). Use of initial and delayed structure in facilitating group development. *Journal of Counseling Psychology, 23,* 92–98.

Davanloo, H. (1980). A method of short term psychotherapy. In H. Davanloo (Ed.), *Short-term dynamic psychotherapy* (pp. 43–74). Northvale, NJ: Aronson.

David, D. S., & Brannon, R. (Eds.). (1976). *The forty-nine percent majority: The male sex role.* Reading, MA: Addison-Wesley.

Diamond, J. (1987). Counseling male substance abusers. In M. Scher, M. Stevens, G. Good, & G. Eichenfield (Eds.), *Handbook of counseling and psychotherapy with men* (pp. 332–342). Newbury Park, CA: Sage.

Douglas, C. (1995). Analytical psychotherapy. In R. J. Corsini & D. Wedding (Eds.), *Current psychotherapies* (5th ed., pp. 95–127). Itasca, IL: Peacock.

Elkins, D. N. (1998). *Beyond religion*. Wheaton, IL: Quest Books.

Erikson, E. E. (1963). *Childhood and society*. New York: Norton.

Fadiman, J., & Frager, R. (1998). Personality and personal growth (4th ed.). New York: Longman.

Farrell, W. (1975). *The liberated man*. New York: Random House.

Fasteau, M. (1974). *The male machine*. New York: McGraw-Hill.

Feldenkrais, M. (1972). *Awareness through movement*. New York: Harper & Row.

Franklin, A. J. (1998). Treating anger in African American men. In W. S. Pollack & R. F. Levant (Eds.), *New psychotherapy for men* (pp. 239–258). New York: Wiley.

Freud, S. (1961). Introductory lectures on psycho-analysis. Part III. In J. Strachey (Ed. and Trans.), *The standard edition of the complete psychological works of Sigmund Freud* (Vol. 16, pp. 243–448). London: Hogarth Press. (Original work published 1917)

Freud, S. (1961). Inhibitions, symptoms, and anxiety. In J. Strachey (Ed. and Trans.), *The standard edition of the complete psychological works of Sigmund Freud* (Vol. 20, pp. 77–178). London: Hogarth Press. (Original work published 1926)

Gjerde, P., Block, J., & Block, J. (1988). Depressive symptoms and personality during late adolescence: Gender differences in the externalization–internalization of symptom expression. *Journal of Abnormal Psychology, 97,* 475–486.

Gold, H. (1966). *Fathers*. New York: Arbor House.

Goldberg, H. (1976). *The hazards of being male*. New York: Nash.

Goldenberg, I., & Goldenberg, H. (2000). *Family therapy: An overview* (5th ed.). Pacific Grove, CA: Brooks/Cole.

Goldstein, W. N. (1991). Clarification of projective identification. *American Journal of Psychiatry, 148,* 153–161.

Gomez, L. (1997). *An introduction to object relations*. Washington Square, NY: New York University Press.

Good, G., Dell, D., & Mintz, L. (1989). The male role and gender role conflict: Relationships to help-seeking. *Journal of Counseling Psychology, 68,* 295–300.

Good, G., & May, R. (1987). Developmental issues, environmental influences, and the nature of therapy with college men. In M. Scher, M. Stevens, G. Good, & G. Eichenfield (Eds.), *Handbook of counseling and psychotherapy with men* (pp. 150–164). Beverly Hills, CA: Sage.

Good, G., & Mintz, L. (1990). Gender role conflict and depression in college men: Evidence for compounded risk. *Journal of Counseling and Development, 69,* 17–21.

Good, G., Robertson, J., O'Neil, J., Fitzgerald, L., Stevens, M., DeBord, K., Bartels, K., & Braverman, D. (1995). Male gender role conflict: Psychometric issues and relations to psychological distress. *Journal of Counseling Psychology, 42,* 3–10.

Good, G., & Wood, P. (1995). Male gender role conflict, depression, and help-seeking: Do college men face double jeopardy? *Journal of Counseling and Development, 74,* 70–75.

Greenacre, P. (1956). Re-evaluation of the process of working through. *International Journal of Psychoanalysis, 37,* 439–444.

Haldeman, D. C. (2001). Psychotherapy with gay and bisexual men. In G. R. Brooks & G. E. Good (Eds.), *The new handbook of psychotherapy and counseling with men* (pp. 796–815). San Francisco: Jossey Bass.

Hamberger, K., & Hastings, J. (1991). Personality correlates of men who batter and non-violent men: Some continuities and discontinuities. *Journal of Family Violence, 6,* 131–147.

Hanna, E., & Grant, B. (1997). Gender differences in DSM–IV alcohol use disorders and major depression as distributed in the general population: Clinical implications. *Comprehensive Psychiatry, 38,* 202–212.

Hart, M. (1990). *Drumming on the edge of magic: A journey into the spirit of percussion.* New York: HarperCollins.

Harway, M., & Evans, K. (1996). Working in groups with men who batter. In M. Andronico (Ed.), *Men in groups: Insights, interventions, and psychoeducational work* (pp. 357–375). Washington, DC: American Psychological Association.

Heifner, C. (1997). The male experience of depression. *Perspectives in Psychiatric Care, 33,* 10–18.

Heppner, P. P. (1983). Structured group activities for counseling men. *Journal of College Student Personnel, 24,* 275–277.

Heppner, P. P., & Gonzales, D. S. (1987). Men counseling men. In M. Scher, M. Stevens, G. Good, & G. Eichenfield (Eds.), *Handbook of counseling and psychotherapy with men* (pp. 30–38). Newbury Park, CA: Sage.

Hesse, H. (1951). *Siddhartha* (H. Rosner, Trans.). New York: New Directions. (Original work published 1929)

Hillman, J. (1975). *Re-visioning psychology.* New York: Harper & Row.

Horne, A., & Kiselica, M. S. (1999). *Handbook of counseling boys and adolescent males: A practitioner's guide.* Thousand Oaks, CA: Sage.

Johnson, N. G. (2001). Women helping men: Strengths of and barriers to women therapists working with men clients. In G. R. Brooks & G. E. Good (Eds.), *The new handbook of psychotherapy and counseling with men* (pp. 696–718). San Francisco: Jossey Bass.

Jones, D. (1999). Evolutionary psychology. *Annual Review of Anthropology, 28,* 553–575.

Jung, C. G. (1958). *Psyche and symbol.* Garden City, NY: Doubleday.

Jung, C. G. (1966). The practical use of dream analysis. In C. G. Jung (Ed.), *The practice of psychotherapy: Collected works* (Vol. 16, pp. 139–161). Princeton, NJ: Princeton University Press. (Original work published 1934)

Jung, C. G. (1968). *Analytical psychology, its theory and practice.* New York: Pantheon.

Karasu, T. B. (1999). Spiritual psychotherapy. *American Journal of Psychotherapy, 53,* 143–162.

Kaufman, G. (1992). *Shame: The power of caring* (3rd ed.). Rochester, VT: Schenkman Books.

Keleman, S. (1971). *Sexuality, self, and survival.* San Francisco: Lodestar Press.

Kennedy, G., Metz, H., & Lowinger, R. (1995). Epidemiology and inferences regarding the etiology of late life suicide. In G. Kennedy (Ed.), *Suicide and depression in late life* (pp. 3–22). New York: Wiley.

Kernberg, O. F. (1985a). *Borderline conditions and pathological narcissism*. Northvale, NJ: Aronson.

Kernberg, O. F. (1985b). *Internal world and external reality*. Northvale, NJ: Aronson.

Kessler, R., McGonagle, K., Swartz, M., Blazer, D., & Nelson, C. (1993). Sex and depression in the National Comorbidity Survey: I. Lifetime prevalence, chronicity, and recurrence. *Journal of Affective Disorders, 30*, 15–26.

Kohut, H. (1971). *The analysis of the self*. New York: International Universities Press.

Kohut, H. (1977). *The restoration of the self*. New York: International Universities Press.

Kohut, H. (1984). *How does analysis cure?* Chicago: University of Chicago Press.

Krugman, S. (1998). Men's shame and trauma in therapy. In W. S. Pollack & R. F. Levant (Eds.), *New psychotherapy for men* (pp. 167–190). New York: Wiley.

Lazur, R. (1987). Identity integration: Counseling the adolescent male. In M. Scher, M. Stevens, G. Good, & G. Eichenfield (Eds.), *Handbook of counseling and psychotherapy with men* (pp. 136–149). Beverly Hills, CA: Sage.

Lazur, R. F., & Majors, R. (1995). Men of color: Ethnocultural variations of male gender role strain. In R. F. Levant & W. S. Pollack (Eds.), *A new psychology of men* (pp. 337–358). New York: Basic Books.

Lee, C. C. (1999). Counseling African American men. In L. E. Davis (Ed.), *Working with African American males: A guide to practice* (pp. 39–53). Thousand Oaks, CA: Sage.

Levant, R. F. (1995). *Masculinity reconstructed: Changing the rules of manhood—At work, in relationships, and in family life*. New York: Dutton.

Levant, R. F. (1998). Desperately seeking language: Understanding, assessing, and treating normative male alexithymia. In W. S. Pollack & R. F. Levant (Eds.), *New psychotherapy for men* (pp. 35–56). New York: Wiley.

Levinson, D. J., Darrow, C. N., Klein, E. B., Levinson, M. H., & McKee, B. (1978). *The seasons of a man's life*. New York: Knopf.

Levit, D. (1991). Gender differences in ego defenses in adolescence: Sex roles as one way to understand the differences. *Journal of Abnormal and Social Psychology, 61*, 992–999.

Lieberman, M. A., Yalom, I. D., & Miles, M. B. (1973). *Encounter groups: First facts*. New York: Basic Books.

Lisak, D. (1998). Confronting and treating empathic disconnection in violent men. In W. S. Pollack & R. F. Levant (Eds.), *New psychotherapy for men* (pp. 214–236). New York: Wiley.

Lowen, A. (1975). *Bioenergetics*. New York: Penguin.

Lowen, A. (1984). *Narcissism: Denial of the true self*. New York: Macmillan.

Lowen, A., & Lowen, L. (1992). *The way to vibrant health: A manual of bioenergetic exercises*. New York: International Institute for Bioenergetic Analysis.

Mahler, M., Pine, F., & Bergman, A. (1975). *The psychological birth of the human infant*. New York: Basic Books.

Majors, R. (1994). *The American Black male: His present status and future*. Chicago: Nelson & Hall.

Majors, R., & Billson, J. M. (1992). *Cool pose: The dilemmas of Black manhood in America*. New York: Lexington Books.

Malan, D. (1976). *A study of brief psychotherapy*. New York: Plenum.

Mann, J. (1973). *Time-limited psychotherapy*. Cambridge, MA: Harvard University Press.

Maslow, A. (1968). *Toward a psychology of being* (2nd ed.). New York: Van Nostrand.

Masterson, J. (1981). *The narcissistic and borderline disorders*. New York: Brunner/Mazel.

May, R. (1961). *Existential psychology*. New York: Random House.

May, R. (1969). *Love and will*. New York: Norton.

May, R., & Yalom, I. D. (1995). Existential psychotherapy. In R. J. Corsini & D. Wedding (Eds.), *Current psychotherapies* (5th ed., pp. 262–292). Itasca, IL: Peacock.

McDargh, J. (1994). Group psychotherapy as spiritual discipline: From Oz to the kingdom of God. *Journal of Psychology and Theology, 22*, 290–299.

Meade, M. (1993). *Men and the water of life*. San Francisco: Harper.

Meyers, H. (1986). How do women treat men? In G. Fogel, F. Lane, & R. Liebert (Eds.), *The psychology of men* (pp. 262–276). New Haven: Yale University Press.

Milton, J. (1951). *Paradise lost, and selected poetry and prose*. New York: Rinehart. (Original work published 1667)

Moore, T. (1992). *Care of the soul*. New York: HarperCollins.

Moreno, J. L. (1946). *Psychodrama*. New York: Beacon Press.

Moscicki, E. (1997). Identification of suicide risk factors using epidemiological studies. *Psychiatric Clinics of North America, 20*, 499–517.

Nolen-Hoeksema, S. (1990). *Sex differences in depression*. Palo Alto, CA: Stanford University Press.

O'Neil, J. M. (1981). Patterns of gender role conflict and strain: Sexism and fear of femininity in men's lives. *Personnel and Guidance Journal, 60*, 203–210.

O'Neil, J. M., Good, G. E., & Holmes, S. (1995). Fifteen years of theory and research on men's gender role conflict: New paradigms for empirical research. In R. F. Levant & W. S. Pollack (Eds.), *A new psychology of men* (pp. 164–206). New York: Basic Books.

Osherson, S. (1986). *Finding our fathers*. New York: Fawcett Columbine.

Osherson, S., & Krugman, S. (1990). Men, shame, and psychotherapy. *Psychotherapy, 27*, 327–339.

Perls, F. (1969). *Gestalt therapy verbatim*. Moab, UT: Real People Press.

Philpot, C. L. (2001). Family therapy for men. In G. R. Brooks & G. E. Good (Eds.), *The new handbook of psychotherapy and counseling with men* (pp. 622–636). San Francisco: Jossey-Bass.

Philpot, C. L., Brooks, G. R., Lusterman, D., & Nutt, R. L. (1997). *Bridging separate gender worlds*. Washington, DC: American Psychological Association.

Pleck, J. H. (1981). *The myth of masculinity.* Cambridge, MA: MIT Press.

Pleck, J. H. (1995). The gender role strain paradigm: An update. In R. F. Levant & W. S. Pollack (Eds.), *A new psychology of men* (pp. 11–32). New York: Basic Books.

Pleck, J. H., & Sawyer, J. (1974). *Men and masculinity.* Englewood Cliffs, NJ: Prentice Hall.

Pollack, W. S. (1990). Men's development and psychotherapy: A psychoanalytic perspective. *Psychotherapy, 27,* 316–321.

Pollack, W. S. (1995a). Deconstructing disidentification: Rethinking psychoanalytic concepts of male development. *Psychoanalysis and Psychotherapy, 12,* 30–45.

Pollack, W. (1995b). No man is an island: Toward a new psychoanalytic psychology of men. In R. Levant & W. Pollack (Eds.), *A new psychology of men* (pp. 33–67). New York: Basic Books.

Pollack, W. S. (1998). Mourning, melancholia, and masculinity: Recognizing and treating depression in men. In W. S. Pollack & R. F. Levant (Eds.), *New psychotherapy for men* (pp. 147–166). New York: Wiley.

Pollack, W. S. (1999). *Real boys: Rescuing our sons from the myths of boyhood.* New York: Random House.

Pollack, W. S. (2000). *Real boys' voices.* New York: Random House.

Pollack, W. S. (2001). "Masked men": New psychoanalytically oriented treatment models for adult and young adult men. In G. Brooks & G. Good (Eds.), *The new handbook of psychotherapy and counseling with men* (pp. 525–543). San Francisco: Jossey-Bass.

Pollack, W. S., & Levant, R. F. (Eds.). (1998). *New psychotherapy for men.* New York: Wiley.

Potash, M. S. (1998). When women treat men: Female therapists/male patients. In W. S. Pollack & R. F. Levant (Eds.), *New psychotherapy for men* (pp. 282–308). New York: Wiley.

Rabinowitz, F. E. (1991). The male-to-male embrace: Breaking the touch taboo in a men's therapy group. *Journal of Counseling and Development, 69,* 574–576.

Rabinowitz, F. E. (1998, August). Process analysis of a long term psychotherapy group for men. In F. Rabinowitz (Chair), *Researching psychotherapy with men: Findings and prospects.* Symposium conducted at the 106th Annual Convention of the American Psychological Association, San Francisco.

Rabinowitz, F. E. (2001). Group therapy with men. In G. Brooks & G. Good (Eds.), *The new handbook of psychotherapy and counseling with men* (pp. 603–621). San Francisco: Jossey-Bass.

Rabinowitz, F. E., & Cochran, S. V. (1987). Counseling men in groups. In M. Scher, M. Stevens, G. Good, & G. Eichenfield (Eds.), *Handbook of counseling and psychotherapy with men* (pp. 51–67). Newbury Park, CA: Sage.

Rabinowitz, F. E., & Cochran, S. V. (1994). *Man alive: A primer of men's issues.* Pacific Grove, CA: Brooks/Cole.

Rank, O. (1947). *Will therapy and truth and reality.* New York: Knopf.

Real, T. (1997). *I don't want to talk about it: Overcoming the legacy of male depression.* New York: Fireside.

Reich, W. (1973). *The function of the orgasm.* New York: Pocket Books. (Original work published 1942)

Reich, W. (1976). *Character analysis.* New York: Pocket Books. (Original work published 1949)

Rinsley, D. (1989). *Developmental pathogenesis and treatment of borderline and narcissistic personalities.* Northvale, NJ: Aronson.

Roberts, J. (1999). Beyond words: The power of rituals. In D. J. Wiener (Ed.), *Beyond talk therapy* (pp. 55–78). Washington, DC: American Psychological Association.

Robins, L., & Reiger, D. (1991). *Psychiatric disorders in America.* New York: Free Press.

Rogers, C. R. (1951). *Client centered therapy.* Boston: Houghton Mifflin.

Rogers, C. R. (1957). The necessary and sufficient conditions of therapeutic personality change. *Journal of Consulting Psychology, 21,* 95–100.

Rogers, C. R. (1961). *On becoming a person.* Boston: Houghton Mifflin.

Scher, M. (1979). On counseling men. *Personnel and Guidance Journal, 58,* 252–254.

Scher, M. (1981). Men in hiding: A challenge for the counselor. *Personnel and Guidance Journal, 60,* 199–202.

Scher, M. (1990). Effects of gender role incongruities on men's experience as clients in psychotherapy. *Psychotherapy, 27,* 322–326.

Scher, M. (2001). Male therapist, male client: Reflections on critical dynamics. In G. R. Brooks & G. E. Good (Eds.), *The new handbook of psychotherapy and counseling with men* (pp. 719–733). San Francisco: Jossey Bass.

Schwartzberg, S., & Rosenberg, L. G. (1998). Being gay and being male: Psychotherapy with gay and bisexual men. In R. F. Levant & W. S. Pollack (Eds.), *A new psychology of men* (pp. 259–281). New York: Basic Books.

Shay, J. J. (1996). Okay, I'm here but I'm not talking: Psychotherapy with the reluctant male. *Psychotherapy, 33,* 503–513.

Siegelman, E. Y. (1990). *Metaphor and meaning in psychotherapy.* New York: Guilford Press.

Sifneos, P. (1987). *Short-term dynamic psychotherapy.* New York: Plenum.

Stewart, S., Stinnett, H., & Rosenfeld, L. (2000). Sex differences in desired characteristics of short-term and long-term relationship partners. *Journal of Social and Personal Relationships, 17,* 843–853.

Strupp, H., & Binder, J. (1984). *Psychotherapy in a new key: A guide to time-limited dynamic psychotherapy.* New York: Basic Books.

Sue, D. (2001). Asian American masculinity and therapy: The concept of masculinity in Asian American males. In G. R. Brooks & G. E. Good (Eds.), *The new handbook of psychotherapy and counseling with men* (pp. 780–795). San Francisco: Jossey-Bass.

Sullivan, H. S. (1953). *The interpersonal theory of psychiatry.* New York: Norton.

Tallman, K., & Bohart, A. C. (1999). The client as the common factor: Clients as self-healers. In M. A. Hubble, B. L. Duncan, & S. D. Miller (Eds.), *The heart and soul of change* (pp. 91–131). Washington, DC: American Psychological Association.

Vessey, J. T., & Howard, K. I. (1993). Who seeks psychotherapy? *Psychotherapy, 30,* 546–553.

Wallach, T. (1994). Competition and gender in group psychotherapy. *Group, 18,* 29–36.

Walsh, R. (1999). Asian contemplative disciplines: Common practices, clinical applications, and research findings. *Journal of Transpersonal Psychology, 31,* 83–107.

Washington, C. S. (1979). Men counseling men: Redefining the male machine. *Personnel and Guidance Journal, 57,* 462–463.

Washington, C. S. (1987). Counseling Black men. In M. Scher, M. Stevens, G. Good, & G. Eichenfield (Eds.), *Handbook of counseling and psychotherapy with men* (pp. 192–202). Newbury Park, CA: Sage.

White, J. L., & Parham, T. A. (1990). *The psychology of Blacks: An African American perspective.* Englewood Cliffs, NJ: Prentice Hall.

Wiener, D. J. (1999). *Beyond talk therapy.* Washington, DC: American Psychological Association.

Winnicott, D. (1965a). *The family and individual development.* London: Tavistock.

Winnicott, D. (1965b). *The maturational processes and the facilitating environment.* New York: International Universities Press.

Winnicott, D. (1971). *Playing and reality.* New York: Basic Books.

Winnicott, D. (1987). *Babies and their mothers.* Reading, MA: Addison-Wesley.

Winnicott, D. (1988). *Human nature.* New York: Schocken Books.

Wolberg, L. R. (1954). *The technique of psychotherapy.* New York: Grune & Stratton.

Wolfert, R., & Cook, C. A. (1999). Gestalt therapy in action. In D. J. Wiener (Ed.), *Beyond talk therapy* (pp. 3–27). Washington, DC: American Psychological Association.

Yalom, I. D. (1980). *Existential psychotherapy.* New York: Basic Books.

Yalom, I. D. (1985). *The theory and practice of group psychotherapy* (3rd ed.). New York: Basic Books.

AUTHOR INDEX

Alexander, F., 52, 54, 70
American Psychiatric Association, 95
Andronico, M. P., 155
Asay, T. P., 70
Aston, J., 15–16

Baumgard, C., 13
Bell, S., 13
Bergman, A., 36
Bergman, S. J., 118
Betcher, R. W., 33
Billson, J. M., 108
Binder, J., 26
Black, D., 13
Blatner, A., 74
Blazer, D., 14
Block, J., 49
Block, J., 49
Bly, Robert, 81
Bohart, A. C., 73, 74
Bowlby, J., 35
Brannon, R., 3, 21, 42
Brooks, G. R., 15, 89, 95, 117, 155, 158,
        159, 160, 176, 185, 187, 190
Burstein, A., 14

Caldwell, L. D., 108, 110, 186
Caldwell, M., 158
Campbell, J., 80
Carlson, N. L., 125, 187
Casas, J. M., 186
Chodorow, N., 17, 38, 39, 43, 45
Cochran, S. V., 14, 16, 19, 26, 39, 47, 48,
        89, 99, 100, 108, 137, 139, 146,
        159, 166
Cook, C. A., 75
Corey, G., 155
Corey, M. S., 155
Crews, C. Y., 166

Darrow, C. N., 95
Davanloo, H., 26
David, D. S., 3, 21, 42
Dell, D., 43
Diamond, J., 16
Douglas, C., 51
Elkins, D. N., 51, 52, 80

Erikson, E. E., 118
Evans, K., 104

Fadiman, J., 79
Farrell, W., 3, 42
Fasteau, M., 3, 42
Feldenkrais, M., 182
Frager, R., 79
Franklin, A. J., 109, 186
Freud, S., 51, 52, 53, 139

Gjerde, P., 49
Gold, H., 177
Goldberg, H., 3, 41
Goldenberg, H., 155
Goldenberg, I., 155
Goldstein, W. N., 119
Gomez, L., 130
Gonzales, D. S., 187
Good, G. E., 15, 21, 43, 108, 190
Grant, B., 13, 16
Green, P., 14
Greenacre, P., 53

Haldeman, D. C., 186
Hamberger, K., 15
Hanna, E., 13, 16
Hart, M., 82
Harway, M., 104
Hastings, J., 15
Heifner, C., 15
Heppner, P. P., 166, 187
Hillman, J., 52, 79
Holmes, S., 21, 43, 108
Horne, A., 190
Howard, K. I., 4, 13, 89

Johnson, N. G., 125, 187
Jones, D., 4–5
Jung, C. G., 52, 58, 59, 139

Karasu, T. B., 79
Kaufman, G., 100
Keleman, S., 182
Kennedy, G., 16
Kernberg, O. F., 36, 37, 118
Kessler, R., 14

Kiselica, M. S., 190
Klein, E. B., 95
Kohut, H., 37, 48, 52, 69, 70, 114, 139, 156
Krugman, S., 4, 89, 99, 118, 119, 130, 137, 139, 146
Lambert, M. J., 70
Lazur, R. F., 16, 109
Lee, C. C., 110
Levant, R. F., 4, 22, 139, 190
Levinson, D. J., 95
Levinson, M. H., 95
Levit, D., 49
Lieberman, M. A., 166
Lisak, D., 139
Loucks, S., 14
Lowen, A., 52, 83, 84, 139, 182
Lowen, L., 84
Lowinger, R., 16
Lusterman, D., 155, 159, 185

Mahler, M., 36, 37
Majors, R., 108, 109
Malan, D., 26
Mann, J., 26
Maslow, A., 52, 70, 71, 79, 132
Masterson, J., 36, 37
May, R., 15, 52, 64
McDargh, J., 159
McGonagle, K., 14
McKee, B., 95
Meade, M., 81, 117
Melnick, J., 166
Metz, H., 16
Meyers, H., 125
Miles, M. B., 166
Mintz, L., 43
Moore, T., 80
Moreno, J. L., 52, 74
Moscicki, E., 16

Nelson, C., 14
Nolen-Hoeksema, S., 49
Nutt, R. L., 155, 159, 185

O'Neil, J. M., 21, 43, 108
Osherson, S., 4, 89, 99, 118, 119, 130, 139, 159

Parham, T. A., 110
Peplau, L., 158
Perls, F., 52, 74, 75
Philpot, C. L., 159, 185

Pine, F., 36
Pleck, J. H., 3, 4, 42, 159
Pollack, W. S., 16, 17, 18, 33, 39, 48, 98, 117, 118, 139, 151, 190
Potash, M. S., 118, 187

Rabinowitz, F. E., 14, 16, 19, 26, 39, 47, 48, 89, 99, 100, 108, 119, 137, 139, 146, 155, 158, 159, 166, 167, 176
Rank, O., 53, 151
Rasco, S., 14
Real, T., 16, 170
Reich, W., 9, 52, 82, 182
Reiger, D., 14
Rinsley, D., 36, 37
Roberts, J., 80
Robins, L., 14
Rogers, C. R., 52, 69, 70, 100
Rosenberg, L. G., 186
Rosenfeld, L., 4–5
Ruiz de Esparza, C. A., 186

Sawyer, J., 3
Scher, M., 4, 95, 99, 117, 118, 129, 187
Schwartzberg, S., 186
Shay, J. J., 4, 99, 100
Siegelman, E. Y., 59
Sifneos, P., 26
Silverstein, L., 15
Stewart, S., 4–5
Stinnett, H., 4–5
Strupp, H., 26
Sue, D., 186
Sullivan, H. S., 154
Swartz, M., 14

Tallman, K., 74
Turner, J. A., 186

Vessey, J. T., 4, 13, 89

Wallach, T., 159
Walsh, R., 52
Washington, C. S., 108, 166
White, J. L., 108, 110, 186
Wiener, D. J., 74
Winnicott, D., 23, 35, 37, 49
Wolberg, L. R., 137
Wolfert, R., 75
Wood, P., 15, 43

Yalom, I. D., 52, 64, 139, 155, 160, 166

SUBJECT INDEX

Abandonment, relational, 185
Abuse
    in case study (John), 20
    in case study (Nick), 10–11
    in case study (Ron), 105, 120
    See also Violence
Active imagination, 59
Active imagination/guided imagery, 62–63
Activity-oriented relationships, 183
Adler, Alfred, 34
Alan (case study), 56–57
Alcohol abuse or addiction
    and grief or sadness, 19
    and men's psychological suffering,
        13–14
    as presenting symptom, 16
    and psychotherapy, 13
Alex (case study), 93
    in early phases, 93–94, 95, 103–105,
        106–108, 109–110, 112–114, 115
    and group therapy, 153–154
    in men's group, 161, 163, 164–166,
        169, 170–171, 172–173
    in working phase, 121–126, 128–130,
        133–134, 135–136
    in working phase through termina-
        tion, 141–142, 144–146, 148–150,
        153–154
Alexander, Franz, 54
Alimony laws, 3
Aloneness, 68
Anger, 103
    in case of Ron, 121
    catharsis of, 53–54
    control through, 104
    as presenting symptom, 16
    as total emotional repertoire, 176
    and women, 186
Antisocial personality
    and doing approach, 23
    prevalence rate of, 14
Anxiety
    and behaviors to provide safety, 5
    and interpersonal conflict, 15
    neurotic, 64
    successful therapy outcomes for, 89
Archetypes, 58
    imaging of, 60

Art, as creative venue, 62
Assessment, 180
    in initial therapy process, 98–100
Attachment model of human develop-
    ment, 35
Attachment shame, 130
Authentic interaction, in therapeutic rela-
    tionship, 72
Autonomy, preference for, 40
Awareness exercises, 77

Being
    and deepening group psychotherapy,
        157
    vs. doing, 5, 23–25, 30, 49–50, 99,
        139
    in case of Ron, 127
    masculine-specific conflicts over, 178,
        182
    and therapeutic relationship,
        182–183
"Big wheel," 21, 42
Bill (case study), 18–19
Binds
    imposed on men, 41–42
    by parents in childhood, 100
Bioenergetics, 83
Bisexuality, as basic set of capacities, 49
Black man
    Alex as, 106–107
    See also Ethnic background or iden-
        tity; Men of color
Bly, Robert, 3, 81
Body language, and portal to deepening
    process, 28
Body memories, 102–105
Body-oriented techniques, 181–182
Body and perceptual awareness, 77
    in case of Alex, 123
Body work, 82–87
    in case of Ron, 132
    in men's groups, 166–167
"Boot camp" exercise, 164
Bowlby, John, 34
Breathing exercises, 83, 84
    as awareness exercises, 77
    in case of Ron, 127
British object relations theory, 34, 35

Bryan (case study), 63
Byron (case study), 85

Carlos (case study), 77
Case studies, 6
    Alan (resistance), 56–57
    Alex, 93
    in early phases, 93–94, 95, 103–105,
        106–108, 109–110, 112–114, 115
    in working phase, 121–126, 128–130,
        133–134, 135–136
    in working phase through termina-
        tion, 141–142, 144–146, 148–150,
        153–154
    Bill (dependence), 18–19
    Bryan (Jungian dream interpreta-
        tion), 63
    Byron (eye exercises), 85
    Carlos (role playing parts of personal-
        ity), 77
    Charlie (mortality), 67
    Christian (mirroring), 71
    Craig (masculine self-structure),
        22–23, 25
    Dave (inner life), 24–25
    George (imaging of archetype), 60
    Gerald (multiple conflict zones),
        29–31
    Greg (staying in present), 75–76
    Henry (exposing of shadow), 60–61
    Herbert (active imagination/guided
        imagery), 62–63
    Ian (authentic interaction), 72
    Jerry (kicking exercises), 86
    Joe (creative expression), 62
    John (prohibitions on grief and sad-
        ness), 20–21
    Ken (exaggeration), 78
    Ken (free association), 54
    Kyle (playing parts of dream), 78–79
    Lance (transference), 55–56
    Lionel (dream interpretation), 54–55
    Louis (false promises), 67
    Luke (feelings beneath words), 72–73
    Marty (aloneness), 68
    Michael (freedom), 68
    Nick (entering psychotherapy), 9–13
    Owen (psychodrama), 76
    Philip (unconditional positive
        regard), 71–72
    Rick (existential questions), 65–66
    Ron, 90

    in early phase, 90–92, 94–95,
        102–103, 105–106, 109, 110–112,
        114, 115
    in working phase, 119–121, 123–125,
        126–128, 130–132, 135, 136
    in working phase through termina-
        tion, 140–141, 142–144, 146–148,
        150, 152–153
    Saul (transference), 56
    Von (internal discrepancies), 66
    Zak (reowning of projections), 61
Catharsis, 53–54, 174
Central or focal conflict, 26
Chameleons, social, 95, 96–98, 125
Character (Reich), 83
Character structure, Reich on, 9
Charlie (case study), 67
Child custody laws, 3
Child-rearing practices, 17–18
Chodorow, N., 34, 38–39, 44, 45
Christian (case study), 71
Client-centered psychotherapy, 4
Clinical material. *See* Case studies
Clinical reports, on psychological prob-
    lems of men, 15–17
Cochran, Sam, 90
Collages, 62, 80
Collective unconscious, 58
Complexes, 58
Compulsive activities, 25
Conflicts
    existential confrontation of, 66
    interpersonal, 15
    masculine-specific, 5–6, 178, 180, 182
    and men in psychotherapy process,
        139
    and men's groups, 159, 169
    as portal to deepening process, 26
    See also Psychological problems of
        men
Connection, in initial therapy process,
    98–100
Control, in case studies (Ron and Alex),
    103–105, 135
Corrective emotional experience, 54,
    57–58, 70
    in case of Ron, 153
Countertransference reactions, 101, 119,
    176, 187
    in case of Alex, 122
    in case of Ron, 132
Couples therapy

and case-study couple (Nick and
Kristin), 9
deepening therapy in, 184–185
Craig (case study), 22–23, 25
Creative expression, 62
Cultural background, 105–110
deepening therapy as examination of,
186
and dependence, 45

Dave (case study), 24–25
Death
acknowledging of, 67
awareness of, 64
Deepening, process of, 8, 51, 178
importance of, 179
and listening, 26
and loss experiences, 189
portal to, 26–28, 178, 180–181 (*see
also* Portal to deepening process)
for women, 186
Deepening group psychotherapy for men.
See Men's groups
Deepening psychotherapy, 7–8, 9, 178
breakthroughs in, 135
as couples work or family therapy,
184–185
Deepening psychotherapy with men (individual), 6, 178–179, 191
development of as therapeutic
approach, 177–178
early phases of, 89–90
assessment and connection in,
98–100
and body memories, 102–105
and case of Alex, 93–94, 95, 103–105,
106–108, 109–110, 112–114, 115
and case of Ron, 90–92, 94–95,
102–103, 105–106, 109, 110–112,
114, 115
and cultural background, 105–110
and influence of gender role socialization, 108–110
and life-damaged men, 95–98
and portal, 100–102
and social chameleons, 95, 96–98
and surfacing of memories and emotional material, 110
and ethnic background, 185–186
goals of, 155–156
vs. group therapy, 184
and managed care, 183

men not helped by, 188
as personal and individualized, 182
practice-oriented foundations of,
51–52
body work, 82–87, 132, 166–167
existential perspective on depth,
64–69
experiential psychotherapy, 73–79
in Jungian approach to depth, 58–63
in psychoanalysis and beginnings of
depth-oriented therapy, 52–58
self psychology and person-centered
deepening, 69–73
transpersonal and spiritual metaphors
of depth, 79–82
research on, 189–190
termination of, 151–156
early, 137–139
theoretical foundations of
and gender role strain viewpoint,
33–34, 41–44 (*see also* Gender
role strain viewpoint)
and psychoanalytic development
viewpoint, 33–41 (*see also*
Psychoanalytic developmental
viewpoint)
psychoanalytic and gender role strain
formulations integrated, 44–50
therapist in, 187
working phase of, 117–119, 137, 146
and case of Alex, 121–126, 128–130,
133–134, 135–136
and case of Ron, 119–121, 123–125,
126–128, 130–132, 135, 136
centrality of treatment in, 142
portal approached, 130–136
working phase through termination
and case of Alex, 141–142, 144–146,
148–150, 153–154
and case of Ron, 140–141, 142–144,
146–148, 150, 152–153
and early termination, 137–139
grief and longing revisited in, 146–150
and investment in process, 139–146
and masculine issues, 139
Dependence, 17–19
in boys and men, 44–46
in case study (Gerald), 30
masculine-specific conflicts over, 178
and therapy for men, 151
Depression, 16
covert, 170

and interpersonal conflict, 15
prevalence rate of, 14
successful therapy outcomes for, 89
Depressive position, 5, 47, 98, 130
Depth psychotherapy, 51
Diagnostic and Statistical Manual of Mental Disorders, 4th ed. (DSM-IV), 95
Dilemma, existential, 66
Doing
vs. being, 5, 23–25, 30, 49–50, 99, 139
in case of Ron, 127
masculine-specific conflicts over, 178, 182
in case studies (Ron and Alex), 115
and deepening group psychotherapy, 157
and therapeutic environment, 185
and therapeutic relationship, 182–183
towel twisting as (case of Ron), 132
Dream(s), 59
in case of Ron, 140, 142
and free association, 52
of group leaders, 161
playing parts of, 78–79
Dream interpretation, 54–55
Jungian, 63
Drug abuse and dependence
and men's psychological suffering, 13–14
and psychotherapy, 13
Drumming, 82

Early phases of deepening psychotherapy with men, 89–90
assessment and connection in, 98–100
and body memories, 102–105
and case of Alex, 93–94, 95, 103–105, 106–108, 109–110, 112–114, 115
and case of Ron, 90–92, 94–95, 102–103, 105–106, 109, 110–112, 114, 115
and cultural background, 105–110
and influence of gender role socialization, 108–110
and life-damaged men, 95–98
and portal, 100–102
and social chameleons, 95, 96–98
and surfacing of memories and emotional material, 110

Early termination, 137–139
Egalitarianism, 3
Elkins, D. N., 52
Emotions
and deepening psychotherapy, 179
suppression of, 19
See also Anger; Feelings; Grief; Shame
Empathy, 70, 71, 101–102, 176, 186
Empty chair dialogues, 75, 181
Entering psychotherapy, 13
case study on (Nick), 9–13
Ethnic background or identity, 108, 185–186. *See also* Cultural background
Exaggeration, 78
Existential issues or concerns, 175, 191
Existential perspectives on depth, 64–69
Existential predicaments, 160
Experiential interventions, 4
Experiential knowing, 73–74
Experiential psychotherapy, 73–79, 135
Eye exercises, 85

Fairbairn, 34
False promises, demystifying of, 66–67
Family. *See* Father(s); Parents
Family re-enactment, 175
Family therapy, deepening therapy in, 184–185
Father(s), 21
in case of Alex, 93, 94, 112–113, 114, 115, 124, 141, 144–145, 148–149, 165, 170–171
in case of John, 20, 21
in case of Ron, 90, 102–103, 105, 111, 115, 120, 121, 140–141, 142–143, 144, 146–148, 150
in imagery exercise, 62–63
men's group discussion of, 81
See also Parents
Fear of flying, 119
in case studies (Alex and Ron), 119–126
Feelings
beneath the words, 72–73
men's distancing from, 4
See also Anger; Emotions; Grief; Shame
Female therapist, 118, 125, 187
Femininity, and being, 23, 49
Feminism, impact of on men, 42
Focal conflict, 26

Free association, 52, 54
Freedom
    confronting of, 67–68
    existentialists on, 64–65
Freud, Sigmund, 7, 34, 51–52
    on catharsis, 53
    and Jung, 51
    Perls and Moreno influenced by, 74
    and Reich, 82
    on repressed traumatic events, 52
    and transference, 53

Gender role conflict, 43
Gender roles
    masculine-specific elements of, 21
    traditional, 21
Gender role socialization, 4
    influence of in therapy, 108–110
    male, 176
    male and female, 185
Gender role strain viewpoint, 3–4, 17,
        33–34, 41, 178
    and early descriptions of problematic
        masculinity, 41–42
    and gender role conflict, 43
    integrated with psychoanalytic per-
        spective, 44–46
    and sex role strain, 42–43
    and social roles, 43–44
George (case study), 60
Gerald (case study), 29–31
Gestalt therapy, 74–75
"Give 'em hell," 21, 42
Good-boy dynamic, 97, 115
Greg (case study), 75–76
Grief
    in case of Ron, 144
    catharsis of, 53–54
    and growth for boys and men, 40
    internal prohibitions on, 19–21, 30,
        46–47
    masculine-specific conflicts over, 178
    and men's group, 170
    and reason (quote), 177
    as therapy theme, 156
    in working phase through termina-
        tion, 146–150
Grounding exercises, 84–85
Group psychotherapy
    and Alex, 153–154
    vs. individual deepening psychother-
        apy, 184

and Moreno, 74
    storytelling in, 81
    See also Men's groups
Guided imagery, 62–63
Guntrip, H., 34

Hard sell, 89
Henry (case study), 60–61
Herbert (case study), 62–63
Hero bind, 42
Hesse, Herman, quoted, 137
Hillman, J., 52
Homer, quoted, 157
Homophobia, 159, 184, 187
Horney, Karen, 34
Human potential movement, 70

Ian (case study), 72
Identity, 40–41
    ethnic and cultural, 108
    male, 118
    vulnerable forms of, 109
Identity development worldview, 4, 33
*I Don't Want to Talk About It: Overcoming
    the Secret Legacy of Male Depression*
    (Real), 170
Imagination, active, 59
Individuation, 58
    in psychoanalytic developmental
        viewpoint, 35–38, 46
Inner life, 23–24
Inspirational passages, 81
Internalization, transmuting, 69
Interpersonal conflict, 15
Interpersonal learning input, 175
Interpersonal learning output, 175
Interpersonal relationships
    activity-oriented, 183
    assessment of, 180
    and dependence, 17–19, 45, 46
    and developmental strains, 39–40
    as presenting concern, 15
    psychotherapy relationship as,
        118–119
    wounding from rejection in, 27
Intimacy
    ambivalence around, 19
    defensiveness about, 40
    and dependence conflicts, 46
    males' disavowal of, 190
    men's avoidance of, 4, 5, 117
    and sexuality, 187

Investment in therapy process, 139–146
Isolation, 65

Jerry (case study), 86
Joe (case study), 62
John (case study), 20–21
Jung, Carl, 7, 51, 52
    and Jungian approach to depth, 58–63
    and Reich, 82

Ken (case study, exaggeration), 78
Ken (case study, free association), 54
Kernberg, O. F., 34
Kicking exercises, 86
Kinetic bind, 42
Klein, Melanie, 34
Knowing, experiential, 73–74
Kohut, Heinz, 7, 34, 52, 69–70
Kyle (case study), 78–79

Lance (case study), 55–56
Laughing, as exercise, 85–86
Legal difficulties, and psychotherapy, 13
Libido, 83
Life-damaged men, 95–98
Limitations, need to face (quote), 33
Lionel (case study), 54-55
Listening, 71
Longing, in working phase through termi-
    nation, 146–150
Loss
    in case of Ron, 146–147
    and deepening process, 189
    and growth for boys and men, 40
    and entering into psychotherapy, 9
    inevitability of (quote), 33
    masculine-specific conflicts over, 178
    separation experienced as, 39
    of son (case of Ron), 91–92
    termination of therapy as, 156
    as therapy theme, 156
Louis (case study), 67
Lowen, A., 7, 52, 83–84, 182
Luke (case study), 72–73

Mahler, M., 34, 36–37, 46
Male gender role, 4–5, 118
    early critiques of, 41–42
    and men's group, 176
    and psychotherapy, 89
    and repression of feelings, 190
    See also Gender role strain viewpoint

Male identity, 118
Male role models, 108
Male sex role identity paradigm, 42
Managed-care model, 183
Marty (case study), 68
Masculine identification, 190
Masculine issues, 139
Masculine socialization model, traditional,
    91
Masculine-specific conflicts, 5–6, 178, 182
    assessment of, 180
Masculine-specific self-structure, 21–23,
    25, 30, 99
    in case of Ron, 106
    conflicts over, 178
    problematic, 47–49
Masculinity
    attitudes emphasized in, 44
    and doing, 23, 49
    as problematic, 41–42
    traditional, 109
    values about, 42
Maslow, Abraham, 52, 70, 79
May, R., 7, 52, 64
Meade, Michael, 81
Meaninglessness, 65
Meditation, 82
Men
    denial or avoidance of emotion in,
        178
    psychology of, 13
    study of, 3–4
    See also at Masculine
Men of color
    and Alex as Black man, 106–107
    experiences of, 108–109, 109–110
Men's doing and being, 23–25, 30, 49–50,
    139. See also Being; Doing
Men's groups, 157–158, 176
    drumming session at, 82
    fathers discussed in, 81
    vs. individual deepening psychother-
        apy, 184
    ingredients for success of, 158–161
    leader's notes on, 161–174
    structure in, 166–167
    suggestions for therapists working
        with, 175–176
    themes and issues in, 174–175
    See also Group psychotherapy
Men's liberation movement, 3
Men's rights movement, 3

Metaphors, 81–82
Michael (case study), 68
Milton, John, quoted, 3
Mirroring, 69, 71
Moreno, Jacob, 7, 52, 74
Mortality, acknowledging of, 67
Mourning, prohibitions against, 46–47
Music, as creative venue, 62
Mythopoetic men's movement, 3

Narcissistic compensatory structures, 48
Narcissistic wounding, 27
Neurotic anxiety, 64
Nick (case study), 9–13
Nonverbal attention, 73
"No sissy stuff," 21, 42

Object relations theory, 34, 35
Odyssey, The (Homer), quote from, 157
Orgasm, Reich on, 83
Owen (case study), 76

Paradise Lost (Milton), quoted from, 3
Paradoxes, imposed on men, 41–42
Parataxic distortion, 154
Parents
    and emotional wholeness of sons, 190
    internalization of judgments from, 101
    reparative parenting, 70
    See also Father(s)
Peak experiences, 79
Perceptual awareness, 77
Perls, Fritz, 7, 52, 74, 75
Perls, Laura, 74
Persona, 58
Personality, role-playing parts of, 76–77
Person-centered deepening, 69–73
Person-centered psychotherapy, 70
Philip (case study), 71–72
Pollack, W. S., 34, 39
Portal to deepening process, 26–28, 178,
    180–181
    different approaches to, 182
    in individual therapy
    early phase, 100–102
    working phase, 130–136
    and men's groups, 158
Postfeminist psychoanalytic constructions,
    38–40
Pounding exercises, 87
    in "boot camp" program, 164
    in case of Alex, 145, 149

Present, staying in, 75–76
Presenting complaints, 14
    in clinical reports, 15–16
    See also Psychological problems of
    men
Prohibitions, internal, 19–21, 30
Projections
    of critical parent onto therapist, 130
    of different images onto therapist,
    125
    reowning of, 61
Psychoanalysis, beginning of depth-ori-
    ented therapy in, 52–58
Psychoanalytic developmental viewpoint,
    3, 17, 33–34, 40–41, 178
    first wave (British object relations
    theory), 35
    integrated with gender role strain per-
    spective, 44–46
    second wave (separation, individua-
    tion and self), 35–38
    third wave (postfeminist psychoana-
    lytic constructions), 38–40
Psychodrama, 74, 76
Psychological distress, externalizing of, 14
Psychological problems of men
    clinical reports on, 15–17
    conceptualizing of, 17, 28–31
    internal prohibitions on grief and sad-
    ness, 19–21, 30
    masculine-specific self-structure,
    21–23, 25, 30
    men's doing and being, 23–25, 30
    (*see also* Being; Doing)
    pull of dependence, 17–19, 30
    empirical findings on, 13–14
Psychology of men, 13
Psychotherapy
    continuation rate of men in, 89
    experiential, 73–79, 135
    men's resistance to, 89, 117
    as path to spiritual growth, 79
    and shame (quote), 89
Psychotherapy with men, 4, 5, 6
    problems keeping men away from, 13
    See also Deepening psychotherapy
    with men

Questions, existential, 65–66

Rabinowitz, Fred, 90
Racism, 109

Reaching and stretching exercises, 87
Real, Terrance, 170
Reason, and grief (quote), 177
Reich, Wilhelm, 7, 52, 82–83, 182
Relationship of therapist and client. See
    Therapeutic relationship
Relationships, interpersonal. See
    Interpersonal relationships
Reparative parenting, 70
Research, on deepening approach,
    189–190
Resistance, 126
    addressing of, 119
    and body-oriented technique, 181
    in case studies (Alex and Ron),
        126–128
    in Gestalt therapy, 75
    hard sell and soft sell against, 89–90
    interpretation of, 56–57
    moving through, 134–135
    to self-exploration, 188–189
    working through, 53, 57
Rick (case study), 65–66
Risk-taking, in being-and-doing case,
    24–25
Rogers, Carl, 7, 52, 69, 70–71
Role playing the parts of personality,
    76–77
Roles, social, 43–44
Ron (case study), 90
    in early phases, 90–92, 94–95,
        102–103, 105–106, 109, 110–112,
        114, 115
    in working phase, 119–121, 123–125,
        126–128, 130–132, 135, 136
    in working phase through termina-
        tion, 140–141, 142–144, 146–148,
        150, 152–153

Sacredness, 79–80
Sadness
    anger as defense against, 103
    internal prohibitions on, 19–21, 30,
        46–47
Saul (case study), 56
Screaming, 85–86
Self, in psychoanalytic developmental
    viewpoint, 35–38
Self-dialogue, in case of Alex, 134
Self-disclosure, by therapist, 72, 176
Self-exploration, resistance to, 188–189

Self-exposure, shame from, 100, 129–130
Self psychology, 69–73
Self-structure
    child with lack of, 69
    masculine-specific, 21–23, 25, 30,
        47–49, 99, 106, 178
Separation
    from mother, 185
    in psychoanalytic developmental
        viewpoint, 35–38, 46
    from therapist, 151
Sex role strain, 42–43
Shadow, 58–59
    exposing of, 60–61
"Shadow work," 167–168
Shame
    anger as defense against, 103
    in boys' expression of emotion, 190
    in psychotherapy (quote), 89
    and reason (quote), 177
    in seeking psychological help,
        117–118
    from self-exposure, 100, 129–130
Shame-based defense, 98, 101
Short-term managed-care model, 183
Siddhartha (Hesse), quote from, 137
Social chameleons, 95, 96–98, 125
Social constructionist world view, 4, 33
Socialization
    gender role, 4, 108–110, 176, 185
    traditional masculine socialization
        model, 91
Social phobia, prevalence rate of, 14
Social roles, 43–44
Soft sell, 90
Soulfulness, 79, 80
Spiritual concerns, 191
Spiritually oriented psychotherapy, 79–82
Storytelling, 80, 81
Stretching exercises, 87
"Sturdy oak," 21, 42
Substance abuse
    and grief or sadness, 19
    as presenting symptom, 16
    See also Alcohol abuse or addiction;
        Drug abuse and dependence

Termination, 151
    and cases (Ron and Alex), 152–154
    early, 137–139
    and goals of therapy, 155–156

as loss, 156
    preparation for, 154–155
Terror position, 143
Therapeutic relationship
    authentic interaction in, 72
    as balance between intrusiveness and
        ignoring of critical issues, 92
    client's testing of, 188
    countertransference in, 101, 119 (*see
        also* Countertransference
        reactions)
    and dependence conflict, 46
    "doing" relationship in, 182–183
    and feelings of engulfment, fear and
        terror, 130
    with female therapist, 118
    and issues of grief and loss, 47
    as male contest, 118
    male posturing in, 92
    parataxic distortion in, 154
    projection in, 61, 125, 130
    Rogers on importance of, 70
    sabotage of, 118–119
    and therapist as authority figure, 99
    and therapist's self-exploration, 176
Therapy. *See* Deepening psychotherapy
    with men; Psychotherapy
Towel twisting, 87
    in case study (Nick), 11
    in case study (Ron), 132
Transference, 53
    interpretation of, 55–56
    working through, 53, 56
Transmuting internalization, 69
Transpersonal and spiritual metaphors of
    depth, 79–82
Twinship, 70
Twisting exercises, 87
    towel twisting, 11, 87, 132
Two-chair technique, in case of Alex, 134

Unconditional positive regard, 71–72
Unconscious, collective, 58
Universality/group cohesion, 175

Violence, 15
    in case study (Ron), 102, 111, 120, 140
    See also Abuse

Vocalizing exercises, 85–86
Von (case study), 66

Weeping, 85–86
Will, 64
Winnicott, C., 34
Women
    absence of in men's group, 159
    deepening process for, 186
    and depressive position, 130
    See also Femininity
Work, failure at, 27
Workaholism, 166
    of Alex, 107, 108, 109
Working phase of deepening psychother-
    apy with men, 117–119, 137, 146
    and case of Alex, 121–126, 128–130,
        133–134, 135–136
    and case of Ron, 119–121, 123–125,
        126–128, 130–132, 135, 136
    centrality of treatment in, 142
    portal approached, 130–136
Working phase through termination of
    deepening psychotherapy with
    men
    and case of Alex, 141–142, 144–146,
        148–150, 153–154
    and case of Ron, 140–141, 142–144,
        146–148, 150, 152–153
    and early termination, 137–139
    grief and longing revisited in,
        146–150
    and investment in process, 139–146
    and masculine issues, 139
Working through, 53
    of transference, 56
Worldviews
    identity development, 4
    social constructionist, 4
Woundings, 178
    as portals to deepening process, 27,
        178
Writing, as creative venue, 62

Yalom, I. D., 7, 52, 64

Zak (case study), 61

ABOUT THE AUTHORS

Fredric E. Rabinowitz, PhD, is a full professor of psychology at the University of Redlands in California. He received his PhD in counseling psychology from the University of Missouri–Columbia in 1984. He has written and cowritten journal articles and book chapters on the topic of men and psychotherapy and has presented at national conferences on this topic. Dr. Rabinowitz has coauthored two books with Sam Cochran: *Man Alive: A Primer of Men's Issues* and *Men and Depression: Clinical and Empirical Perspectives*. He has received the Outstanding Teaching Award and Professor of the Year award at the University of Redlands. Dr. Rabinowitz has served several years as the Psychology Department chair and has also been the clinical director of the local community mental health center in Redlands. His private psychotherapy practice is primarily focused on work with men. He founded and has been coleader of an ongoing men's therapy group in Redlands since 1987.

Sam V. Cochran, PhD, is director of the University Counseling Service and clinical professor at the University of Iowa in Iowa City. He received his PhD in counseling psychology from the University of Missouri in 1983. Since that time, Dr. Cochran has worked with men in therapy, written about men's issues, and researched depression in men. He has coauthored two books with Fredric Rabinowitz: *Men and Depression: Clinical and Empirical Perspectives* and *Man Alive: A Primer of Men's Issues*. In addition to these two books, Dr. Cochran has published several papers and book chapters on assessing and treating depression in men and on psychotherapy with men. In 2000 he received the Distinguished Service Award from the Society for the Psychological Study of Men and Masculinity (APA Division 51). He is a Fellow of the APA and is currently president-elect of Division 51. Dr. Cochran lives with his family in Iowa City.